THE COMPLETE
Trauma
Treatment
Guide

Over 150 Clinical Worksheets, Exercises, and Interventions to Identify, Assess, and Treat Traumatic Stress

CBT • EMDR • IFS • Somatic Psychology
Polyvagal Theory • Trauma-Informed Yoga
Havening • Attachment • Mindfulness
Psychodrama • Energy Psychology
Complementary and Alternative Medicine

PESI Publishing
pesipublishing.com

THE COMPLETE TRAUMA TREATMENT GUIDE
Copyright © 2025 by PESI Publishing

Published by
PESI Publishing, Inc.
3839 White Ave
Eau Claire, WI 54703

Cover design by Emily Dyer
Interior design by Amy Rubenzer

ISBN 9781683738053 (print)
ISBN 9781683738060 (ePUB)
ISBN 9781683738077 (ePDF)

PESI Publishing
pesipublishing.com

Table of Contents

Chapter 4

Yoga-Based Tools 87

Chapter 5

Polyvagal Tools 121

Chapter

6

Chapter

7

Chapter

8

Chapter

9

Internal Family Systems Tools..225

Chapter

10

Eye Movement Desensitization and Reprocessing Tools 249

Introduction

As a clinician, you know that trauma is a complex and multifaceted issue. It can range from more acute and isolated stressors, such as a car accident, natural disaster, or physical assault, to more pervasive and ongoing events, such as childhood abuse or neglect, cultural genocide, and racial oppression and discrimination. It can affect the young and the elderly, the privileged and the oppressed. It can come in many forms and be experienced in a variety of ways.

It should come as no surprise then that treatment for trauma is equally complex and multifaceted, often requiring a multidisciplinary and targeted approach to address the needs of each individual client. While some clients will only need time-limited support to resolve their distress, others will suffer from intractable symptoms that require more extensive and ongoing care. With so many available treatment options out there—ranging from well-established interventions with proven success to cutting-edge therapies that show incredible promise—it can be difficult to know where to begin.

That is where *The Complete Trauma Treatment Guide* can help. Compiled from a variety of resources written by leading experts in the fields of trauma, neuroscience, somatics, and more, this book contains over 150 interventions that are foundational to the art and science of trauma recovery. Organized by treatment modality, you'll find everything you need to fill your therapeutic toolbox, including tools from the fields of cognitive behavioral therapy (CBT), eye movement desensitization and reprocessing (EMDR), internal family systems (IFS), somatics, neuroscience, polyvagal theory, complementary and alternative medicine (CAM), and more. All of these tools have been carefully curated with a trauma-informed lens in mind, allowing you to have easy access to the most up-to-date and tried-and-true interventions—all in one place.

In **chapter 1**, you'll find a variety of CBT-based tools that approach trauma from a top-down perspective. This includes cognitive interventions to challenge the counterproductive beliefs that clients have developed as a result of their trauma (e.g., cognitive restructuring, Socratic questioning), as well as behavioral interventions to reduce avoidance of trauma-related triggers (e.g., exposure, fear hierarchies).

Chapter 2 shifts to a bottom-up perspective with experiential tools that promote an inward focus and help clients develop their sense of interoceptive awareness, such as breathwork, meditations, and body scans. These exercises help clients grow the mind-body connection and allow them to better manage difficult memories, sensations, and emotions as they arise.

Chapter 3 presents more active body-based tools that invite clients to explore the power of movement in connecting to the body and healing from trauma. With the somatic practices in this chapter, clients can reestablish body boundaries, release long-standing protective patterns held in the body, and access a felt sense of safety.

Chapter 4 provides trauma-informed yoga interventions to shift clients out of states of protection and into states of connection. Within this chapter, you'll find calming yoga practices to reduce autonomic nervous system arousal, balancing yoga practices to facilitate more fluid movements between nervous system states, and energizing yoga practices to release any lingering states of fight, flight, or freeze held in the body.

Chapter 5 looks at trauma recovery through the lens of polyvagal theory, with particular attention to the role of the vagus nerve in nervous system regulation. The tools in this chapter allow clients to identify symptoms of hypoarousal and hyperarousal, stimulate the vagus nerve, increase vagal tone, and move out of states of immobilization and mobilization.

Chapter 6 provides tools to help clients process any relational and attachment wounds from their past. These interventions empower clients to look deeper at their attachment history, identify problematic relational styles, and grieve relational losses. Remember that relational repair can occur in the context of the therapeutic relationship as well when you offer your clients a co-regulating and attuned presence.

Chapter 7 examines the neuroscience of trauma with brain-based tools that encourage clients to consider how the brain remembers trauma and to uncover their own symptoms of autonomic reactivity. They'll also learn how to interrupt and redirect amygdala-activating thoughts with activities that involve distraction, sensory input, and mental containment.

Chapter 8 includes additional brain-body tools drawn from the burgeoning fields of tapping and self-havening. These psychosensory interventions involve the use of self-touch and other tactile input to calm the nervous system and reduce the intensity of emotional distress. The power behind these healing mechanisms lies in their simplicity, as clients can easily practice on their own between sessions.

Chapter 9 delves into parts work with a variety of IFS-informed interventions that invite clients to get curious about the various parts within themselves. Whether clients are struggling with self-critical, dissociative, or neglectful parts, the tools in this chapter will allow them to resolve extreme polarizations between parts, distinguish between parts and their core Self, and resolve traumatic wounds held by more vulnerable parts.

Chapter 10 discusses how to facilitate memory reprocessing through the lens of EMDR. Within this chapter, you'll find interventions to help clients build positive resources in preparation for processing; identify beliefs, emotions, and sensations related to their trauma; and desensitize to target memories that are the source of their distress.

Chapter 11 looks at how the field of CAM can amplify the therapeutic benefits of traditional trauma therapy. In particular, this chapter explores the connection between nutrition, digestion, herbal supplements, biological rhythms, nature, and hydrotherapy in mental wellness, allowing you to provide a more holistic and integrative approach to trauma treatment that addresses the needs of the whole person.

Chapter 12 focuses on the use of mindfulness to help clients recognize and attend to their emotional and physical needs in the moment. This includes guided visualizations that teach clients how to settle into a more relaxed state, develop more balanced thinking, and build tolerance for difficult emotions.

Finally, **chapter 13** provides exercises from the world of psychodrama, sociometrics, and addictions treatment. Designed for group work but easily adapted for individuals, the experiential interventions in this chapter are meant to help clients repair, rather than reenact, painful relational trauma dynamics in their lives through real-time healing in connection with others.

Working through trauma takes considerable courage—for both you and your clients—but with the tools in this book, you can feel confident in your ability to help clients process unresolved traumatic wounds, strengthen their resilience, and transform into their full potential. As you read through the interventions in the chapters that follow, remember that different interventions will resonate with different people, so pick and choose what works for you (and your clients). Whether you end up choosing more brain-based cognitive tools or more somatic body-based practices—or something in between—rest assured that the expert advice you'll find within these pages has you covered.

Remember, too, that trauma treatment is a continually evolving field, with innovative tools and techniques emerging all the time. Think of this resource as "the best of what we know so far"—your go-to guide for helping clients heal from trauma and live authentic, meaningful, connected lives. Thank you for the work you do each and every day.

CHAPTER 1

Cognitive Behavioral Tools

Cognitive Reappraisal

Engaging clients in *cognitive reappraisal* invites them to explore the beliefs that they have constructed about themselves or the world and helps them identify when they have adopted thinking errors. Negative beliefs from trauma are often related to a sense of being defective or damaged, an inaccurate sense of over-responsibility for the traumatic events, an impaired sense of safety, or a pervasive feeling of helplessness. These "thinking errors" are often due to overgeneralizations, all-or-nothing thinking, catastrophizing, and emotional reasoning.

Once you have identified clients' negative beliefs, you can invite the client to construct new, accurate beliefs. Often this process involves Socratic inquiry, in which you ask the client a question that they have the ability to answer, even if they do not yet realize it. For example, when working with a client who experienced abuse as a child, you might say, "You were just a child. Do you really believe that you could have been responsible for your father's behavior?" This can empower the client to see new possibilities, question their assumptions, develop new beliefs, and form a new outlook for the future (Heiniger et al., 2018). This facilitates cognitive dissonance, creates a new emotional response, and allows clients to form new meanings about the events of their lives (Tryon, 2014). For example, the client may realize that they were never to blame for their abuse and that they were always deserving of kindness and respect. Often, this evokes a grief process that involves letting go of limiting beliefs or behaviors with which they have overidentified.

You can use the next two interventions, *Garden of the Mind Metaphor* and *Invite Cognitive Reappraisal*, to facilitate this process of cognitive appraisal. The first focuses on helping clients recognize the importance of cultivating a healthy mind through a garden metaphor. The second practice helps clients identify negative beliefs, explore counterevidence to these beliefs using Socratic inquiry, and form new beliefs they would like to adopt.

Garden of the Mind Metaphor

Trauma recovery is like creating a garden. You begin by tending to the soil—adding in the right amount of nutrients, sun, and water that create an optimal environment for growth. When planting the garden of your mind, remember that you have a choice about what seeds you are planting. You can think of kindness, compassion, and wisdom as flowers that come from a well-tended garden of the mind.

You must, at times, also pull up the weeds. These are the thoughts that tell you that you are unworthy of love, not enough, or helpless to change your circumstances. In your garden, you can take the weeds and place them into the compost. There, they can be safely held and, in time, transformed into the rich, fertile earth.

What new seeds would you like to plant in the garden of your mind? What would you like to believe about yourself now? Perhaps you want to grow a new sense of self rooted in the knowledge that you are worthy of love, kindness, and respect. You get to choose what you want to grow and flourish in yourself and in your life.

_____

_____

_____

_____

_____

_____

_____

_____

_____

_____

It is important to take care of the new growth in your garden. The seeds you planted may still be fresh, green sprouts that require protection and careful tending. Ultimately, with the sunlight of your awareness, you can guide yourself to bloom into your full potential.

Invite Cognitive Reappraisal

Let's take a look at the following list of common negative beliefs. Are there any you identify with? If so, do you have a sense of where this belief comes from as related to your history?

- ❏ I am not good enough.
- ❏ I am a bad person.
- ❏ I cannot trust myself.
- ❏ I am not lovable.
- ❏ I am worthless.
- ❏ I am weak.
- ❏ I am damaged.
- ❏ I should have done something.
- ❏ I should have known better.
- ❏ I did something wrong.
- ❏ It is my fault.
- ❏ I am not safe.
- ❏ I can't trust anyone.
- ❏ I can't protect myself.
- ❏ I am not in control.
- ❏ I am powerless.
- ❏ I am helpless.

Pick one negative belief that you identified on the previous list, and examine this belief by asking yourself a few questions.

Do you know for sure that what you feel or believe is true?

_____

_____

What evidence do you have for this negative thought?

_____

_____

Can you find any evidence that suggests this belief is not true?

_____

_____

Are you holding yourself to an unrealistically high standard?

_____

_____

[*If the traumatic event happened in childhood*] You were just a child. Do you really believe that a child could be blamed for…?

_____

_____

Is the belief that you carry about yourself helpful for you?

_____

_____

Will this thought allow you to achieve your goals?

_____

_____

If a close friend of yours knew that you were having this thought, what would they say to you?

_____

_____

If someone you love was having this thought, what would you tell them?

_____

_____

Imagine receiving advice from your future self. What would the future you like to tell you? How does this information change your thoughts or beliefs about yourself?

_____

_____

Now let's take a look at the following list of positive beliefs. What would you like to believe about yourself now?

- ☐ I am good enough.

- ☐ I am a good person.

- ☐ I can trust myself now.

- ☐ I am lovable.

- ☐ I am worthy of love.

- ☐ I am strong.

- ☐ I am healthy and whole.

- ☐ I did the best that I could.

- ☐ I am doing the best that I can now.

- ☐ I can learn from difficult experiences.

- ☐ It was never my fault.

- ☐ It is over and I am safe now.

- ☐ I can choose whom to trust now.

- ☐ I can protect myself and take care of myself now.

- ☐ I have choices now.

- ☐ I can stand up for myself now.

- ☐ I am empowered.

Assessing Your Own Patterns of Thinking

It is possible to change thoughts that aren't serving you well or that are blocking you from your goals. But before you can do this, you need to become aware of the underlying thought patterns that you have in the first place. On this worksheet, you'll find a series of checklists that will help you to assess your typical patterns of thinking. You may find that you interpret situations in ways that may not make sense or may not be necessary in your current life. Then you can consider and observe how these thoughts affect your life.

Pessimism

One of most common patterns of thinking that increases worry, stress, and anxiety is *pessimism*. If you tend to expect the worst to happen, you are causing yourself to suffer, even before anything distressing has actually occurred. Read through the following statements to gauge the extent to which you engage in pessimistic thinking, checking off those that apply to you.

❑ When someone is late, I often imagine that something has gone wrong.

❑ I often believe that there is no use in trying. Things will never work out for me.

❑ When I want to make a request of someone, I expect that they will say no.

❑ When I need to accomplish something, I frequently expect to have difficulties.

❑ To prepare myself, it is best to expect that something is likely to go wrong.

❑ It is just my luck that things are not going to work out for me.

❑ I often prepare myself for bad things that never happen.

❑ I have found that most people will let you down in the end.

❑ It is hard for me to try because things seem so hopeless.

If you checked off more than three of these statements, you may have a tendency toward pessimistic thinking. But you don't have to interpret situations according to these expectations. You can replace these thoughts with coping thoughts, which allow you to experience less anxiety and distress. Coping thoughts for pessimism include statements like "I don't know what is going to happen," "Let's wait and see before assuming anything," or "I can handle whatever happens." These thoughts are less likely to cause distress. Even if the situation does turn out badly, you will have reduced the amount of time you had to suffer. Why start suffering before you even experience anything negative?

Anticipation

Another common thought pattern you may experience is *anticipation*, in which you spend a great deal of time thinking about an upcoming event, considering different outcomes, and rehearsing how you could respond. While anticipation can be helpful in planning, it can lead you to focus too much time on potential problems that may never be relevant. Anticipation so often feels worse than the anticipated event itself! Check off any of the following statements that apply to you.

☐ I frequently find myself considering a problem from a variety of angles.

☐ It is difficult to stop myself from thinking about things that make me anxious.

☐ I try to have solutions for a variety of outcomes, no matter how unlikely.

☐ I need to think about an upcoming situation in detail in order to prepare myself.

☐ I frequently prepare responses to criticisms I expect (but don't receive) from others.

☐ When an important event is coming up, my thoughts about it interfere with my sleep.

☐ I am never sure that I have prepared myself enough for an upcoming event.

☐ I know that I dwell on upcoming events, but it seems necessary.

☐ When I daydream, it is almost always about negative events, not positive ones.

If you checked off more than three of these statements, you may be overusing anticipation. You may benefit from coping statements like "I have thought about this enough, and I will get through it" or "I can figure out what to do once I'm in the situation." Another way to replace anticipatory thoughts is to keep yourself engaged with other situations, activities, or topics that have a present-moment focus. This helps ground you to what is happening *right now* so you can stop thinking so much about the future. Engage in activities that are entertaining so you can enjoy each day as you experience it.

Mind Reading

Some people spend a great deal of time trying to figure out what other people are thinking in the hopes that they can please others or manage their reactions. While it is important to be considerate of what others might be thinking, it's easy to go too far and make assumptions that are based more on your own worries. This type of *mind reading* can increase distress because it focuses your attention on critical or negative thoughts that others *may* have about you or about something that concerns you. When you spend time trying to determine what is happening in another person's mind, you often make incorrect assumptions in the absence of any real evidence. To determine how much you may be mind reading, consider if any of the following statements apply to you.

❐ I often hear other people's criticisms of me in my mind, even when they've said nothing.

❐ I frequently prepare responses to people's statements before they have spoken.

❐ I expect others to have a negative view of me and am surprised by compliments.

❐ I frequently get the sense that I am a disappointment to others.

❐ I often assume that others are irritated with me, even when they deny it.

❐ I want to be prepared to defend myself against other people's opinions of me.

❐ I hesitate to ask for anything from others because I expect rejection.

❐ When I hear that someone is upset, I tend to assume I have something to do with it.

❐ I often don't believe what other people tell me they think, especially about me.

If you checked off more than three of these statements, you may have a tendency to engage in mind reading. Humans are social creatures, so we are often very concerned with the possibility of others criticizing or rejecting us. However, when there is no evidence to suggest that someone else has negative thoughts about you, you could benefit from replacing mind-reading thoughts with thoughts like "I can't know what they are thinking without discussing it with them" and "I can't please everyone, and it is not my job to do so anyway." You can also ask yourself, "Did the other person really say that, or am I just assuming?" Sometimes we worry too much about pleasing others, even people we barely know or may never see again! Although there are some people we need to be concerned about, like our work supervisors or family members, it is really unnecessary (and impossible) to be liked and approved of by everyone. It's not always worth it to worry about what others think.

Catastrophizing

Catastrophizing involves responding to a small setback or minor difficulty as if it is a catastrophe. When your expectations are not met or when something goes wrong, it makes sense to feel frustrated or disappointed, but it doesn't mean your whole day has to be ruined. If you have ever lost your temper when you've been stopped by a red light, or completely panicked when you couldn't find your keys for several minutes, you have catastrophized. Catastrophic thoughts like "I'm going to be late and be seen as incompetent!" or "I won't be able to drive my car all day!" are just the kind to cause distress because they present the situation as one that is very threatening. Consider the following statements to see if you have a tendency to catastrophize.

- ❒ When something goes wrong, I tend to imagine the worst possible outcome.

- ❒ I tend to overreact to small setbacks.

- ❒ I often feel like giving up when I hit a snag in something I am working on.

- ❒ When something breaks, I have a tendency to see it as disastrous.

- ❒ I often feel like I can't cope with even one thing going wrong.

- ❒ I frequently get infuriated when someone makes a mistake that affects me.

- ❒ I admit that I can often make a mountain out of a molehill.

- ❒ I notice that other people interpret problems more calmly than I do.

- ❒ People have told me that I overreact to minor difficulties.

If you checked more than three of these statements, you may have a tendency to catastrophize. To calm yourself, try replacing catastrophic thinking with more realistic thoughts, like "Getting stuck at this traffic light will only make me arrive a minute later, and I can handle that" or "This is not the worst thing that could happen." The next time you encounter a difficulty that makes you want to catastrophize, take a breath and give yourself a few moments to adjust. Try not to jump to the conclusion that all is lost when you could be more hopeful about what the rest of the day will bring.

Perfectionistic Thinking

Although you might not realize it, *perfectionistic thinking* puts you in a constant state of fear: the fear of being imperfect. However, no one is perfect, so perfectionism creates a standard that is impossible to achieve. We will all inevitably fail, mess up, or have setbacks at times, and the immense self-criticism and disappointment that result from perfectionism create a sense of danger. Look over the following statements to consider whether you have a tendency toward perfectionistic thoughts.

- ❑ I have a great deal of difficulty admitting or accepting my mistakes.

- ❑ I believe there is a best way to do things, and I don't want to compromise.

- ❑ I try to hold myself to very high standards.

- ❑ It's important to expect a lot of myself and not allow any excuses.

- ❑ I want to be a careful, conscientious, and hard worker every day.

- ❑ I expect myself to be a high achiever in everything I undertake.

- ❑ I rarely am satisfied with my performance.

- ❑ It is hard to forgive myself for errors. Even minor ones haunt me.

- ❑ I expect myself to perform better than others in most situations.

If you checked off more than three of these statements, you may have a tendency toward perfectionistic standards. Many of us have been raised to believe that we should always do our best, and we may equate that with perfectionism, which is an exhausting and unreasonable ideal. Often, perfectionism involves the constant need to outshine others, do everything correctly, and know more than others. It comes with the expectation of complete and utter flawlessness, which is simply unsustainable. The reality is that we all have strengths and weaknesses. Further, you don't *always* need to do your best. If you were to give 100 percent when performing every single task (e.g., brushing your teeth, making your bed, preparing breakfast), you would be exhausted from the constant pressure by the end of the day. It's healthier to choose what to do your best at.

Perhaps the most obvious coping statement to replace perfectionistic thoughts is the simple reminder that "no one is perfect." When you catch yourself criticizing your imperfections or mistakes, let yourself off the hook and say, "I have talents and skills, but I can't be perfect." It is healthy to see mistakes and imperfections as a normal part of being human.

Cognitive Fusion

When we take our thoughts too seriously—becoming so "fused" with them that it's hard to disentangle them from reality—we are experiencing *cognitive fusion*. We worry that simply thinking about something means that it will definitely happen, either through our own or others' actions. For example, someone might have the thought that their partner is cheating on them, and then believe that having this worry makes it true. However, it is actually very common for people to have random thoughts pop into their minds, and overestimating the importance of those thoughts is the source of the problem. For instance, someone who has intrusive thoughts about how deadly it would be to drive in front of a semitruck on the highway may be surprised to learn that most people experience thoughts like this—and having these thoughts does not mean they are in danger of killing themselves. Here are some statements to help you determine whether you experience cognitive fusion.

❑ When I have a worry, I often think that my worry is very likely to come true.

❑ I take my anxiety to be a clear indication that something is going to go wrong.

❑ Some of my thoughts truly frighten me.

❑ I often worry that I may act on thoughts that I have, even though I don't want to.

❑ When I think something will go wrong, it usually means that it will.

❑ I worry about what certain thoughts mean and what I will do as a result of them.

❑ If I think I can't do something, I know it's best to just give up.

❑ When images come into my mind, I can't help but think they will come true.

❑ I think it is important to take my thoughts very seriously.

If you checked off more than three of these items, you may have a tendency to overvalue your thoughts. To cope with the effects of cognitive fusion, remember not to accept thoughts without verification. Instead of taking them at face value, ask yourself, "What evidence supports this thought?" Remind yourself that simply having a thought doesn't mean that it will come true. Label your thoughts as only thoughts—for example: "I'm having the thought that I'm going to fail, but that doesn't mean I will." Try to be observant of your thoughts and approach them with a healthy skepticism: "Although I'm aware of this pesky thought, I have no reason to put faith in it." Remind yourself that these thoughts have been wrong in the past.

Shoulds

When you frame your goals as *shoulds*, you are putting pressure on yourself that is not necessary for change to occur. These should statements can come in the form of thoughts about the need to behave in a correct way ("I *should* always be patient with my child and never lose my temper") or be a better person ("I *should* be more organized"). Because these statements increase guilt and shame, they typically increase distress rather than supporting the change process.

If the should statement is focused on something a person did that was objectively wrong ("I *should* not have said hurtful things to my friend in the heat of the argument"), the ensuing guilt can be helpful in encouraging the person to seek forgiveness, correct the behavior, and make a commitment to not repeat it. But guilt can be unhealthy when it comes from should statements that impart unrealistic self-blame or rigid, high standards. And should statements that cause shame are never healthy, as they simply make you believe that you are worthless or hopelessly flawed, while offering no clear way to resolve the situation or feel more positively about yourself. Consider the following statements to see if you have a tendency to "should" yourself.

- ❑ I know I should be a better person.

- ❑ I frequently tell myself what I should do or how I should be.

- ❑ While I don't necessarily say "I should…" out loud, I frequently think it to myself.

- ❑ I beat myself up when I've hurt someone's feelings.

- ❑ I have high expectations for myself.

- ❑ When I set a goal for myself, I can be very hard on myself.

- ❑ I tend to be harder on myself than on other people.

- ❑ I hate it when I feel like I've let someone down.

- ❑ It is difficult for me to tell someone no.

- ❑ I often suspect that others are disappointed with me.

❐ If someone wants something, it's easy for them to guilt me into doing it for them.

❐ I feel ashamed about who I have become.

If you checked off more than three of these statements, you may often feel like you are not measuring up to some standard. However, it's important to ask yourself where this standard came from. Oftentimes, we set unreasonable expectations for ourselves that only serve to perpetuate anxiety, guilt, and shame. While expectations can motivate you to improve yourself and your relationships with others, when you are constantly "shoulding" yourself, you are holding on to guilt and shame that will increase your suffering. Part of you may believe it would be wrong to stop suffering, but do guilt and shame lead to beneficial results for you and others, or are you stuck in a useless cycle of suffering?

One way to overcome self-critical should statements is to replace "I should" with a preference statement, such as "I want to," "I would prefer it if," or "I would like to." These statements are less emotionally charged and don't get you stuck in the same cycle of anxiety, guilt, disappointment, frustration, and shame. For example, instead of berating yourself by saying "I should exercise more," see what it's like to use a preference statement instead: "I would like to exercise more."

In addition, if you find that you are "shoulding" yourself in response to some healthy standard—for example, perhaps you didn't treat someone as kindly as you would have liked to—you can benefit from making reparations and then practicing thoughts that focus on the present and future: "The best thing I can do is commit myself to engaging in better behaviors today and in the future" or "Guilt and shame keep me focused on the past. What do I want to do *today* that makes a difference in someone's life?" You can also work to let go of the guilt and shame by replacing should statements with coping statements, such as "When I acted that way, I did not intend to create the harm I did" or "I was not the only cause of the situation; other people's decisions and actions played a role too."

Combating Negative Automatic Thoughts

To get into the habit of challenging negative automatic thoughts, read through the following example, which takes you through the steps involved in modifying a distressing thought and replacing it with a more useful coping thought. Then practice applying the steps to a negative automatic thought of your own using the blank template.

Negative automatic thought	When I attend the church potluck, I'll say something that will make people laugh at or criticize me.
Has this ever happened? How many times? What was the situation?	This has happened, but not at church. Several times I was laughed at and criticized in a group setting like this. That was in high school.
Evidence that this is (or is not) likely to occur	The people at church tend to be kind with me and with one another. I chose this location for this step because I know that.
Actual chance of this happening (0%–100%)	I think I can be cautious about what I say, and because they are kind, the probability is only about 5%–10%.
How to cope	If someone does laugh or criticize, I can laugh along at myself or I can listen to them and say, "That's a good point."
Coping thought	I don't have to be perfect, and I can handle possible criticism. I just need to stay there and get through it and I'll have succeeded.

Combating Negative Automatic Thoughts

Negative automatic thought	
Has this ever happened? How many times? What was the situation?	
Evidence that this is (or is not) likely to occur	
Actual chance of this happening (0%–100%)	
How to cope	
Coping thought	

Socratic Questioning

Socratic questioning is a method you can use to question the evidence and assumptions behind your negative automatic thoughts. When you take a closer look at the facts, you will often find that there is very little evidence to support your negative automatic thoughts. In fact, you might even find evidence to the contrary. The next time you have a negative automatic thought, write it down in the space provided, then go through the following series of Socratic questions to see whether or not the thought holds up.

Negative automatic thought: _____

_____

Socratic questions to ask yourself:

1. Is this thought realistic?

   _____

   _____

   _____

   _____

2. Am I viewing this situation as black and white when it's really more complicated?

   _____

   _____

   _____

   _____

3. Am I having this thought out of habit, or do the facts support it?

   _____

   _____

   _____

   _____

4. Am I basing my thoughts on facts or on feelings?

_____

_____

_____

_____

5. What evidence do I have to support this thought?

_____

_____

_____

_____

6. What evidence do I have that contradicts this thought?

_____

_____

_____

_____

7. Could I be misinterpreting the evidence?

_____

_____

_____

_____

Thought Log

A thought log is an effective tool to recognize how your thoughts, feelings, and behaviors affect one another. With enough practice, it will become natural to identify these connections, which will give you the power to begin challenging your negative automatic thoughts in real time. Complete the following thought log by describing an experience that caused distress, making sure to provide as much detail as possible in each category.

Thought Log

Date/Time	Situation (Trigger) *What was going on before the distress escalated?*	Negative Automatic Thought *What were you thinking at the time?*	Emotions *What were you feeling at the time?*	Body Sensations *What physical symptoms did you experience?*	Behaviors *How did you respond? Did it make you feel better?*	Examine the Evidence *Does the evidence support the thought?*
		How strongly do you believe this thought (1–10)?				
		What cognitive distortion(s) are present?	How intense were these feelings on a 1–10 scale?			What is a more realistic or helpful thought instead?

Creating an Exposure Hierarchy

In order to take back control of your life, it's important to become more aware of what triggers your distress and then take steps to gradually confront those triggers so that new learning can occur. Whether your trigger is a spider, an attentive audience awaiting your performance, or the sound of explosions, you can learn to stop reacting to that trigger. This process of exposing yourself to a trigger is called *exposure*.

First, consider the specific trigger you have decided to work on, and think of the most anxiety-provoking situation you want to be able to tolerate with regard to that trigger. This won't necessarily be the most terrifying experience you can possibly imagine; it should be something you actually want to accomplish. For example, Simone, a landscape architect, is afraid that a snake will fall off a branch and onto her shoulder as she tags a tree, which is a routine task in her job. Therefore, she might write, "Having a snake on my shoulder." This is a realistic goal that would greatly reduce her anxiety in the field (unlike, say, "Being trapped on an airplane with hundreds of snakes," which is terrifying, but not realistic or necessary for her!). Using the template provided, write down your most anxiety-provoking (but realistic) situation in step 7 of the hierarchy.

Next, focus on a behavior or situation that would elicit some anxiety but that you feel you could readily accomplish if you were to push yourself. Simone might say, "Seeing a snake in a cage is stressful, but I could handle that." Write down this least anxiety-provoking situation as step 1 in your exposure hierarchy.

Now you're ready to list other anxiety-provoking activities that could come in between these two anchoring points. Write down between 5 and 10 different situations, objects, or behaviors that would cause you to experience distress in relation to the trigger. Don't worry about putting these steps in order yet—just brainstorm. Some of the steps could look pretty similar, except for an important detail that would increase the level of anxiety you would feel. Simone may experience differing levels of anxiety if she stands 10 feet away from a caged snake versus just one foot away. Describe each step clearly to show how it is different from the others.

After you've completed your list, rate the distress you would feel in each situation using a scale of 0 to 100, where 0 is no distress and 100 is the worst distress you can imagine. This is known as your subjective units of distress (SUDs) level, and it takes into account any anxiety, physical discomfort, or distressing thoughts you would experience in response to these situations. SUDs ratings reflect how you personally react to each situation, so your ratings are unique to you.

After you have rated each activity, write them down on your exposure hierarchy in order from lowest to highest SUDs. The order of these activities will not necessarily be logical; it is based on your reaction to each situation. After completing your hierarchy, look at your SUDs ratings in the right-hand column. If you find a large increase from one step to the next, see if you can think of a situation or behavior that would get a SUDs rating in between those steps, and insert that step between the other two. This helps you avoid having a large "jump" in difficulty as you work through the hierarchy. The number of steps in an exposure hierarchy can vary, but you should aim for 10 or fewer.

Here is Simone's exposure hierarchy as an example, followed by a blank template for your own use.

Step	Activity	SUDs (0–100)
1	Seeing a snake in a cage from 10 feet away	20
2	Seeing a snake in a cage from 1 foot away	35
3	Seeing a snake outside its cage while someone else holds it	45
4	Seeing a snake outside its cage on the ground, moving around	60
5	Holding a snake in my hands while someone else holds it too	75
6	Having a snake in my lap without touching it	85
7	Having a snake on my shoulder without touching it	95

Exposure Hierarchy

Step	Activity	SUDs (0–100)

Space to Brainstorm Activities

_____

_____

_____

_____

Exposure Guidelines

In order to make exposure sessions effective, here are some helpful guidelines to remember during the process.

Carefully plan and monitor your progress throughout the exposure process. You and your therapist can use your exposure hierarchy to design exposures that will retrain you to stop reacting to the trigger. The goal is to gradually expose yourself to the steps in this hierarchy, working from lower levels to higher levels, until the trigger no longer causes you distress. Although you can start with the lowest activity on your hierarchy, I recommend starting with an activity that has a SUDs level around 40, if possible, for a couple of reasons: (1) Most people can handle getting through situations rated below 40 without much trouble or special training, and (2) activities at this level have a high enough SUDs rating to allow you to clearly feel a decrease in distress when new learning begins to occur. It is very empowering to feel, as you get through the steps, that you are teaching yourself to respond differently and making a lasting change in your brain.

The SUDs rating is also a very helpful measure *during* the exposure process. You can use it to identify and communicate what level of distress you are feeling during the exposure at any given time, as well as how it changes over time. Rate your distress every couple of minutes so you and your therapist are aware of how the exposure is progressing. Although your distress level may go up beyond what you expected when you first rated the situation, *it is essential that you do not leave the situation until your anxiety has decreased*. Otherwise, you are teaching yourself that escape is needed, which will cause you to experience even greater distress the next time you encounter the trigger.

The goal is to stay in the situation until your SUDs rating comes down to *at least half* of the highest rating you experienced in the session. That means if your highest rating is a 50, getting to a 25 is sufficient. You may choose to stay in the exposure longer, but it is never necessary for your SUDs rating to go to 0 since the effects of adrenaline or muscle stiffness may linger for a while.

Continue to work through each step of the hierarchy over multiple exposure trials until you can complete that step with confidence and little to no distress. Make sure you plan in advance to give yourself *multiple* opportunities to practice each step in the hierarchy. Exposures must be done repeatedly for you to learn most effectively. Repeated exposures help your brain build new neural circuits that no longer associate the trigger with distress. Each time you repeat the exposure, you will likely find that the particular step becomes easier.

Make sure you are properly and directly experiencing the trigger. It's important that you don't distract yourself from the feared situation or object during the exposure. You need to allow yourself to fully experience the trigger—directly looking at, listening to, and sometimes even feeling or smelling it—so you can learn not to associate it with any danger. When you feel your heart pound or your muscles tense up, know that the exposure is going well. One of my clients, who was working to overcome his fear of heights, told me during his exposure session that he wanted to look over the ledge of the top floor of the parking garage. He was really going for the whole experience.

Use relaxation skills as needed. Relaxation skills—like deep breathing and muscle relaxation—will help you handle the stress of the exposure. However, it's unlikely you will be able to relax yourself completely, given that you will naturally experience the fight, flight, or freeze response in reaction to this trigger. In addition, you *want* to remain somewhat activated so your brain can generate new neural connections. That means that until your brain learns to respond differently, you will experience distress each time you encounter the trigger. Your therapist can coach you through the process of using relaxation skills to keep your distress at a manageable level so you can stay in the situation.

Consider using imaginal exposure. If you're having difficulty trying an actual step in your hierarchy, you can begin by *imagining* yourself in the situation instead. This process is known as *imaginal exposure*. For example, Justin was so worried about doing exposures with an actual dog that he first needed to imagine himself being in the presence of a dog until he reduced his distress enough to try real-life exposures. If you're working with a therapist, they may guide you through this process by describing the imagined situation in great detail. You can also do imaginal exposure by simply picturing yourself in the anxiety-provoking situation, taking care to imagine specific sights, sounds, and smells you might encounter. When you can successfully imagine situations without much distress, you are building new neural connections in your brain.

In some cases, imaginal exposure is the only way to do exposure. For example, I have used imaginal exposure when working with Gulf War veterans who were trying to cope with nightmares of combat experiences and with clients who had fears I couldn't recreate in session, like becoming pregnant, losing a child to cancer, or asking the boss for a raise. There are also some situations where real-life exposure would not be ethical (e.g., asking a pharmacist with a fear of dispensing the wrong medicine to do so). Sometimes I'll record an exposure script that the client can listen to repeatedly. Although imaginal exposure can be an effective treatment that builds confidence and reduces distress, when possible, the best treatment still involves *directly* experiencing the trigger in a safe environment.

Carefully monitor and manage your thoughts during the exposure session. Do not unnecessarily increase your distress by engaging in thoughts that are self-defeating ("I'll never be able to do this!") or catastrophizing ("I'm going to lose control of the car and get in an accident") because they increase your SUDs level rather than helping decrease it. When you engage in these thoughts, you are not teaching yourself that the situation is safe; you are doing just the opposite. Stay focused on what is happening and what you are experiencing *in the moment*, rather than anticipating what could possibly occur. Here are some general coping thoughts that will be useful during exposure:

- "Keep breathing deeply. This won't last long."

- "I expect my distress to rise, but I can manage it."

- "Release the tension; just relax my muscles as much as possible."

- "This won't last too long. If I wait, my brain will learn."

- "I'm taking control by teaching myself that there is nothing to fear."

- "I don't like this, but I can handle it."

- "When I get through this, I won't always react this way."

- "Stay focused on this situation. This is all I have to deal with right now."

Mindfulness can help you fully experience and benefit from exposure. When you are mindful during exposures, you notice and describe how your body is reacting: "My heart is pounding harder. I'm getting slightly nauseous." Be curious, observant, and accepting of what you are experiencing, rather than trying to fight or judge the process. Don't expect to stay in control of your bodily responses; it is not your goal to keep the body from reacting. Let your body do whatever it does and just wait. Remember that although your body's fight, flight, freeze reactions make sense in a dangerous situation, this situation is safe. By staying in the exposure, you are teaching yourself that it is not necessary to react this way in response to the trigger. Notice also when you feel a decrease in the level of activation you are feeling: "I'm finding it easier to breathe deeply. I'm starting to recognize this isn't such a big deal."

Be aware of the danger of safety-seeking behaviors. Safety-seeking behaviors are actions you engage in to help you get through a difficult situation but that prevent you from learning. For example, if you bring a bottle of tranquilizing medication with you to the mall so you can take a pill in case you feel overwhelmed, having that bottle of medicine (even if you don't take any) may prevent you from learning that the situation is safe. You are learning to go to the mall *with the bottle of medication*, not to reduce the fear of going to the mall.

Other examples include having a friend or family member with you (or on the phone with you) during the anxiety-provoking experience, carrying a lucky charm or object that helps you feel safe, always sitting near the door, or wearing sunglasses or avoiding eye contact with others. Safety-seeking behaviors provide a temporary crutch instead of changing how you respond to the trigger, so it's important that you do not resort to these behaviors during exposure.

Response prevention may be necessary. If you have learned certain responses, rituals, or checking behaviors to cope with your fears, worries, or distress, you need to eliminate these from exposure sessions. For example, Lorraine was able to drive on busy streets as long as she held her hands in a certain position on the steering wheel; driving with one hand, even for a moment, felt unsafe. If you have learned to perform a particular response in order to feel safe, and you use that in exposure, it only strengthens your assumption that the trigger is dangerous. Not performing the response is the only way you can retrain your brain. When you prohibit the use of a specific ritual or response during exposure, it's called *exposure with response prevention*. This kind of exposure is often used to effectively treat obsessive compulsive disorder (OCD), such as when a person is asked not to use hand sanitizer every time they touch money.

Avoid medications that can interfere with exposure. Medications such as benzodiazepines can interfere with exposure because they inhibit (or sedate) neurons in various parts of the body, including the amygdala, which prevents it from being activated. While this can block the stress response (which is often why people take benzodiazepines), it also prevents your brain from making any new neural connections. In other words, no learning occurs. You are likely to get through the exposure session with less distress, but the exposure will not be effective in changing how you respond to the trigger.

Avoid seeking reassurance. The goal of exposure is to teach you that you are safe in the situation, so it is counterproductive to repeatedly seek reassurance when you are in the presence of the trigger. It undermines all the hard work you are doing. If someone is constantly reassuring you during the exposure, what will you do when you encounter the trigger on your own? What you need is not for someone to tell you that you're safe but, rather, for them to tell you that you can handle what you are going through. For example, if during the exposure you ask, "The dog won't get too close?" your therapist might say, "We agreed the dog wouldn't touch you this time, but it could come close. You just handle whatever comes." I should also note that the need for reassurance is often connected to a need to have certainty, and we all need to learn to cope with the uncertainty of life instead of pretending we can know how everything will turn out.

You are allowed to complain. As you are going through the exposure process, you can verbalize how much you hate it or how hard it is. You do not have to pretend that it is easy or that you have no discomfort. You are deliberately allowing yourself to experience distressful—and sometimes overwhelming—emotions and sensations, and even though they are not dangerous, you are enduring a dreadful situation. I find that I need to acknowledge to my clients that exposure is definitely difficult and unpleasant and that they are doing a great job sticking with it. I remind them that courage is not the absence of fear; it is acting in the face of fear. Remember that no emotion lasts forever. It will eventually pass if you endure it.

Resist any temptation to leave the presence of the trigger until your distress goes down. If you end the exposure while you are still feeling a strong stress response, it reinforces the idea that escape is the right response and keeps you from learning that the situation is safe. You need to experience a reduction in distress *while still in the presence of the trigger* in order for learning to occur. Wait for your discomfort to decrease, remembering that this is an opportunity to put yourself in the driver's seat.

If you do need to leave the exposure, commit yourself to coming back and getting through the situation. It is normal to have a setback or two. You still have the opportunity to learn. Remember, the goal is not just about overcoming distress in this specific moment. You are staying in the situation to make long-lasting changes in your neural circuitry that will allow you to achieve your goals.

Work toward being independent in exposure situations. The goal of exposure is to help you become comfortable with the trigger. This means that, ultimately, you will need to handle exposure situations on your own, without the help of a therapist, family member, or friend. (An exception would be if the trigger itself involves being in a situation with someone else, like when my client's goal was to fly on a plane to the Virgin Islands with his new wife on their honeymoon.)

Therefore, you should plan to get through certain exposure steps by yourself, which means you will need to do homework assignments between therapy sessions. My clients have accomplished a variety of exposures without my being there, including driving independently, going to movies with friends, interviewing for jobs, and attending drag shows in a bar. Make plans to carry out exposures by yourself out in the real world so you can follow your own goals.

When you complete each step in the exposure hierarchy, take some time to consider what you learned. After you get through an exposure experience, ask yourself if your worries came true and, if so, how you handled them. Look for changes in how you responded, and consider what you learned about yourself. What did you do that worked? What would change next time? What surprised you about the experience? Your therapist can also provide feedback on what you did well and what strategies you can use to improve next time.

Reward yourself. Doing exposure is hard work, so you should celebrate your achievements along the way. When you complete a step in your exposure hierarchy, congratulate yourself and treat yourself to something special. You deserve it!

Build on your success. Once you successfully complete the last step on your exposure hierarchy—the one with highest SUDs rating—you are typically ready to work on the life goal you set for yourself. Since you have made changes to the way your brain and body react, you should find that your trigger no longer blocks you from achieving this goal. After seeing how exposure helps you achieve this specific goal, you can choose another goal to work toward, using exposure to keep your worry, distress, or anxiety from blocking you from living the life you want to live.

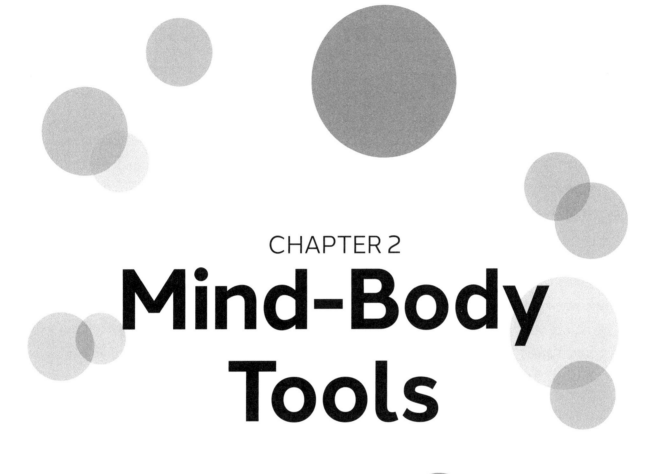

CHAPTER 2
Mind-Body Tools

Focusing on Sensations: Awareness of the Felt Sense

There is no right or wrong approach to this focusing exercise; it is a process piece. Whatever you create will be right and appropriate.

On the body map, color in the areas where you most often experience discomfort, tension, tightness, or pain. Color in the areas where you are presently experiencing discomfort, tension, tightness, or pain. Use those colors and the type of strokes that you feel best represent the particular body sensation that you are experiencing in each area of the body. For example, if you feel jittery and nervous in the stomach, you might pick a bright color and draw something that represents electricity in the stomach area. If you feel flighty and not really present, you might choose a light color and draw wispy lines wherever that sensation is noted.

Once you have completed the body map, use your nondominant hand to label the colored areas with emotion word(s). Finally, on the next page and with your dominant hand, write down any observations you have about your body map.

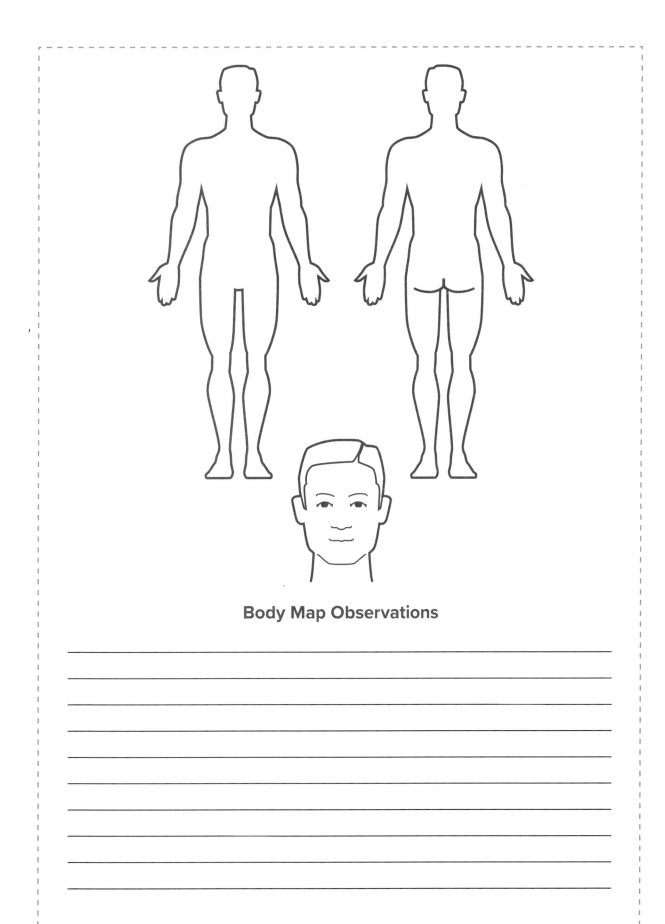

Body Map Observations

_____

_____

_____

_____

_____

_____

_____

_____

_____

_____

Body Scan Body Map:
Awareness of the Felt Sense

Part One

Allow yourself to be comfortable . . . either lying down or sitting up with your back, neck, and spine fully supported. Knowing that you will not be interrupted for the next little while, begin by gently closing your eyes. Now begin to bring your attention to your breath—the direct experience of your breath—however it is . . . and however it changes. Allow yourself to softly focus your awareness on to the breath that is arising right now . . . the in-breath and the out-breath . . . the rising and the falling. If you can, try to follow one full cycle of the breath from the beginning of the in-breath and through its entirety the beginning of the out-breath and through its entirety. Allow yourself the time and the space to be in direct contact with the breath throughout one entire cycle.

Now, starting at the crown of your head, gently guide your focus down your entire body, noticing and then noting any and all sensations. Notice any tension, tightness, and any pressure; notice any sensations of warmth, coolness, pain, or areas of numbness, feelings of softness or pleasure and relaxation. Just note what is. Continue to scan, noticing any other identifiable sensations. Allow yourself to label them, and then gently bring your attention back to the direct experience of the sensations themselves. When you've completed the journey through the entire body, bring your attention back to the room.

Using the following body map, color in all areas of the body that were calling to you—any signals of pain, pressure, tension, tightness, calm, relaxation, etc. Use those colors and the type of strokes that you feel best represent the particular body sensation that you are experiencing in each area of the body. For example, if you feel jittery and nervous in the stomach, you might pick a bright color and draw something that represents electricity in the stomach area. If you feel flighty and not really present, you might choose a light color and draw wispy lines wherever that sensation is noted.

Part Two

Choose the area that was signaling the loudest—the one with the strongest sensations of pain, tension, or tightness. In the outline below, mark that body area.

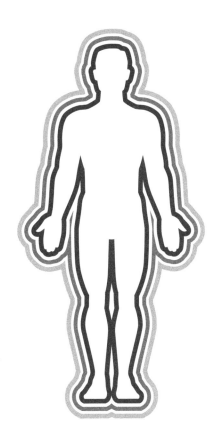

Part Three

In the following table, write out a dialogue between you and that body part. You will be using both hands, therefore both hemispheres of your brain. Write out the following questions with your dominant hand, and then answer the questions using your nondominant hand:

- What are you?

- How are feeling?

- How long have you been feeling bad?

- What has you feeling like that?

- Is there something you want or need from me? Is there something I can do to help you?

- Is there something I need to know from you?

- Is it okay to stop now?

- Should I check in again?

Dominant Hand Questions	Nondominant Hand Answers

Grounded Breath and Centering

Grounding is the act of connecting to the earth beneath you and feeling the steadiness of its support. Centering is the act of orienting your awareness inward, toward your experience of you. The following practice supports both grounding and centering, which are foundational to the development of interoceptive awareness.

To begin, make sure you are settled into your safe place. Take a moment to scan your location, noticing the doors, windows, or landscape and addressing anything that might interfere with your practice. Find a comfortable seat, and support your legs and back as needed so you feel well supported by the earth below you. This is the grounding component of the practice. Your body is well grounded and you are safe in this space, in this moment.

Next, you will move into the centering component of the practice. Place one hand on your stomach and one hand over your heart as you focus on breathing in and out. Breathe using your typical breathing pattern for three breaths, then begin to slowly extend the inhalation and exhalation by counting—inhale 1, 2, 3, 4 . . . exhale 1, 2, 3, 4. Inhale 1, 2, 3, 4 . . . exhale 1, 2, 3, 4. Continue to take these deeper and longer breaths.

As you breathe deeply in and out, notice your hands as they move with your chest and your stomach. You might notice that as you inhale, your chest rises and your stomach expands, and as you exhale, your stomach contracts and your chest falls. Breathe here and simply notice.

Next, bring your awareness to your rib cage. You might feel your rib cage expanding with each inhalation and moving back to its neutral shape with each exhalation. Breathe here, noting your rib cage movement. Remember here to allow for the possibility that it may be difficult to notice sensations or that you might not notice anything. You are simply being with your breath and being aware.

Next, notice your nose and your nostrils. Notice the temperature of the cool air moving in and the warm air moving out. See if you notice the air moving down through your windpipe, into your bronchial tubes, and then into your lungs. Maybe open up to the possibility of noticing the air move into your lungs and back out. Breathe here and notice.

Continue breathing with a hand on your heart, and turn even deeper inward toward your heart. Perhaps you can feel a thump-thump of your heart beating with your hand, through the breath as you breathe, maybe in your chest. Remember here to allow for the possibility that it may be difficult to notice sensations or that you might not notice anything. You are simply being with your heart and noticing.

As you notice your breath and your heartbeat, perhaps say to yourself, *I can be aware of and connected to my body*. Breathe and repeat this statement to yourself: *I can be aware of and connected to my body*.

It can also be nice to add a message to your heart and your body, like *I am taking time to know you, breath* or *I am taking time to know you, heart*. Try different self-statements and see which ones align best with your embodied experience. Take as much time as you'd like there breathing, connecting to your heart.

When you are finished, use the space here, or write in a journal, to record what you noticed, including any inner and outer sensations, feelings, and thoughts.

_____

_____

_____

_____

_____

_____

_____

_____

Sensate Focus for Distress

This practice adds to your growing set of resources as an additional tool to shift your current state back into the window of tolerance. It helps you focus on your senses and orients you away from escalating thoughts and feelings. Use this practice when the *Grounded Breath and Centering* practice is insufficient, or when you are feeling very escalated and triggered.

Before you start, think of something that really helps you feel grounded and that you know with certainty to be true, such as *I love my dog*, *The sun always shines behind the clouds*, *Right now, I can breathe and that matters*, or *I am worth the effort*. For this to work, the statement must be something that you 100 percent believe to be true.

My one positive, grounding thing that I know to be true is:

_____

_____

Once you have developed your grounding statement, make sure that your body is well grounded. Find a seat and press your feet into the floor and your sitting bones into your seat.

Then orient toward your breath, placing your hands on your belly to help you slow your breath, and take three cycles of a calming breath:

Breathe in 1, 2, 3, 4 . . . and out 1, 2, 3, 4, 5.

Breathe in 1, 2, 3, 4 . . . and out 1, 2, 3, 4, 5.

Breathe in 1, 2, 3, 4 . . . and out 1, 2, 3, 4, 5.

Once you are done with three breath cycles, continue by tuning into your senses:

Name five things you can see (pause).

Name four things you can hear (pause).

Name three things you can touch (pause).

Name two things you can smell (pause).

Say your one grounding, positive statement that you know to be true: "_____."

Pendulation

This pendulation practice is a wonderful resource for managing difficult memories, sensations, emotions, or reactions as they show up. The next time these difficult experiences arise, follow these steps.

Pause and find your breath. Sit or lie down in a way that feels grounded and well supported. Then bring your awareness to your body and notice where you feel the difficult memories, sensations, emotions, or reactions the strongest. Notice the intensity, size, and boundaries of this location in your body. Where does it end? Where are its edges? Then breathe gently and intentionally—breathing in for 1, 2, 3, 4 . . . and out for 1, 2, 3, 4, 5—as you notice this area of your body. Spend about four breath cycles here.

Now, scan your body and find a spot that feels neutral. It might be a toe, your hands, or the crown of your head. If you don't think you have a neutral spot, consider the area right outside of your body, whether it's one inch around your body, six inches around your body, a foot around your body, or two feet around your body. Notice where you begin to feel a neutral space. Bring your awareness to this neutral space, wherever it is. Breathe here for about four breath cycles— breathing in for 1, 2, 3, 4 . . . and out for 1, 2, 3, 4, 5.

Next, move back to the place where you felt the difficult memories, sensations, emotions, or reactions the strongest. Breathe here for about four breath cycles, breathing in for 1, 2, 3, 4 . . . and out for 1, 2, 3, 4, 5. Then pendulate back to your neutral space. Breathe here for about four breath cycles, breathing in for 1, 2, 3, 4 . . . and out for 1, 2, 3, 4, 5. Do this a few times, pendulating from one spot to the other.

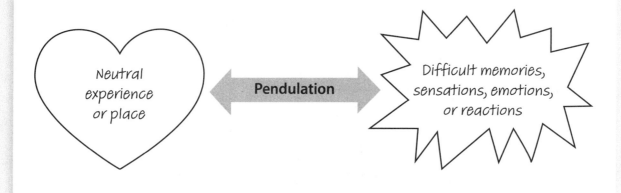

Last, bring your awareness to the place in your body where you felt these memories, sensations, emotions, or reactions most strongly and *simultaneously* hold an awareness of the neutral place in your body. Breathe while you hold this dual awareness of both places for about four breath cycles, breathing in 1, 2, 3, 4 . . . and out 1, 2, 3, 4, 5.

In a journal or in the space below, write what you noticed during this practice. You can describe the place where you felt memories, sensations, emotions, or reactions the strongest; describe your neutral place; reflect on the process of pendulating itself; or describe what it was like to hold both places within your awareness.

_____

_____

_____

_____

_____

_____

_____

_____

Describing a Sensation

The next time you are having a noteworthy sensation, pause and notice. Perhaps you feel a little triggered or the sensation is connected to a big feeling or trauma memory. Notice where in your body you feel the sensation most intensely. Using the qualities listed in the following table, describe what you feel and experience. Begin with the fundamental characteristics that align with what you are experiencing, such as the size, shape, solidity, color, smell, taste, and sound of this sensation. Next, explore its secondary qualities, including its organization, pain, and movement. Finally, notice the qualities associated with body states, including its intensity and how this affects your breath, muscles, and consciousness.

Qualities of Sensations You Might Notice

Fundamental Qualities			
Size: tiny, small, medium, large, gigantic, all-encompassing, bloated, puffy	Shape: round, square, triangular, oval, octagonal, even, uneven, thick, thin, tall, short	Solidity: dense, firm, soft, squishy, formable, misty, ethereal, airy, bubbly, empty, flaccid	Temperature: boiling, scalding, scorching, hot, warm, balmy, cold, frozen, chilly, cool
Color: colorless, flushed, colorful, faded, bright, blue, gold	Smell: fruity, flowery, spicy, putrid, burned	Taste: spicy, mild, sweet, sour, salty, savory, bitter, tart, acidic	Sound: high, deep, rich, low, loud, quiet, pulsating, near, far
Humidity: clammy, fluid, dripping, damp, moist, sweaty, slimy, dry, soggy, soaked, dank, teeming	Weight: heavy, light, bulky, pressure, deadweight, lightweight, weightless, top heavy, unbalanced, leaden	Sharpness: stabbing, shooting, sharp, tingly, stinging, prickly, smooth, faint, penetrating	Texture: fuzzy, smooth, rough, goose bumps, itchy, prickly, tickly, gritty, lumpy, grainy, bristly, slimy, velvety

Secondary Sensation Qualities			
Pain: achy, burning, dull, electric, pins and needles, tingly, weak, strong, persistent, enduring, acute, throbbing, cramping, stabbing, sharp, shooting	Stability: static, changing, waving, pulsing, brief, enduring, steady, jerky, weak, strong, balanced, sturdy, firm, permanent, lasting	Organization: knotted, jumbly, tight, loose, ordered, concentrated, regular, irregular, systematic, unsystematic	Motion: still, fast, slow, blocked, expanding, contracting, radiating, drawing in, moving, churning, buzzy, constricted, fluttery, floaty, vibrating, pushing, pulling
Qualities Associated with Body States			
Intensity: mild, subtle, strong, severe, fierce, violent, extreme, energized, weak, strong, powerful, concentrated, acute, harsh, forceful, vigorous	Breath: congested, airy, smooth, choppy, constricted, suffocating, weak, strong, wheezy, gasping, gentle, short, extended	Muscle state: clenched, tense, relaxed, constricted, paralyzed, quivery, sore, stiff, tight, trembling, twitchy, weak, strong	Conscious state: dizzy, nauseous, numb, paralyzed, quaking, shivery, shuddering, trembling, floaty, wobbly

Fundamental qualities that I notice:

_____

_____

_____

_____

Secondary qualities that I notice:

_____

_____

_____

_____

Qualities associated with body states that I notice:

_____

_____

_____

_____

Overall reflections:

_____

_____

_____

_____

_____

_____

_____

_____

Physical and Energetic Boundaries Meditation

Consider doing this meditation when you feel like you have lost track of your physical and energetic boundaries, or when you feel like you have not been given enough space.

To begin, find a comfortable seated position in a safe and private location. Make sure you have a few feet on all sides of you so you have a sense of space. Sit with your feet and sitting bones grounded, engage your core, lift through your spine, and soften your shoulders, jaw, and eyes. Then orient your awareness to your breath and breathe three to five gentle breath cycles.

As you are ready, orient your awareness inside of you—to the space contained by the boundary of your skin. Consider your bones, your muscles, your cardiovascular system, your organs, and all the amazing parts of your body. You might send the beautiful inside of you a warm energy of loving-kindness. You might add some compassion for all the work your body does for you inside, like digesting food and helping you heal and recover. Consider that this energy—the energy that is you—is powerful.

Now, move your awareness to the space outside of your skin, perhaps two to four inches outside of your body. See if you can get a sense of that space and the energy that radiates from you. What would it be like if someone reached into that space? Even if your eyes were closed, do you think you might notice? What would you notice, sense, or feel? Consider that this space is still you. You can sense it, and it is filled with warmth and energy.

Now, extend your awareness to the space about 12 inches away from your body. You might sense it as a sphere or layer of energy around you. With your eyes closed or softened, see if you can get a sense of that space. Consider that this space is still energetically you. What if someone reached into this space. What would you notice or feel?

Then, become aware of an even larger space radiating about two feet around you, maybe a little more. Consider that this space is still energetically you or may be yours. For a moment, open your eyes and consider this space. Then reach out your arms, as they are probably just a little over two feet on each side. Reach your arms out wide, then overhead. Move them around to get a good sense of this energetic boundary around you. As you are ready, settle in and close or soften your eyes. What would it be like if someone reached into this space? What might you notice, sense, or feel? Consider that this is still energetically your space.

As you bring this meditation to a close, slowly bring your awareness in through the two-foot layer, the one-foot layer, and the two-to-four-inch layer. Bring your awareness to your skin and then all the way into your heart. Gently breathe, aware of your lungs and your heart as you breathe. If you'd like, place your hands on your heart and say, *This is my physical body*. With a sense of your energetic space, you might say, *This is my energetic space* and *I have boundaries*. If you'd like, take out a journal and note anything you noticed that you'd like to process further.

Note that you can informally continue the practice as you go through your day. Notice the effect others might have as they move in and out of your physical and energetic space. Consider that resting might mean having time when no one is in that space. Maybe you remember your boundaries.

Relaxing Rest

This exercise facilitates opening your body to a deep level of relaxation by not "doing anything." To fully rest in the body is not that easy. Usually we think we need to "do something," and "be productive," and we don't learn to trust the body. The body needs space and time to "talk" to you. Learning to truly relax and rest is to tune into the body on a deep level, rather than a thinking level.

1. Lay down on your back. Make sure you are on a comfortable, supportive surface.

2. Have your knees bent, feet flat on the ground.

3. Rest your body completely into the ground. You can use a pillow underneath your knees, if you need more support under your legs. The same goes for the rest of your body—if you need more pillow support, you can accommodate your body.

4. Rest your arms alongside your body or across the lower belly.

5. Connect with your breath, and slow the breath down.

6. Melt the body into the floor. Notice the tensions in the body and see if you can melt them by placing the breath in the area you are working with.

7. Allow the weight and tensions to melt away.

8. See if you can relax the hot spots of the body (jaw, shoulders, belly, chest and legs).

9. Melt and see the resting quality coming forth.

10. Imagine a "lazy" animal, such a relaxing lion or a dog, and see yourself melting just as they do.

11. Let go of any worry and thinking. If you are noticing the thinking, come back to the breath.

12. Examine the "doing" parts coming up. When you notice that, respond by melting the body again.

13. Allow yourself to be alert while you relax. If you get sleepy you can notice this and focus again on the back of your body and melting the body into the ground.

14. Pay attention to how your body lets go and aligns naturally. Allow yourself to simply be here in your body without a goal.

Simple Earth Mindfulness

This exercise was designed after working with a client who said she was tightly bound and trapped inside. She could not trust anyone or open up to anyone. She loved being in nature, loved the Earth, but could not trust people. When it is challenging to trust others, it can be helpful to work with trusting nature. This meditation reminds you to trust the Earth and connects you again with your own innate goodness.

1. Lie on the floor. (This can also be done reclining.)

2. Consider the ground beneath the body.

3. Conceptualize how the ground is holding you up. Think "the Earth is always there for me" or any other positive phrase that suits you.

4. The heaviness you feel is gravity gently pulling you to, and holding you on, the Earth.

5. Focus your senses on the back of your lungs.

6. Let yourself breathe into the back of your lungs.

7. Imagine the Earth is meeting you here.

8. Then let the Earth breathe with you. Imagine the Earth is a giant lung breathing into your lungs, rejuvenating you.

9. The Earth is kind, gentle, and taking her time to breathe with you and into you.

10. Let the exchange between you and the Earth happen; allow your breathing to interact with the Earth's.

11. Notice how you slow down, how your breath expands, how the belly softens.

12. Notice how your mind slows and how your sense of well-being returns.

13. Track your experience.

Reflection

I trust the Earth to _____.

I trust my body to _____.

Identifying Body Themes

If your body could talk, what would it say? This exercise moves you systematically through the different areas of the body and shows you what answers you get. This exercise helps identify the themes of your body that you already know about, in addition to the themes that are hidden. By tuning into the body in a mindful way, you can deepen the answers and insights you will get.

Do an initial pass-through by regularly asking yourself, "If my body could talk, what would it say?" in your ordinary state of mind. Then switch into a state of mindfulness by slowing down, closing your eyes, and asking the question again. There might be a phrase, an image, or a word that comes up.

Body Area	If my body could talk, what would it say? *Ordinary state: What I know now.*	If my body could talk, what would it say? *Mindful state: What I know from the inside out.*
Front of body		
Back of body		
Head		
Neck		
Shoulders: Back of shoulders		

Body Area	If my body could talk, what would it say? *Ordinary state: What I know now.*	If my body could talk, what would it say? *Mindful state: What I know from the inside out.*
Shoulders: Top of shoulders, joints		
Front of chest		
Heart area or center		
Mid-back		
Lower back		
Solar plexus		
Belly		
Lower abdomen		
Pelvis		
Upper thighs		

Body Area	If my body could talk, what would it say? *Ordinary state: What I know now.*	If my body could talk, what would it say? *Mindful state: What I know from the inside out.*
Lower legs		
Knees		
Ankles		
Feet		
Soles of feet		
Upper arms		
Elbows		
Forearms		
Wrists		
Hands		

Body Area	If my body could talk, what would it say? *Ordinary state: What I know now.*	If my body could talk, what would it say? *Mindful state: What I know from the inside out.*
Inner palms		
Fingers		
Front of neck		
Whole face		
Mouth		
Around the eyes		
Ears		
Front of skull		
Back of skull		
Top of the head		

Somatic Beliefs of Self

We have different bodies. This includes our skeletal, muscular, and fascia bodies, as well as our emotional, thinking and spiritual bodies. The way we move, hold our postures, and use our muscles and faces can reflect our emotional and thinking life. There is a connection between how we feel and think and how we are; this presents in our bodies. This exercise helps you identify these beliefs and the ways in which they show up in the body.

Use the following body graph to chart your body areas and associated beliefs.

- Start with the physical body and note what you are sensing in the body. You can write on the body graph or circle the areas you feel and sense.

- Now focus on the emotional beliefs that stem from the physical experience of the body, such as "My tense shoulders feel like I am carrying rocks and burdens for my family."

- Then move to the thinking body. This is what you believe about the physical and emotional experience. For example, "I carry these rocks because I feel responsible for what happened to my family. It's my fault."

- Pick two to three core beliefs that are most familiar and govern your daily experience. Reflect on these beliefs and look for how your body and your mind are interconnected.

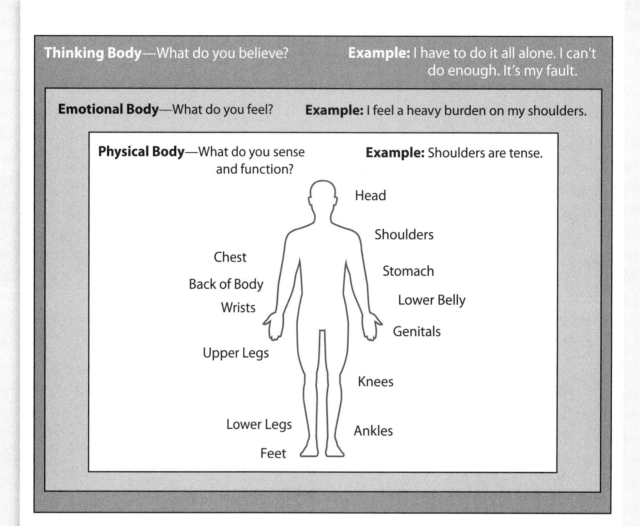

Thinking Body—What do you believe?   **Example:** I have to do it all alone. I can't do enough. It's my fault.

Emotional Body—What do you feel?   **Example:** I feel a heavy burden on my shoulders.

Physical Body—What do you sense and function?   **Example:** Shoulders are tense.

Head
Shoulders
Chest
Stomach
Back of Body
Lower Belly
Wrists
Genitals
Upper Legs
Knees
Lower Legs
Ankles
Feet

My core beliefs are:

1. _____

2. _____

3. _____

Personal Space in Relation

This exercise brings awareness to your body boundary in relation to how you position yourself to another.

Start by visualizing a person whom you have an easy time with, and imagine sitting across from them. How close or far would you sit from them? What is the optimum distance? How do you know that this is the optimum space between you?

Now imagine a person you have a more difficult time with. Where is the optimum space between you? Is it easy to set that boundary? Difficult? What makes it difficult? What is in the way?

Draw your ideal relationship distance. The box is the relationship you are in. Where do you position yourself in relation to the other person?

What would you need to set this boundary?

_____

_____

_____

What stands in the way of setting the boundary?

_____

_____

_____

What can help you in learning to set the boundary?

_____

_____

_____

Take a look at the drawing; sense into this new boundary you just set. What do you notice in your body? What words go with the experience you are having right now?

_____

_____

_____

Journal about the boundaries you know have been invaded and not treated with respect. Write down some key moments that you remember. What do these key moments have in common?

_____

_____

_____

_____

_____

_____

_____

_____

_____

_____

_____

_____

_____

Write down ONE aspect you can change regarding your boundary setting. A word? A sentence you want to say to yourself inside? A feeling in the body you want to remember and come back to?

Remember, learning to set boundaries starts with a clear and concise statement of what you are not willing to do or be anymore.

I will change my boundaries by saying/doing:

_____

_____

_____

I will take a stand for my boundary with this statement:

_____

_____

_____

CHAPTER 3

Somatic Movement Tools

Progressive Muscle Relaxation

Progressive muscle relaxation is a practice that helps you notice any tension you are holding in your body and then guides you through a gentle practice of releasing it. You can do this practice after a difficult therapy session, whenever you feel tense, to assess if you are holding tension, or when trying to fall asleep. If you'd like, it can be helpful to create a recording of this practice on your phone so you can relax and listen to your own voice taking you through the steps. This can also help develop your calm and supportive inner voice.

To begin, find a place where you feel safe and won't be interrupted. You can either lie down or sit in a chair. If you are feeling very unsafe, orient yourself near a wall and face the entrance to the room. Scan the room, and only when you are ready, soften or close your eyes. Allow your breath to move naturally in and out as you briefly scan your whole body from your head to your toes. In a gentle and curious manner, you might ask yourself, *Am I holding tension or stress?* as you scan your body. Breathe gently, allowing the question to orient you toward your body and any tension you may have.

Now, bring your awareness to your feet. Curl your toes and contract the muscles in your feet, scrunching them up as if you can make them smaller than they are. Hold this for 1, 2, 3, 4, 5 . . . then release your feet, letting go of any tension. Breathe here for three to five breath cycles, inhaling and exhaling. With each exhale, release a little more tension in your feet. Maybe you even think to yourself, *It's okay to let go.*

Next, engage your ankles by flexing your feet. Let your calves engage too, tensing everything from your knees down. If your toes want to join in, let them. Keep breathing while you engage your ankles, calves, and shins. Hold this tension for 1, 2, 3, 4, 5 . . . then release your ankles, calves, and shins, letting the tension go. Breathe here for three to five deep breath cycles, inhaling and exhaling. Notice the difference between holding tension and letting go. With every exhale, see if you can let go a little more. There is no pressure to let go. You can simply give your body permission to let go if it would like.

Now, engage your entire legs, from your feet through your glutes, drawing your muscles toward your bones. Keep breathing and tensing your legs and hips. Hold this tension for 1, 2, 3, 4, 5 . . . then release your legs and hips, letting the tension go. Breathe here for three to five deep breath cycles, inhaling and exhaling. Notice the difference between holding tension and letting go. With every exhale, see if you can let go a little more. You might offer your legs permission to let go, saying softly to yourself, *It's okay to let go*.

Bring your awareness to your core. Engage the muscles in your belly and back into a whole-core contraction. It's okay if your legs, shoulders, and even jaw also engage. But your focus is on your core. Draw everything into the center of yourself. Hold this tension for 1, 2, 3, 4, 5 . . . then release your core. Soften your body and breathe. Take five breath cycles here, letting each inhale lift your belly and each exhale lower your belly. Pause here and notice the difference between tension and letting go.

Next, bring your awareness to your shoulders, arms, and hands. Scrunch your shoulders up to your ears, clench your hands into fists, and engage your biceps by bending your elbows and upper arms toward your body. Keep breathing as you squeeze your hands, arms, and shoulders. Hold this tension for 1, 2, 3, 4, 5 . . . then release your shoulders, arms, and hands. Take five breath cycles here, letting your arms and hands rest on the floor or on your thighs, and allowing your shoulders to soften and move away from your ears.

Last, scrunch your face into itself. Close your eyes really tight, furrow your forehead, squeeze your jaw shut, purse your lips, and scrunch your cheeks. Keep breathing as you hold this tension for 1, 2, 3, 4, 5 . . . then release as you soften your jaw, mouth, eyes, cheeks, and forehead. Take 10 deep breath cycles, noticing how your body feels now. On every exhale, think of the word *release*.

When you are finished, you may want to journal about what you noticed. Did you notice any tension in certain areas of the body? Was it easier or more difficult to tense versus release in certain areas? Were there areas in which it was difficult to feel at all? What about the practice felt most helpful? How do you feel after practicing the first time, a few times, many times?

Exploring Directions in Movement

Find a seated position in a safe and comfortable place where you can practice exploring different forms of movement. This can be in a chair or well supported on the floor. You will want to be able to move your belly, shoulders, and arms freely. Here you will be practicing four simple movements that involve your core, hands, and breath. Begin with your hands resting on your thighs.

> **Up:** Press into your sitting bones, engage your belly, and extend through your spine. As you breathe in, lift your hands in front of you to shoulder height, your palms facing down with your elbows somewhat extended and slightly bent.
>
> **Out:** Now, extend your wrists so your palms are facing forward and away from you. On your exhale, push your hands away extending fully through your elbows.
>
> **In:** Then, turn your palms toward you, and slightly overlap your hands so there is a sense of holding. On your inhale, bend your elbows and draw your soft, inward-turning hands toward your heart.
>
> **Down:** On your exhale, press your hands down, allowing your elbows to extend and your hands to separate and move down to the sides of your body.

Repeat this series of movements for several sets: inhaling up, exhaling out, inhaling in, and exhaling down. As you do this, notice what each direction feels like. Which direction feels most aligned with you? Which one is most uncomfortable? Do any make you feel agitated or upset? Do any make you feel a sense of calm or groundedness? There are no right or wrong answers, just notice. If you do this practice while you are feeling different emotions, see if you notice changes in how you experience the different directions.

Moving Through and Honoring Your Body

It can be difficult to work through traumatic experiences when your body is primed to mobilize into a state of fight or flight, immobilize into a state of shutdown, or freeze into a state of attentive immobility. When this happens, movement and stillness that you generate while being connected to yourself and your body can be regulating. In fact, body and movement-oriented interventions can be helpful in trauma recovery. Therefore, while the following embodiment practice is not a trauma-processing practice per se, it can help you honor your body's resilience and strength as you move through the experience of listing your traumas.

This practice has two phases: (1) move through and (2) rest and honor. Note, if you feel you are moving out of your window of tolerance at any point, take a break and engage in a calming or grounding practice before moving forward.

Moving Through

Find a place where you have some privacy and space to move (a circle of about five feet). It is helpful to wear clothes that allow you to move freely, such as comfortable shoes or no shoes with your socks off. Make sure there are no other distractions present—turn off the TV or radio and silence your phone.

To begin, get into a standing position and make sure you are settled into your safe place. Then take a moment to scan your location, noticing the doors, windows, or landscape, and address anything that might interfere with your practice.

In the center of your space, place your feet a little more than hip distance apart. Then begin to gently rock side to side. You can let your hands flow freely by your sides or wrap them arm under arm just below your chest. Bring your awareness to your feet on the floor as one foot and then the other presses. You can track this with your words, saying or thinking, *My feet can connect with the earth*. Repeat this for one to two minutes, moving and reminding yourself, *My feet can connect with the earth*.

Next, add a bit of a twist, releasing your hands and allowing them to swing. Keep your feet where they are. As you twist to the left, release your right heel and let your arms swing to the left. When you swing to the right, lift your left heel and let your arms swing to the right. You might notice the twisting and swinging sensations in your body and the air on your arms and hands as they move from side to side. Swinging and twisting gently side to side, you can track your movements with your words, *I can move my body*. Repeat this for one to two minutes or so, moving and reminding yourself, *I can move my body*.

Pausing at the center, bring your hands to your sides and take a few breaths. Notice your feet on the floor. Notice your knees and allow a gentle softness or bend. Notice your hips, shoulders, and jaw. Allow for the release of any tension or holding. Slowly begin to walk around your space, letting your feet move one ahead of the other with your arms swinging naturally at your side. You can play with your footsteps by making them smaller or bigger. You can create different types of walks, such as a business-person walk, a toddler walk, a someone-with-big-floppy-shoes walk, or a stuck-in-the-snow walk. Play around a little bit and create different kinds of walks. Tip toe. Stomp your feet. Walk lightly. Walk with heavy feet. As you play, you can track this with your words, *I can move my body*. Repeat this for one to two minutes or so, moving and reminding yourself, *I can move my body*.

When you are ready, return to a regular and then a slow walk. You might try synchronizing your breath with your footsteps, breathing in step, step . . . and breathing out step, step. As you breathe and walk, you can track this with your words, *I can move my body*. Repeat this for one to two minutes, reminding yourself, *I can move my body*.

Come back to the center of the room and pause. Take your feet back to hip distance apart, pressing them into the earth with your knees soft. Notice your hips, shoulders, jaw, and eyes. Allow for softness and the release of tension or holding.

Breathing in, lift your hands up toward the ceiling. During a deep exhale, fold forward, allowing your hands to move to the floor. Repeat this several times. Do this at a softness or intensity that feels okay with your body. As you breathe in and raise your arms, track your movements with thoughts like *Rising up*, *Reaching up*, or *Nourishing*. As you exhale and fold forward, track your actions with your thoughts, thinking something like *Letting go* or *Releasing*. Find the words that make sense for you as you reach up (breathing in) and fold forward (breathing out). Depending on how it feels, you can repeat this up to 10 times.

Coming back to standing, begin to slowly rock back and forth. You can let your hands flow freely by your sides or wrap them arm under arm just below your chest. Bring your awareness to the feeling of your feet on the floor as one foot and then the other presses. You can track this with your words, saying or thinking, *My feet can connect with the earth*. Repeat this for one to two minutes, moving and reminding yourself, *My feet can connect with the earth*.

When you're done, find a comfortable seat, and support your legs and back as needed. Your body is well grounded and you are safe. Next, place one hand on your stomach and one hand over your heart as you focus on breathing in and out. Breathe using your typical breathing pattern for three breaths, then begin to slowly extend the inhalation and exhalation by counting—inhale 1, 2, 3, 4 . . . exhale 1, 2, 3, 4. Inhale 1, 2, 3, 4 . . . exhale 1, 2, 3, 4. Then allow your breath to return to normal. With your hand over your heart, bring your awareness to your heart and notice any sensations there or the feeling of your heartbeat. Maybe remind yourself that this does not need to be any certain way.

Honoring Your Body

For this next step, you might want to take a moment to adjust your position so you feel well supported and comfortable. Rest your hands in your lap. As you are ready, soften your gaze or close your eyes. From a distance, imagine you can see your list of traumas, the experiences you and your body have endured. Now, move your awareness back to you, right now. Imagine a sphere of loving-kindness all around you. Imagine your protector is there, making sure you are safe. Acknowledge to yourself, to your body, all that it has endured to get to this point: *You have been through so much. I see you. You are resilient and strong.*

Then bring your awareness to your feet. Imagine a sense of loving-kindness all around your feet and say to them, *You have been through so much. I see you. You are resilient and strong.*

Move your awareness to your legs and hips. Imagine that same loving-kindness all around your legs and hips and say to them, *You have been through so much. I see you. You are resilient and strong.*

Move your awareness to your hands. Imagine the energy of loving-kindness surrounding your hands and say to them, *You have been through so much. I see you. You are resilient and strong.*

Move your awareness to your arms and shoulders. Imagine that radiant loving-kindness all around your arms and shoulders and say to them, *You have been through so much. I see you. You are resilient and strong.*

Move your awareness to your neck and head. Imagine the sphere of loving-kindness on your neck and head and say to them, *You have been through so much. I see you. You are resilient and strong.*

Move your awareness to your belly, lungs, and heart: the core of you. Imagine loving-kindness radiating all around your center as you breathe, as your heart beats. You might want to move your hands, placing one hand on your belly and one hand on your heart, as you breathe. Say to your belly, lungs, and heart, *You have been through so much. I see you. You are resilient and strong.*

Finally, expand your awareness to your whole body. Allow the sphere of loving-kindness to surround your whole body. Breathe a few gentle breaths here. Close the practice by saying to your whole body, *You have been through so much. I see you. You are resilient and strong.*

Self-Holding

Self-holding is a healing practice that can help you be with your experiences as you move through this trauma work. It combines comforting touch with a self-hug to bring about a calming shift in your body.

To begin, close your eyes or gently soften your gaze. Then place your hands on the area where you are noticing the feelings, sensations, or action urges most intensely. Gently press your hands on the area, hand over hand. Engage in gentle, slow breathing here. If you'd like, you can gently move your hands in soft circles. Breathe here and notice.

Next, take your right hand, place it under your left arm (holding your side just under your arm), cross your left arm over the right, and place your left hand on your right shoulder like you are giving yourself a hug. Then gently squeeze in toward your body. Self-hugs can help remind you that your body is a container and that the feelings and sensations are not as overwhelming because they are being contained or well held (Levine, 2010). Breathe here and notice.

Now place one hand on your forehead and the other on your upper chest. Notice what happens in your body between your hands. You might notice an energy flow, a temperature change, certain feelings, or other sensations. Keep your hands in place until you feel some kind of a shift. When you are ready, take the hand on your forehead and move it to your belly, keeping the hand on your chest in place. Again, simply breathe and notice what happens in the area of your body between your hands.

In this process, offer your body the experience of being seen and listened to. When you are ready, use the following figure to draw or write about what you noticed. You can include arrows to show shifts in energy or movement or use colors to represent different types of sensations or aspects of feelings. This process can help you symbolically represent the experience of your body. In this way you are saying, *Body, I see you. Body, I hear you.*

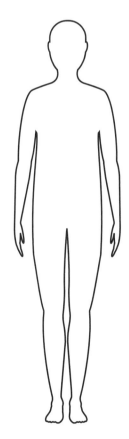

The Kinesthetic Body*

This exercise introduces gentle movement that explores the physical body and the kinesthetic body. The kinesthetic body (also called the energetic or imaginal body) calls on your active imagination—your inner felt sense of where you begin and where you end, your matter and your motion, inside and outside of the physical definitions you call your body. This sense allows you to imagine your body moving when you are not moving at all.

Beginning movement with the kinesthetic body will help you identify the range of your physical body. While you may think you know where your body begins and ends, those boundaries are very subjective. Consider how your body feels after you have a shot of anesthetic, or if you have too much alcohol, or during feelings of dissociation. So much mental distress—pain, addictions, dysmorphia—involves feeling outside of the body or not feeling comfortable in the body. The kinesthetic body can help you explore these sensations and variations.

It will be difficult to do this activity while reading the instructions, so have someone (therapist, friend, family member, etc.) to read the instructions out loud to you or make a recording.

1. Stand with your weight evenly balanced on both your feet. Notice all your muscles—is there any unnecessary tension, particularly in your shoulder and neck area? If so, relax this tension.

2. Raise your real right arm and stretch. Feel the stretch in your fingers, your hand, your shoulder, your torso. Now lower your arm. Repeat this several times.

3. Now stretch your kinesthetic right arm. To do so, keep your real arm still but imagine, as vividly as possible, that you are raising your arm. Recall all the same sensations. Try to experience your kinesthetic arm with as much reality as your real arm.

4. Stretch again with your real right arm, then your kinesthetic right arm. Alternate several times between stretching with your real arm and your kinesthetic arm.

---

* Adapted from *The Possible Human* (Houston, 1997)

5. Do the same thing with your left arm: Stretch your real left arm several times, then keep your real left arm still and stretch your kinesthetic left arm. Alternate several times between stretching with your real arm and your kinesthetic arm.

6. Let your real arms and shoulders circle in a round forward movement. Then do the same thing with your kinesthetic arms and shoulders. Then alternate between your real and kinesthetic arms and shoulders.

7. With your real body, lunge to the right. Come back to the center. Repeat this several times. Now lunge to the right with your kinesthetic body. Come back to the center. Alternate several times between your real and your kinesthetic body.

8. Do the same thing to the left: With your real body, lunge to the left, then come back to center. With your kinesthetic body, lunge to the left, then come back to center. Alternate several times.

9. Follow this sequence:

    a. Real body lunges right, then comes back to the center.

    b. Real body lunges left and comes back.

    c. Kinesthetic body lunges left and comes back.

    d. Real body lunges left and comes back.

    e. Kinesthetic body lunges right and comes back.

    f. Real body lunges right and comes back.

    g. Real body lunges left and comes back.

    h. Now, *at the same time*, your kinesthetic body lunges right and your real body lunges left.

    i. Come back to the center.

    j. Now lunge with your real body to the right and your kinesthetic body to the left.

    k. Come back to center.

10. Rest for a moment.

11. Raise both of your real arms over your head and hold them there.

12. At the same time, feel your kinesthetic arms hanging at your sides. *Slowly* lower your real arms while you raise your kinesthetic arms.

13. Then lower your kinesthetic arms while you raise your real arms.

14. Lower your real arms while you raise your kinesthetic arms.

15. Continue with this until the raising and lowering of your kinesthetic arms becomes almost indistinguishable from the movement of your real arms.

16. Rest for a moment.

17. Be aware of the space several feet in front of you. Now, with your real body, jump as high as you can into that space. Then jump back. Do it again with your real body, jumping as high as you can, forward and back.

18. Do the same thing with your kinesthetic body, jumping forward and back, as high as you can.

19. Repeat with your real body. Jump forward and back three times in a row.

20. With your kinesthetic body, jump forward and back once.

21. Jump with your real body.

22. Jump again with your kinesthetic body.

23. Jump forward with your kinesthetic body and stay there.

24. Now, jumping as high as you can, jump with your real body *into* your kinesthetic body!

25. Standing still, notice how you feel. Scan your body. Is there greater awareness now in your body?

26. Begin to walk around. Notice your awareness.

27. Opening your eyes, see if your perception of the external world and others has changed.

The "Ha" Breath Wood Chopper

This is a fun, active exercise that reduces anxiety and enhances breath. It integrates movement and sound to engage and activate the diaphragm and release emotion. It is especially useful to teach to children or teens, who may find it difficult to express and release feelings such as anger and frustration.

1. Stand with your feet shoulder-width apart, your feet pointing outward, and your knees slightly bent.

2. Imagine yourself to be chopping wood. Breathing in, lift your arms over your head as if you were holding an ax. Your pelvis should tip forward so that your back is arched slightly. Take care not to overextend your shoulders backward.

3. As you breathe out, bring your arms forward while simultaneously bending forward, tilting the hip, and curving your head down as if you were chopping wood. On the downward thrust, make a loud "Ha!" sound. Let your arms swing toward the ground and through and between your legs.

4. Repeat each movement 5–10 times. You can do this exercise more slowly or quickly according to your comfort level.

Shaking to Safety

Body tremors are a common symptom associated with anxiety and fear. The body's flight, fight, freeze system is designed to help the body react quickly and efficiently during duress and threat. Once the threat has subsided, the body uses the shaking movement to process the threat and restore its equilibrium. Body tremors occur naturally during the stress response of hyper-stimulation. The amount of stress can't be fully processed, and the body seeks relief. This nervous system activity is often experienced as an involuntary response, but you can use this natural system in a conscious way by gently initiating this movement to entice the body toward relaxation and restoration.

Shakes come in waves and can vary in intensity. This exercise purposefully allows shaking, and directing the shaking, so you can experience a release and restoration. It contains three phases, each of which takes about five minutes: (1) evoking, (2) moving through, and (3) cooling down. Do this exercise standing, with your legs at a wide stance so you feel supported by your legs. Close your eyes if you are comfortable; you want to see your body from the inside.

A word of caution: Too much shaking that does not go toward restoration of equilibrium can be emotionally activating, resulting in the opposite effect. You are looking to promote a safe release in the body, not activation and more anxiety. It's important to pause and notice, and not just shake for a long time. You want to bring mindfulness to the shaking, not just shake without any awareness—which can lead to feeling overwhelmed and more anxious. If you notice this is not being beneficial, stop.

1. **Evoking**

    a. Notice your body standing and tune into your physical spine.

    b. Let your arms hang by your sides; your head will be moving along with the rhythm you initiate.

    c. Begin to gently move your legs rhythmically up and down, bending them slightly. This results in a gentle, wave-like motion through the spine.

    d. Start with a gentle and rhythmic shake that feels comfortable to your body.

    e. Allow this movement to be the same rhythm the whole time until it becomes second nature and you don't think of "doing the movement."

2. **Moving Through**

   a. In this second phase, you might notice how the body is moving by itself. You are not thinking about the movement anymore; just allowing it to move you.

   b. There might be feelings such as sadness, grief, or anxiety floating through. Allow them to be there without amplifying them.

   c. The rhythm of the movement is how you can process through the body. The body will remember how to do this for you.

   d. Trust the movement.

   e. Let the body shake be even and rhythmic, allowing whatever comes up here. The more relaxed you can be in your body, the better.

3. **Cooling Down**

   a. There is a natural winding down as you listen to your body.

   b. Slow the movement down, making it gradually smaller.

   c. You might notice a release in your body, small tremors, an emotion, or sensations that feel good or pleasurable.

   d. You want to initiate the body into the cooling-down phase to rest.

   e. Let the body come to a standstill and notice what is there.

   f. There are often small inner shakes that release, and you want to be present for that.

   g. Stand firm and still and notice the waves of release subsiding.

   h. Once you feel clear and calm, or a shift in the activation, end the exercise.

Gentle Head Lift

The head is a heavy part of our body. It weighs between 9 to 11 pounds for the average person. Headaches, aches, and tiredness are common stressors and are felt in the head and neck area. Through the face, head and neck we engage the world. When working with the head, use very small (I mean very small) movements. You want to avoid straining the muscles in the neck.

1. To begin, notice your head in a neutral position. Note any tensions in the head or associated areas, such as the neck, jaw, and face.

   Name the tension: My head feels _____ right now.

2. Ever so slowly (as if you are moving at snail speed), and while imagining floating in water or air, lift the head.

3. Close your eyes; feel the lifting inside.

4. Come back to neutral.

5. Now bow the head toward the heart; have your inner gaze look toward the heart.

6. Come back to neutral.

7. Repeat three times *very slowly*. This is the key element. It's not a stretch or getting out the tension; this is moving the head in a new and light or fluid way.

8. Make sure you don't overstretch or add anything. Simply lift-neutral-bow-neutral-repeat.

9. Then pause and notice.

   Name the change: My head feels _____ right now.

Unfurling

This exercise uses awareness of the spine to work with themes of coming out of a shell, shyness, and coming toward something that is unsure. The skill of slowly and gently finding a movement through the spine helps awaken your awareness of the core and spine. The slow and deliberate movement can add more confidence in facing life's uncertainties.

Picture the image of a fern. The fern in its developmental stages unfurls a very tightly coiled leaf. Slowly, it unwraps itself until it expands to the fullness of the leaf. Imagine your body unfurling like a fern leaf.

1. Start standing or sitting. Don't lean your back against anything. If you're sitting, come to the edge of your seat.

2. Keep in mind the theme you are working with, such as feeling tight, afraid to open up, or unsure what it means to be open and vulnerable. Write down your answers on the baseline inquiry before you start.

3. Start with your head bowed down toward your chest. Curl into a ball—imagine being a tightly-wrapped fern leaf.

4. Notice your breath in this position.

5. Gently find an impulse that wants to open and unfurl.

6. Move very slowly! Make the unfurling motion that opens the spine and lifts the head. Savor this slow motion.

7. Imagine you are the fern leaf that takes a long time to unwrap its tight coil.

8. Go ahead and do this movement again. Make sure not to coil inwards, as if you are closing the fern bud again.

9. You can repeat this motion a couple of times. Be careful to go slowly and deliberately and feel the moment of the spine.

10. After the movement, rest in the openness or a coiled position (whichever feels more appropriate) and notice what has changed.

11. Write down your thoughts and answers to the "after the movement" inquiry questions.

Baseline: Before the Movement

How tight do you feel on a scale of 1–10? _____

What holds you back? _____

_____

What is making you recoil or shut down? _____

_____

What are you afraid of if you open up? _____

_____

Baseline: After the Movement

How are you feeling in your body after the movement? _____

_____

On a scale of 1–10, how willing are you to open to the issue/topic at hand? _____

What do you know about what makes you close down now? _____

_____

What do you notice in your body after the movement?_____

_____

What is your perception now on the topic/theme? _____

_____

Describe the experience with one word: _____

Wet Sandbag

This is an excellent exercise for anyone wanting to explore safety and their body's boundaries. It will help reestablish where the body begins and ends. In this exercise, the whole body will have contact with the ground, which will provide a sense of connection between your body and the Earth. Gravity connects a sense of grounding and belonging. For this exercise, it is important to encourage slowness in movement and awareness of breath. Since this is a body-roll exercise, you will need floor space. You can place a blanket or mat on the floor for comfort.

> **Therapist Note:** In this exercise, you will be guiding the client to roll like a "wet sandbag," shifting the weight of their body to imitate the shifting movement of wet sand. It is important to move slowly to feel and sense the weight shifting. If a client gets dizzy or uncomfortable, stop and ask them to pay attention to their body. You do not want to disorient the client, but rather tune them in to their sense of body gravity and feeling grounded. The slower they perform the exercise, the more present they can be with their body.

1. Lay down on one side. Take note of your body against the ground; feel the support. Take a moment to connect with the ground beneath you.

2. Allow your body to shift slightly and observe the gravitational pull that is guiding the movement.

3. Visualize that you are a wet sandbag rolling on the floor. Very slowly, shift the sand in the bag to initiate the movement. Imagine each grain of sand shifting as gravity pulls it in the next direction; your body simply follows the pull of gravity.

4. Notice how the weight rolls you on your back. Allow yourself to rest a moment, and then initiate the next shifting of the sand's weight onto your other side.

5. Don't force the movement, but let the shifting, wet sand do the work.

6. Keep rolling from one side to another as long as you feel motivated and comfortable.

7. When done, slowly sit up and make note of how your body feels.

8. Do you feel connected? Do you have a sense of where your body is in relation to the floor and the space around you?

9. What awareness of your body did this exercise elicit?

Defending Arms

This tool is helpful in establishing a safe body boundary, as well as the expression of saying "no" with a powerful gesture. Using your arms to defend is an instinctive movement that can be used consciously to feel the "no" that the mind wants to express.

> **Therapist Note:** You will want to teach the client the following sequences of arm defenses, instructing them to "rehearse" these possibilities, and coaching them to remember these movements as intrinsic, instinctual, and necessary. When you observe impulses involving the arms, such as pushing, or a split-second halting motion of the hands, have the client slow down and connect with these impulses. Notice where they stop and get stuck, and gently talk them through completing the movement. It is important to work slowly and repeat the instructions. Have the client follow the movements. Track carefully when the client becomes dissociative or collapses—they need to pause and resource at that moment. Throughout the exercise, track for:
>
> - Sequence of the movement: Is there a beginning, middle, and end?
>
> - Any time you observe a client giving up, collapsing, becoming stuck, or exhibiting repetitive movement, slow down immediately or interrupt and resource.
>
> - The whole body supporting the movement.
>
> - Images, memories flooding in, or feelings of being overwhelmed. Remember, it is important to move slowly.
>
> - When fast movement is needed; have the client rest frequently and observe for elevated heart rate, which needs to be felt, but not overwhelm.

Defending Sequence

1. Use the "halt" position of your hands to signal a "no" or "stop."

2. Have your arms stretched out as if to brace against something or to push someone away.

3. Notice if you feel strength or power in your body. See if you can maintain that body feeling. What can support this?

4. If you had a word to express this posture, what would that be?

Protecting Sequence

1. Cross your arms in front of your face as your body leans away. It's another way to say "no" or set a boundary.

2. Tune into the protective quality that your arms are giving you.

3. You can protect your body.

4. What words could go with this body stance?

Action Sequence

1. Push your hands, palm to palm, against each another. This will help you feel the strength of your own hands.

2. Imagine pushing your hands against a person who you want to say "no" to or set some kind of boundary with. You can use a repetitive movement, stretching the arms outward, or hold the position of your arms stretched out.

3. Notice how you can support this strong movement with the rest of your body. Do you have your legs firmly under the rest of your body?

4. Let this movement be dynamic and active. Push the arms forward and notice how YOU are making the action happen.

5. Notice your breath. It's not uncommon to feel a faster breath rhythm.

6. Stay mindful of this movement so you stay connected with the action of the movement. Take little breaks and sense into the change of your body.

7. What do you notice?

8. When you feel you've had enough or it's done, take a break and sense into your body.

9. What does the body have to say now?

Lean Back to Lean In

This exercise is a short two-minute practice to work with irritation, impatience, or emotional agitation in the moment. It is designed to help you work with any impulse-control issues. If you have a tendency to quickly jump into a conversation or an action, you will benefit from practicing this tool. The outcome is a calmer and more rational manner of engaging without being reactive.

Practice this exercise with your therapist first to help establish a good habit. After a few practices, you will be able to do this on your own. Repetition is important. This is a powerful yet simple self-regulation tool you can add to your daily life.

1. Notice the feeling of irritation, impatience, or tension in the body.

2. Check into your body posture: Are you leaning forward? Are the muscles in your belly clenched? Is your face straining or tense? Are your eyes straining or tense? Is your voice hurried or high pitched? Is your head down as if you are fighting a strong wind?

3. Time to lean back!

4. Stop what you are doing and shift your body posture into a leaning-back posture. This can be sitting back or shifting your weight backwards while standing. If you are standing, sense your heels rather than the balls of your feet. If you are sitting, feel the back of the chair; sense your sitting bones.

5. Let your gaze be relaxed. Imagine you are looking from behind your eyes, as if you are dropping backward into your eyes. This will allow you to take in the whole vista in front of you without straining forward. You might gently look around and move your eyes and head slowly as if you are scanning the horizon.

6. Do this for one to two minutes.

7. Notice what changes. Was there a small mood shift? Did you notice a detail you hadn't before? How is your mood now? Do you still want to react? Or can you pass on that urge?

8. Now that you've learned how to lean back, you can choose what to lean in to!

Cueing Hands

Placing your hands on your body is a cueing of attention. By touching your own body with intention, awareness, and focus, you are directing attention toward the area of inquiry. This works well if you have an area of tension or discomfort, or have a place in the body that you want to learn more about.

When you place your hands on your body, make sure your touch is gentle, kind, and open. The best way to touch an area of your body is to slowly place your hand and "cup" the area. For example, you can cup your tight jaws by placing your hands around the face and jaw. Or you can cup your hands around a tense arm or leg. Quality of touch matters: By doing this slowly and softly, you will experience more heightened sensations and information.

Be receptive and inquisitive. It's important to wait and be with the touch so you can drop into your experience. Notice your breath and "send your breath" to the area of your touch. You should feel a change in your tissue, tension, or level of discomfort in a few minutes. Be patient and wait for your body!

1. Identify an area of the body that needs attention.

2. Slow down and notice that area first.

3. Slowly place your hand on that area. Make sure your touch is soft, slow and receptive, as if you are "listening with your hands."

4. Stay with your touch and be present to what your experience is as you are self-touching.

5. Now breathe slowly and consciously into this area. "Send" your breath into the place you are working on. It can help to imagine the breath traveling to the area and the area being receptive to it.

6. Stay mindful and inquisitive.

7. Are you noticing any change? Is the tension lessening?

Somatic Repatterning

Before you were able to stand, walk, or talk, you began to explore the world through your body. Your natural reflexes such as sucking, curling, reaching, and grasping movements allowed you to know yourself. The ways in which you were held, spoken to, and touched also shaped your felt sense of self. For example, if as a child you knew that you were safe to explore your environment and that you could reach for (and obtain) what you wanted, this provided you with a deep sense of accomplishment and gratification. Growing up in this type of environment, you were also empowered to know that you could move away from or push away unpleasant experiences. However, when there is early childhood trauma, our basic instincts are often blocked. You can imagine a child who was threatened and wanted to kick, scream, or run away but wasn't able to do so for fear of making a bad situation worse.

When it comes to healing from any trauma, it is important to recognize that the body holds memories of what happened and provides tremendous feedback regarding the impact of the trauma on your physical being. *Simply put, your body keeps the score* (van der Kolk, 2015). For example, you might carry tension in your body that makes it difficult to relax, or your posture might be a reflection of your emotions. You might close off your chest to protect your heart from events that occurred years ago. You might continue to freeze or collapse in response to current events that trigger feelings related to your traumatic past. Or you might notice how trauma from your past obstructs your willingness to look someone in the eyes, stand up tall, or speak with confidence.

Importantly, your body does not just hold the memory of what happened—it also holds the memory of what it *wanted* to happen. For example, if you were neglected, you may have given up on physically reaching out for the support of others. In this case, reclaiming your ability to express your longing for connection can be guided by experiencing the sensations in your body. A tightness in the throat might resolve by making a sound or crying out for connection. Or following an impulse to reach out through your arms can open up a new possibility of reaching out to others in the world now. This new movement pattern can help to create boundaries in your life today with greater success.

Healing from trauma involves increasing your awareness of these habitual patterns of tension in your body. Once you develop this awareness, then you can start to experiment with small changes in your breath, posture, eye contact, and body movement. For example, if you tend to keep your arms in tight to your body, then you might experiment with how it feels to take up more space. Or you might explore lengthening your spine and lifting your gaze, and notice how these subtle changes impact your sense of self.

As you continue to explore your somatic experience, you might begin to notice various movement impulses. Although it can take time to learn to trust your instincts and intuition, this process can eventually help you find resolution in body and mind. Explore trusting your body and following sensations that help you to unwind tension. If you tend to have tension in your jaw, then you might exaggerate your sensations by scrunching your face tightly and then opening your jaw into a wide yawn. Or if you tend to hunch your shoulders, then you could follow that impulse until you curl into a small ball. Eventually, you can allow yourself to freely associate, noticing any thoughts, memories, or images that arise as you honor your sensations and movement impulses.

Sometimes this process of somatic repatterning can cause trembling or shaking in your arms and legs as you release long-held tension from your body. Within somatic psychology, this process of discharging tension from the body is referred to as *sequencing* (Aposhyan, 2007). In sequencing, you aim to allow feelings to move all the way through your body—out your arms or legs—until you feel a sense of relief or satisfaction. As you release tension from your body, you have an opportunity to discover a greater sense of freedom in your body and mind. Your body gives you feedback about when the events of the past no longer define your life in the present.

Often, working with a therapist is instrumental to any embodiment practice because habitual somatic patterns can be difficult to recognize; they are fundamentally integrated into the fibers of our identity. A somatically trained therapist can offer a compassionate reflection of your embodied self-expression.

Healing Through Movement

Take some time to bring your attention to a difficult memory. As you reflect upon this time in your life, notice the sensations in your body. Perhaps scan your body from head to toe and notice any areas of tension. Are these feelings and sensations familiar? What happens if you explore subtle movements that increase your awareness of these areas of your body? Maybe you tighten an area of your body or breathe more deeply into your sensations.

Notice if you feel any urge to move your body. Perhaps you notice a desire to push into your arms or your feet. Maybe you feel an impulse to reach out with your hands. Or you might notice a desire to move your legs as if you were running away or kicking. You can also explore making a sound that matches the feeling in your body. Give yourself as much time as you need to find any movements or sounds that match the sensations you have in your body. Allow any spontaneous movements to sequence out your arms or legs.

When you feel complete, take a few moments to come into stillness and notice your connection to your body. Reflect upon the distressing memory that you started with and observe if anything has changed. Perhaps you sense a feeling of satisfaction or resolution. Releasing tension in the body is a vulnerable process. If you notice a lingering sense of frustration, then you may choose to work through this memory in therapy.

When you feel ready, take some time to write about your experience, knowing that you can repeat this process with other sensations or areas of tension.

_____

_____

_____

_____

_____

_____

_____

_____

_____

_____

_____

_____

_____

_____

_____

_____

_____

_____

_____

_____

_____

_____

_____

_____

_____

I can learn to trust my sensations and movement instincts. I am embodied.

CHAPTER 4

Yoga-Based Tools

Basics of a Trauma-Informed Yoga Practice

Choice. Always give choices using invitational language. Giving someone choices regarding a pose or breathing exercise should also include the freedom to not do the pose or breathing exercise at all. This way, you help students learn to trust their own judgment about what is appropriate for them to do in that moment. The following are some examples of invitational language:

- "I invite you to…" (instead of "I want you to…")
- "If you want to, join me in raising your arms on your next inhale."
- "Would you like to try?"
- "I invite you to sit in a comfortable position."
- "If you would like, join me in linking your breath to your movement. Inhale, lift your arms. Exhale, lower them."
- "As you start to notice your breathing, feel free to have your eyes open or closed, whichever feels more comfortable to you."

Knowing the suitability of a yoga pose or breathing exercise often comes from practicing and being able to feel the effect of that practice. Noticing the effect of a pose or breathing practice is particularly helpful in certain situations. For example, if you want to use a calming practice to prepare for bed and a good night's rest, choose a practice that has made you calm in the past rather than a practice that has energized you. There are no hard and fast rules that always apply, mostly because each person's nervous system responds differently to different practices. As you gain experience in the practices, you start to know yourself better. You become aware of what calms you and what energizes you.

Emphasizing a client's choice is particularly important if you are working in an institutional setting, like a VA, or in a restrictive setting like a juvenile detention center, where people are used to being told what to do. In these cases, I suggest explicitly acknowledging the choice they have in the practice of yoga by saying something like:

Perhaps you have been exposed to an environment where following orders or mandatory rules are the norm. Yoga is different from that. I cannot make you do anything, let alone move and breathe in a particular way, unless you want to. In this class today, you have my permission and complete freedom to decide what you want to do or not to do. You can engage or not engage, for any reason. Yoga is about self-care and self-awareness. You are the expert on you and your needs, not me. I am here to guide you with helpful instruction. Of course, I practice yoga myself, so I know its power and the effect it has had on my own mind and body, so I am hoping you will give it a try. But it is completely up to you to decide what is best for you today. And I will honor and respect your choice.

The use of such emphatic language, repeated over time, gives people the confidence to tune in to themselves and to start trusting that they can make good decisions for themselves, even if that is simply deciding whether they want to lift their arms over their head and breathe. If you can point them to their own agency—highlighting that they do have some control over some things—you are headed in the right direction.

Your Audience. Consider the population of people you are teaching. Are you teaching in a yoga studio in the suburbs? Or are you teaching in a juvenile detention center? Or perhaps an after-school program in the inner city? Context matters. The yoga-based practices that follow will work across a very diverse range of environments. Your job is to know your people and to educate and equip yourself to be culturally competent to teach the people in front of you.

Your Position in the Room. Put your back to the door, not theirs. Someone with a history of trauma often wants to see where the exits are or to sit near them.

Awareness. Read the body language of the people around you. How are they breathing? Over time, you can train your eyes and mind to notice the subtleties of someone's breathing. It is helpful to keep in mind that you may be in a room of highly anxious individuals. Often, they will need to move frequently to dissipate some of their nervous energy. Although slow movement may be challenging, any movement will help and will eventually allow them to enjoy a slower, quiet practice. If someone is mostly quiet and has a flat affect, then start with a quiet practice, like breathing, and build to more energizing breathing and movement to elevate the mood. In LifeForce Yoga, we call this *meeting the mood.*

Pause. Practice creating an intentional space of silence after you say something. It is not necessary to fill up every space with words. Take time to pause, and pause often. Let silence be your friend.

Tone of Voice. When you speak, think of thick, sweet honey coating your vocal cords. As an example, notice how you usually talk to small children and animals. Often, your intonation, pitch, and pace softens—that is the tone of voice that will be helpful for you to use. Record yourself talking so you know how you sound. Do you sound angry even when you are not (or don't realize you are)? The state of your nervous system affects your tone of voice, and it is very hard to sound genuinely calm and kind if you are not feeling calm and kind. Being able to identify your inner state and what you need to calm this state before you teach a class continues to be of paramount importance. What works for you will depend on your life stage and circumstances. For some, it involves taking deep breaths during the two-minute walk from the car to the studio before teaching. For others, it may involve taking at least an hour before a class to plan, refresh, and focus. The point here is to do the best you can with what you have available. Sometimes that will be a whole hour and sometimes not. I always like to have a back-up plan or my "tried and true" practices if my usual prep has not worked or has been hijacked in some way.

Your Own Presence. Make sure you are present and accounted for every class you teach. That means getting enough rest, staying hydrated, fueling your body with proper nutrition, and so forth. In polyvagal terms, it means being in a ventral vagal state, which is a state of relaxation and social engagement. Other people's nervous systems will take their cues from your nervous system. Therefore, if there is only one person in the room in a ventral vagal state, let it be you (Dana, 2018).

No Hands-On Adjustments. Learn how to use your body language, gestures, and vocal tone to offer comfort or empathy. Use your words, and perhaps demonstrate using your own body, to show someone how to adjust themselves even if you trained in a lineage that teaches hands-on adjustments. For example, if you see someone's face contort when they try to follow your cue to lift both hands over their head, it might be helpful to say (and to remind them), "Let's lift our arms to the natural stopping point, in our pain-free range of motion." And then demonstrate moving your arms only halfway. A follow-up cue may be, "Soften your jaw and your face muscles. Find your breath. Do a little less if you are not breathing smoothly." Or, as yoga teacher and author Max Strom (2017) likes to say, "Relax your face like you are on vacation . . . for the rest of your life."

Slowness. Slow down your movement, your breath, and the pace of your speech. Create a vibe characterized by "We have all the time we need" versus "Let's hurry up and relax." When we slow down, it helps create present-moment awareness, and this awareness is the key to learning so that change becomes possible.

Client Exercise

Chair Mountain

Chair Mountain is a pose you should practice daily, or anytime you find yourself in a chair, because its benefits are so profound and far reaching. Daily practice will allow you to experience these benefits. Of note, *Chair Mountain* requires more from you than initially meets the (inner) eye. When done attentively, *Chair Mountain* helps you maintain good posture and supports good biomechanics, whether you are at your desk or behind your steering wheel. At the same time, sitting for hours on end will tax your body no matter how good your posture is. The spinal load is greater while sitting than standing. Alternating between sitting and standing throughout your day, if possible, is a good way to support or heal the spine.

A kitchen chair or a metal folding chair is best for this practice. It is fine to use the back of the chair for support, but over time, you and your back will not need the constant support of the chair. Your abdominal muscles and quadriceps will help support the spine.

Script

Sit straight in your chair . . . feet hip-width apart . . . scoot forward on your chair so there is a space between your back and the back of the chair . . . the support of the chair is always there when you need it.

Move your belly button toward your spine to engage the abdominal muscles . . . let your muscles do the work, not your breath . . . see if you can let the breath be smooth and flowing while maintaining this slight engagement.

Press your feet into the floor and pretend that you are slowly straightening your spine. Notice if you can engage your quads (the muscles on the front of your thighs) . . . place your hands on your quads so you can feel when your quads are engaging . . . the muscles will feel harder . . . if your back needs a rest . . . it is always okay to use the back of your chair to support your spine.

Notice the effort of sitting upright . . . now relax and soften everything . . . good, observe the difference. Now engage the quads again . . . soften the face . . . breathe . . . and relax.

Your homework is to practice *Chair Mountain* for a few minutes each day until it becomes effortless and comfortable.

Client Exercise

Grounding

There are times when we are anxious or feeling the early stages of being overwhelmed with our thoughts, and we get so caught up in our minds that we lose awareness of the body. Finding a way to physically ground ourselves and reconnect to the body is empowering. It helps us to metaphorically tether ourselves to the present moment. We can do so by drawing attention to the fact that our head and feet are indeed connected by the body. This factual information is literally grounding—*Ah, yes! My head is attached to the rest of my body. My feet are on the ground, and it's all connected*—which can be a very powerful antidote to overwhelming thoughts.

If you notice that your client is having difficulty focusing, then this practice may be a good one with which to start. Encourage your client to keep their eyes open, as it is not necessarily a good idea for them to close their eyes if they are not feeling grounded. Keeping their eyes open will help them remain in the present moment, instead of being distracted with their thoughts, and can increase their sense of safety. Grounding is a standing practice, so make sure there is room to swing the arms freely. If you prefer to do this exercise sitting, there is a seated variation that omits the arm movements and body twisting.

Script

Standing Variation

Let's begin the practice of grounding. Begin by noticing the breath . . . no need to make changes . . . what is the texture of your breath today? . . . is it smooth and soft? . . . or is it rough and raggedy? . . . or something else?

Take a glance down at your feet. Notice them . . . notice the support of the floor under your feet . . . now bring your awareness all the way to the crown of your head.

Now pretend that you are drawing an imaginary line from your head down your center, all the way to your feet.

Look at your feet on the floor again. Lift your toes if you can . . . then relax the toes.

Shift your awareness back to the crown of your head . . . again, focus your awareness to the imaginary line that runs from your head to your feet.

Your head and feet are connected through your body . . . observe the connection . . . your feet are on the ground. Return to observing the sensations of your breath . . . notice your inhale and your exhale.

Now begin to shape your breath . . . inhale for a count of three, and sigh it out. Inhale, two, three. Exhale.

Sigh—with your mouth slightly open—making the sigh audible.

Let's try that again. Inhale, two, three, and exhale. Sigh it out. One more time. Inhale, two, three, exhale, sigh it out.

Now let's move the body gently from side to side.

Demonstrate moving the body left to right and right to left, simply shifting your weight from one foot to the other.

Do a slight twist, letting your arms hang by your sides, gently twisting from side to side. Your feet are still and your knees are soft. Your body is leading the movement and your arms are just going along for the ride—as if you are moving empty coat sleeves.

Shake your hands a little . . . notice how you are feeling . . . when you are ready, take a seat.

Seated Variation

Sit up straight in your chair . . . let's begin the practice of grounding. Begin by noticing the breath . . . no need to make changes . . . what is the texture of your breath today? . . . is it smooth and soft? . . . or is it rough and raggedy? . . . or something else?

Take a glance down at your feet. Notice them . . . notice the support of the floor under your feet . . . now bring your awareness all the way to the crown of your head.

Now pretend that you are drawing an imaginary line from your head down your center, all the way to your feet.

Look at your feet on the floor again. Lift your toes if you can . . . then relax the toes.

Shift your awareness back to the crown of your head . . . again, focus your awareness to the imaginary line that runs from your head to your feet.

Your head and feet are connected through your body…your feet are on the ground.

Return to observing the sensations of your breath . . . notice your inhale and your exhale.

Now begin to shape your breath . . . inhale for a count of three, and sigh it out. Inhale, two, three. Exhale.

Sigh—with your mouth slightly open—making the sigh audible.

Let's try that again. Inhale, two, three, and exhale. Sigh it out. One more time. Inhale, two, three, exhale, sigh it out. Gently shake out your hands . . . stomp your feet a few times . . . notice how you are feeling.

Client Exercise

A Restorative Reset

As you explore this yoga nidra practice, you are welcome to adapt it in any way that best supports you. You can vary the length of the time that you engage in the practice, remain seated instead of lying down, or choose to keep your eyes open the entire time. I recommend recording the practice for yourself or having someone you trust record it for you so you can experience the gift of effortlessly being guided through yoga nidra.

Script

Orienting and Centering

I invite you to begin by choosing whether you would like to lie down on your mat or find a comfortable and supported seated position. If you are lying down, you might choose to place a bolster under your knees, rest your head on a pillow, or cover yourself with a blanket for warmth. As you settle in, take a moment to notice your sensations, emotions, thoughts, breath, and level of energy. If you would like, perhaps set aside any thoughts or items from your to-do list so you can be fully present for this restorative reset for your body and mind.

Intention Setting

Now take a moment to reflect on a time when you felt connected to yourself in a positive and loving manner. Where were you? Who helped you developed this deep sense of connection to yourself? How do you feel in your body as you recall this time, place, or supportive person? As you sense this feeling in your body, is there a word or short phrase that matches this feeling? Here are some examples: content, peaceful, expansive, open, safe, flowing, connected, at ease, comfortable, secure, balanced, relaxed.

Once you have found a word that matches this deep feeling of connection and support, you can create a short phrase by adding "I am" to your chosen word. For example, if your word is *balanced*, you would simply say to yourself, "I am balanced." Once you have arrived at your chosen intention for today, I invite you to repeat your intention several times to yourself as you sense the associated feeling in your body. You can also repeat your intention at any time throughout this practice to help you return to a peaceful felt sense of connection, ease, and support.

Guided Awareness of Your Face and Neck

At this point, I will guide you to bring your attention to your body, one area at a time. To begin, I invite you to bring your attention to your face by noticing the sensations in your jaw, mouth, ears, nose, cheeks, eyes, forehead, and scalp. Draw your attention to the back of your neck, your chin, the front of your neck, and the inner sensations of your throat. While you might choose to remain still, you are also welcome to create small movements in your face and jaw or soft sounds to increase your sensory awareness of your face and neck. If you would like, create a gentle squeeze to contract the muscles in your face and neck and then let the tension go. Repeat this if you would like, and then take two or three additional breaths while noticing the sensations in your face and neck.

Guided Awareness of Your Arms

Now I invite you to bring your attention to your left shoulder, left arm, left palm, and left fingers. Then shift your awareness to your right shoulder, right arm, right palm, and right fingers. While you might choose to remain still, you are also welcome to create small movements by gently tensing and releasing the muscles in your shoulders and arms, opening and closing your hands, or wiggling your fingers if this helps you sense and feel your arms and hands. Then take a few breaths as you notice the sensations in your shoulders, arms, and hands.

Guided Awareness of Your Torso

Now I invite you to bring your attention to the sensations in your torso. Become aware of your front and back side as you notice the sensations in your upper back, lower back, chest, and belly. Notice your pelvis and sacrum. While you might choose to remain still, you are also welcome to take a deep breath in as you lift and stretch your belly and chest, and then release this stretch as you exhale. Then take two or three breaths while noticing the sensations in your entire torso.

Guided Awareness of Your Legs

Now I invite you to bring your attention to your left hip, left leg, left foot, and left toes. Then shift your awareness to your right hip, right leg, right foot, and right toes. While you might choose to remain still, you are also welcome to create small movements by gently tensing and relaxing the muscles of your legs or by wiggling your toes if this helps you sense and feel your legs and feet. Then take two or three breaths while noticing the sensations in your hips, legs, and feet.

Guided Awareness of Your Entire Body

Finally, bring your attention to the sensations in your entire body. Allow yourself to notice the front, back, top, bottom, and sides of your body. Notice the wholeness of your body. Sense your breath moving through your entire body. Every inhalation invites you to sense your body, and every exhalation invites you to release any lingering tension from your entire body. Welcome yourself just as you are in this moment, without trying to change anything. Sense the deepest connection that resides within your heart. Sense how this deep connection allows you to reside within the peace that lives in the very core of your being. This is always here for you.

Completion

Return your attention to your intention—the words that help you connect to a felt sense of connection, ease, and support. Once again, repeat this phrase to yourself two or three times. As you prepare to complete this practice, take a few moments to reflect on your experience. Slowly, when you are ready, begin to transition your full awareness back to your surroundings. If your eyes were closed, open them to notice the space around you. Bring your awareness to the sounds around you and to the sensation of the air on your skin. If you are lying down, slowly press back up into a comfortable sitting position. Take several breaths here, and when you are complete, notice what you are aware of now in your body, mind, emotions, and level of energy. Take some time to write down any observations, knowing that you can return to this practice as often as you would like.

Client Exercise

Neck Surrender

The neck and shoulders are very common places where we hold tension in the body. Therefore, paying some regular attention to these areas can go a long way toward combating chronic tension. This practice involves very slow neck movements, coordinated with the breath. That's it! Even though we know this type of practice is good for us, it can still be hard to remember to do it. My suggestion is that you set an hourly timer to remind yourself to get up from your chair, or whatever activity you are engaged in, and move your body. Take a few deep breaths. Then do this practice at least once a day. Try doing this practice slower than slow (whatever that is for you). It really does take practice to move this slowly. Underwhelm yourself a little. I recommend that you introduce this practice into session as needed. When you feel comfortable adding movement, you may want to add this one early on to help relieve neck tension that is common with so many of us.

Script

Begin by sitting comfortably in your chair . . . back straight . . . feet on the floor . . . chest lifted in *Chair Mountain* . . . notice your neck and shoulders.

We are going to give your neck a little treat for a few minutes. Think about the work it does supporting your head and your brain. The average head weighs seven to eight pounds. That is a lot of weight to hold up every day.

Decide whether it is better for your back today to use the back of the chair for support, or to sit on the edge of your chair letting your back support itself with help from your legs and abdominal muscles . . . either is fine . . . if you choose the first option, make sure that your bottom is all the way against the back of the chair so you are not tempted to slouch.

Choose one posture or the other.

Before we do this movement, let me demonstrate so you don't need to look up when your gaze should be toward the floor instead. I am dropping my chin toward my chest . . . the movement is the same as if I were drawing a smiley face across my chest with my chin . . . Begin with an inhale . . . Move your chin toward one shoulder, always moving within your pain-free range of motion . . . pause if you feel some resistance . . . exhale . . . chin back to center . . . then inhale . . . chin toward the other shoulder . . . exhale back to center.

Demonstrate this movement with your neck.

We will repeat this movement. A note of instruction . . . you don't have to feel any sensation when you move your neck . . . in fact, it is best if you don't. Simply breathe and move . . . even if you experience no sensation at all.

Find your breath . . . lower your chin to your chest . . . and inhale . . . shift your chin toward one shoulder, moving within your pain-free range of motion . . . exhale back to center.

And again . . . inhale . . . chin travels toward the other shoulder . . . and exhale . . . return to center.

One more time . . . inhale . . . chin travels toward the shoulder . . . and exhale . . . return to center.

Good . . . gently bring the chin up . . . put your hand under your chin, with your palm facing down . . . Check that your palm is parallel to the floor . . . good.

Demonstrate putting your hand under your chin, palm down. Then relax your hand, placing it back at your side.

Now inhale and rotate your head to the right . . . exhale and return center . . . inhale and rotate your head to the left . . . exhale and return center . . . and again, nice and slowly . . . inhale right . . . exhale center . . . inhale left . . . exhale center.

These are your last directions for movement. Again, underwhelm yourself . . . this is your neck. Remember all the weight it bears to support your head . . . be kind to it . . . inhale and tilt your right ear toward your right shoulder . . . don't force it . . . just head (pun intended) in that direction . . . exhale and return to center.

Inhale and tilt your left ear toward your left shoulder . . . very gently . . . exhale and return to center.

Notice how your neck is feeling . . . do you notice any difference?

Movements of the Spine: Spinal Twists

We can often overlook the need to rotate the spine since we don't do much twisting in our typical getting up, getting dressed, and out-the-door activities. However, this is worth intentionally adding to your daily movement so your spine gets used to what safe, gentle rotation feels like while twisting, as opposed to jerking or pushing movements. You can do this practice anytime, other than after you have just eaten, given that it may be uncomfortable to twist the spine while you are digesting food. The instructions for this practice are for sitting in a chair. But the practice could easily be done standing or sitting on the floor, much like other movements of the spine. In a one-on-one session, you can sit across from your client or beside them, whichever feels more comfortable to your client. If you are teaching a small group where clients are sitting in a circle or horseshoe shape, place yourself where everyone can see you and you can see everyone.

Script

Sitting comfortably in your chair, the spine is straight, the chest lifted slightly. Begin by placing your feet hip-width apart on the floor. Or you can make a one or two fist-size space between your knees.

Notice the feeling of breathing in your body . . . are you breathing through your nose or your mouth? . . . is it a short breath? . . . or a long breath? . . . if you are not already breathing in and out through the nose, do so if you can.

If you are congested today or cannot breathe in and out through your nose, just do the best you can.

Let's begin two movements of the spine . . . twisting the spine to the right and to the left . . . it doesn't matter which way you start. We will practice a very slow twist, and it doesn't need to be much . . . try it like this . . . inhale and lift the chest . . . exhale and rotate your spine . . . not just your head and shoulders.

Demonstrate a gentle twisting action.

When you get to the end of your exhale . . . pause and hold the twist . . . explore here for a few breaths . . . find a satisfying, natural in-and-out breath . . . good . . . now let's unwind the spine . . . coming back to center.

Twist on the exhale. It doesn't need to be much. Demonstrate restraint in the action.

Now for the other side . . . inhale and lift the chest . . . and exhale turn . . . find a natural stopping point in your twist and pause . . . now breathe a pleasant, natural in-and-out breath.

Remember, you are holding the pose . . . not your breath . . . and unwind . . . coming back to center.

You have now done a seated spinal twist. Let's check in here and notice how you are feeling.

Repeat the twist on both sides if you have more time.

Seated Pigeon

Seated Pigeon is an accessible modification of a more challenging version that is done on the floor. The point of doing the pose from a chair is to externally rotate one hip at a time, an important action that is missing from regular standing and sitting activities. Many people (myself included) are not particularly aware of their hips, but functional hip mobility is essential to many daily activities, such as getting dressed and moving around. Therefore, rotating your hips is certainly a helpful action to assist you in putting your pants on in the morning. Keeping your ball-and-socket joint mobile may be good for your emotional health too. For many years and from different teachers, I have heard the phrase "negative emotions are stored in the hips." I haven't seen a study corroborating this possibility, but I have practiced yoga long enough to know there is so much more than I can possibly study. The ancient wisdom of the yogis may be on to something.

Seated Pigeon can be introduced or practiced anytime during session. Daily practice is recommended. Many people have tight hip flexors and will not have a huge range of motion in their hips. Others will have hypermobility. Often these folks do not feel the pose. Reassure them that it is fine if they do not feel the pose. Simply being in the pose, even without feeling sensation in doing so, is a good practice. Whether someone is feeling sensation or not, the point is that the hip is externally rotating.

Script

Begin by sitting straight in your chair with your feet flat on the floor in *Chair Mountain* . . . your feet are hip-width apart . . . toes tracking forward.

Notice your hips . . . feel your sitting bones on the chair . . . direct your attention into the hip joints themselves . . . how do they feel right now? . . . it's okay if you don't notice anything in particular.

Now lift your right ankle and rest it on your left knee . . . don't strain . . . if it doesn't go there easily, then let your foot slide down onto your shin.

Demonstrate both options.

Observe the pace of your breath . . . if you want to explore your hip joint a bit . . . put your right hand on your right knee and ently guide your knee slightly toward the floor.

Remember, we always move in our pain-free range of motion. The movement we are doing will bring some awareness to your hip joints.

Look for tension in the face or holding of the breath.

Return to observing your breath . . . don't force the movement . . . take five natural breaths here.

Now uncross the foot, and place it back on the floor . . . notice how the hip you just externally rotated feels.

Let's try it on the other side . . . from your *Chair Mountain* . . . lift your left foot and place it on your right knee . . . if that position is available to you. If not, try resting your foot on your shin.

Demonstrate both options.

Notice your breath . . . just as on the other side . . . if you want to explore your hip more deeply . . . you can put your left hand on your left knee and gently move your knee toward the floor, externally rotating the joint.

Focus again on the flow of your breath . . . don't force the movement in your hip . . . take five natural breaths here.

Now uncross the foot, and place it back on the floor.

Notice if there were any differences between the range of movement on the left and the right side . . . notice sensations of increased circulation.

Fluid Movements for a Flexible Spine

One way to improve autonomic nervous system functioning is to engage in a variety of yoga practices that focus on enhancing spinal flexibility and correcting common spinal imbalances. Yoga practices often involve moving through postural transitions in a repeated, rhythmic manner that allows you to alternately increase and decrease your heart rate. Because these postures have a strong impact on vagal tone, you can think of this as strengthening the resilience of your nervous system in addition to the physical endurance required in these actions. The poses in this exercise are not intended to align your body into perfect symmetry but, rather, to facilitate a flexible and resilient spine that will help you respond and adapt to the inevitable challenges of life. This exercise guides you to move your spine while seated in a chair or cross-legged on the floor.

Script

Orienting and Centering

To begin, find a comfortable seat in a chair or on the floor. Notice your body sensations, your breath, and any emotions that are present for you in this moment. This will serve as a baseline and will allow you to notice subtle changes in how you feel throughout the practice.

Seated Spinal Flexion and Extension

Take a moment to notice how you are sitting in your chair or on your yoga mat. Imagine your pelvis as a bowl of water. If your pelvis is tilted forward or back, the water will run over the rim of this bowl. Notice the tone of your spine and whether you feel any natural tendencies for your pelvis to tilt forward or back. Now, I invite you to roll your tailbone back, which will lengthen your torso and lift your chest up. Here you can roll your shoulders back and gently lift your chin. Perhaps you exaggerate the shape by puffing out your chest with a deep inhalation. What do you notice in this shape?

Now, on the exhalation, begin to curl your tailbone forward as you roll your shoulders and bring your gaze down. Once again, exaggerate this rounding of your spine. What emotions or sensations do you notice in this shape? Now, if you would like, begin to move your spine back and forth with your breath, inhaling as you lengthen your spine and exhaling as you curl forward. You might place your hands on your shoulders as you continue to move back and forth, moving with the pace and rhythm of your breath. Open your elbows wide as you lift your spine, and draw your elbows together as you exhale forward. After about five to ten breath cycles, slowly bring yourself back to center to find an open but supportive posture, lifting the crown of your head so your head feels supported and centered above your spine and core.

Seated Side Bend

Now begin to lean your upper body to the right. You can use your right hand against the chair or floor to support your weight. Notice how it feels to contract the right side of your body as you simultaneously lengthen the left side of your body. Then switch sides, bending toward the left and lengthening the right side of your body. Take your time moving side to side, and when you feel complete, return to center.

Seated Twist

This next set of movements invites a gentle twist to each side of your body. Begin by lifting your arms up above your head and draw your right arm back behind you. You might place your right fingertips on the chair or floor behind you and your left hand on your right knee. Find the range of motion that is right for your body. There is no need to add force into the twist. Honor your body and move slowly and gently.

If it feels comfortable, allow your head to gently turn toward your right shoulder, and if you would like, allow your eyes to move toward the right, gazing behind your right shoulder. It can be lovely to move with your breath by backing out of your twist as you inhale and deepening into the shape as you exhale. Take several breaths here, and when you feel complete on this side, slowly return to center. Pause here for a moment prior to taking your twist to the left. Once again, find a natural and unforced twist while staying connected to your breath.

Eagle Wings

There are two versions of this pose. Both involve crossing the arms at the midline of the body, though the second variation also creates some space between the shoulder blades. Some studies suggest that crossing the midline of the body activates the opposite hemisphere of the brain, so cross-lateral movement might promote balance via this activation (Hannaford, 1995). This action doesn't have to be particularly energetic but can consist of simply crossing the midline of the body from side to side. The action can be done with the arms or the legs. I find this practice useful when my clients feel stuck, physically or emotionally. If you do this practice while standing and you cross your feet, it can be difficult to find balance even though both feet are on the floor.

Despite the simplicity of the movement, it can be surprisingly challenging if someone's ability to perceive where they are in space is compromised. Therefore, if your client is eager to try the practice and starts to fumble with arm or wrist crossing, be prepared to pause the action and guide them through the movements step by step. The finger, wrist, arm, and shoulder movements can also raise awareness of tender spots in these areas that might be the result from prolonged screen time or time behind the driver's wheel.

Script

First Variation

Begin sitting in *Chair Mountain* or standing tall . . . notice the pace of your breathing . . . bring awareness to your fingers . . . wrists . . . arms and shoulders.

If you have never tried this pose before . . . let's begin moving step by step until your body gets the hang of it . . . let's lift the arms straight out in front of you to chest height, arms straight . . . Pretend that you are holding a doorknob in each hand, and turn the knobs to the left and to the right . . . inhaling turns the knobs to the left . . . exhaling turns them to the right.

Demonstrate the movement. Arms should be straight, with wrists and shoulders rotated slightly to simulate the action of twisting a doorknob.

We don't usually have our wrists and arms in these positions . . . so at first it may take a little conscious maneuvering . . . we may get information from our body along the way about muscle tightness or stiffness in the joints of the arms, shoulders, and wrists . . . Think of all the new ways we now use our hands, wrists, and fingers with how we interact with screens.

Now cross your wrists in front of your body with your arms extended . . . your palms are facing down . . . now rotate your palms inward toward one another and interlace your fingers together.

Bending your elbows, draw your interlaced hands and fingers toward your heart.

Demonstrate the movement.

Good . . . breathe . . . notice your fingers, wrists, arms, and shoulders.

Second Variation

Begin by sitting or standing straight and tall . . . cross your arms in front of your chest and hold on to the opposite elbow.

Demonstrate crossing arms in front of chest and holding elbows.

Now move your fingers up your arms a little . . . if you are able . . . and give your biceps and triceps a little squeeze.

Now keeping your arms crossed, move your fingers up toward your shoulders . . . if you can . . . until it feels like you are giving yourself a hug.

Demonstrate squeezing biceps and triceps and then moving hands toward the shoulders.

Good . . . now notice if you have room to lift your elbows a little . . . how are your shoulder blades doing? . . . how does it feel to be held? . . . you can move your body a little . . . perhaps a little rocking motion . . . notice your ribs expanding as you breathe in and out.

Notice which arm is on top . . . uncross the arms, and put the other arm on top.

Demonstrate uncrossing the arms and putting the other arm on top.

Massage those biceps and triceps . . . now move the fingers up the shoulders . . . and hug yourself . . . Receive your own hug . . . feel your ribcage expanding in and out with your breath.

Uncross your arms.

Client Exercise

Bee Breathing

As the name suggests, the sound of this breath is like that of a bee buzzing. Although *Bee Breathing* takes a little more time to teach and practice, I have found that it is well worth the effort. Certain added components of the breath—such as whether your lips are partially open or closed, or whether you incorporate a hand gesture—determine the intensity of the practice. The practice is designed to reduce sensory input, particularly through the eyes and ears. By closing both the eyes and ears, the *zzz* sound is intensified and reverberates in your head. It heightens your awareness inside your head without turning on your thoughts.

I have found that *Bee Breathing* has an immediate and deep calming effect, but at the same time, it is quietly energizing. It also is a breath that can interrupt obsessive and compulsive thoughts. This breath has a refreshing quality to it. One client rather poetically described its effect as: "This breath feels like splashing cool mountain water on my face . . . so refreshing and restorative." Introduce *Bee Breathing* after you have established a comfortable familiarity with simpler practices.

Script

We are going to learn *Bee Breathing* because it is often a refreshing practice that can lift your energy . . . let's try it and see if that rings true for you.

I am going to teach it in two parts. First, we will learn the breathing part. Then we will learn the hand gesture part. Let's begin by simply making a zzz sound on the exhale . . . inhale and…

Make the zzz sound as you exhale through your mouth.

Good . . . you may notice that it feels a little ticklish on the lips as the sound vibrates the skin. Now let's try it with the lips slightly apart. Like this…

Make the zzz sound on the exhale with your lips closer together.

Notice the breath goes from sounding like one bee to a hive of bees . . . let's try it once again.

Make the zzz sound on the exhale with your lips closed.

Now we are ready to practice the hand gesture. Put your hands on your head like a helmet.

Demonstrate putting your hands on your head.

Let's try it together. I will provide cueing to set us up. When we are ready to go, we will do three rounds of zzzs. Since your exhale will be different, when you are done with your three, place your hands in your lap . . . any questions so far?

Make the zzz sound three times while your hands are on your head. Keep your eyes open so you can "peek" at your client or the group. When you notice they are on their third zzz, place your hands in your lap.

When you are finished with your third zzz . . . taking all the time you need . . . relax your hands in your lap.

Notice when their hands are in their lap.

Sense your right hand, sense your left hand, sense your right foot, sense your left foot. Perhaps you notice the glow of the honeybee . . . open your eyes if they are still closed.

Notice what expression you see.

Notice what you notice . . . if you have one or two words to describe your experience of this breath . . . you may share it now if you want to.

Sharing is completely optional. Sitting in silence for a minute or two may also be an appropriate choice.

Energizing
Practices

Half Salute

Generally speaking, a practice like the *Half Salute*—which activates the large muscle groups as you bend your knees, sweep your arms overhead, and fold your body forward—is energizing and helps the blood circulate. At the same time, the movement is slow and thoughtful. I often offer a series of half salutes at the beginning of a session in order to help clients feel grounded and centered.

When this practice becomes familiar to you, the simple rhythmic movement will lend itself well to the addition of affirmations or a prayer. But it can be too much for many people to take in at once if you teach new movements with the words. The idea is to be present with any sensations that arise in the body. If clients need to think about or remember new words at the same time, one action tends to compromise the other. This may sound surprising because neither the movement nor the affirmation is necessarily complex. I think the challenge arises from our cultural deconditioning of not regularly moving our bodies or joints within their range of motion each day. It becomes easy to forget that the body has a bigger role than simply carrying around our head and brain all day.

If you haven't been moving much and you start doing this practice daily for even five minutes, you will feel it. Receive this felt sense of your body as encouragement. *I can feel my body as a result of consistent, mindful movement. This is good.* And try not to overdo it. Stopping before you feel fatigued is key.

The *Half Salute* is a very handy practice because it can be done while standing or sitting, and it can be done without a yoga mat and without prior knowledge of yoga. Given that the practice involves sweeping the arms out wide, make sure that there is ample room to do so.

Script

Standing Variation

Let's check in with how your body is feeling in this moment . . . notice the pace of your breathing.

The *Half Salute* involves some sweeping arm actions and big body movements . . . let me demonstrate the movement . . . it begins with inhaling the arms up to the sky . . . exhaling and hinging at the hips and reaching down . . . inhaling up halfway, like an L shape . . . exhaling down into forward fold . . . inhaling all the way back up, pressing through the feet . . . it's okay to bend the knees here . . . sweeping the arms wide and bringing them back to heart center.

Demonstrate the movement.

Let's try it together . . . inhale . . . sweep the arms up . . . exhale . . . hinge forward into forward fold . . . inhale, come up halfway . . . exhale . . . forward fold . . . inhale, press your feet into the floor to come up . . . sweep the arms up . . . then exhale . . . hands returning to heart center.

Cue with words and now watch their movement.

Let's try it together . . . inhale . . . sweep the arms up . . . exhale . . . hinge forward into forward fold . . . inhale, come up halfway . . . exhale . . . forward fold . . . inhale, press your feet into the floor to come up . . . sweep the arms up . . . then exhale . . . hands returning to heart center.

Soften your face . . . notice how you feel . . . do you want to do a few more, or is this a good resting place?

Seated Variation

Let's check in with how your body is feeling in this moment . . . as you sit comfortably in your chair, notice the pace of your breathing.

The seated *Half Salute* involves some sweeping arm actions and big body movements . . . let me demonstrate the movement . . . it begins with inhaling the arms up to the sky . . . exhaling and hinging at the hips and reaching down while sitting . . . inhaling up halfway . . . exhaling and folding forward in your chair . . . inhaling all the way back up, pressing your feet into the floor . . . sweeping the arms wide and bringing them back to heart center.

If you are unable to hinge forward . . . you can lift one knee toward your chest . . . using your hands under the knee to support the movement . . . then place your foot back on the floor and bring the other knee toward your chest . . . again using your hands under your knee to aid in the movement . . . and then returning that foot to the floor.

Demonstrate the movement.

Let's try it together . . . inhale . . . sweep the arms up . . . exhale . . . hinge forward into forward fold . . . inhale, come up halfway . . . exhale . . . forward fold . . . inhale, press your feet into the floor to come up . . . sweep the arms up . . . then exhale . . . hands returning to heart center.

Cue with words and now watch their movement.

Let's try it together . . . inhale . . . sweep the arms up . . . exhale . . . hinge forward into forward fold . . . inhale, come up halfway . . . exhale . . . forward fold . . . inhale, press your feet into the floor to come up . . . sweep the arms up . . . then exhale . . . hands returning to heart center.

Soften your face . . . notice how you feel . . . do you want to do a few more, or is this a good resting place?

Client Exercise

Shaking

The practice of shaking helps to circulate blood and lymph in the body and has an overall effect of elevating mood and energy levels. The practice is more energetic than you may initially think, and it will require your focused attention and sustained movement in your pain-free range of motion. Start small with your hands and feet. If you are standing, you obviously will not be able to shake both feet at once. It may feel awkward as you work your way through the process of shaking the legs, hips, torso, and shoulders. But the movements get smoother and more comfortable with practice. This shaking practice should be done very gently, and I recommend starting out for about three minutes when you try it the first few times. This is a favorite practice among young adults I teach. They appreciate the awake and alert feeling they get from the practice. At the same time, I have witnessed older veterans successfully doing this practice from a chair and enjoying it. It is a fun practice to do early in a session if a client has low energy.

Although this practice can be done sitting, it is more effective when done standing (if this is possible given your client's physical abilities and the space you have available). I often use music for this practice, although I am careful not to choose songs with too many beats per minute. I want to encourage slow and gentle movement, not fast movement.

Script

Whether you are sitting or standing, start by noticing your breathing . . . where are you noticing your breath in your body?

Can you transition to a slow, even breath? . . . perhaps you are there already.

Once we achieve that slow, even breath, we can begin. Start by gently shaking your hands and wiggling your fingers . . . get the elbows involved. We are going for a jiggling effect. Eventually, we will move every body part that is able to move.

Demonstrate gently shaking the hands and fingers, then the elbows.

If it all feels like too much, just do one body part at a time.

Demonstrate shaking one hand at a time.

Start to shake your shoulders . . . if you can. If not, move on to your torso . . . and then your hips.

Demonstrate gently shaking the shoulders, torso, and hips.

Begin shaking your legs . . . knees . . . feet. Pause if you are starting to overdo it . . . no pain . . . no throwing your back out . . . that wouldn't look good for either of us.

Now that you've gotten your groove going, see what you can sustain for a few minutes . . . perhaps it will be just your hands and arms with an occasional shoulder shimmy . . . or maybe you want to focus on your legs and knees.

Watch for fatigue. Encourage pausing. Look for a natural stopping point. Keeping shaking for at least four minutes.

Allow yourself to come to stillness . . . what is your breath doing? . . . how is your body feeling? . . . is there one word that characterizes how you feel right now? Feel free to share it.

Make a mental note to yourself—in which pocket of my toolbelt does this practice belong?

Client Exercise

Flow for Your Fascia

This practice guides you through a series of exploratory, natural movements while seated on your yoga mat, from a tabletop position, from a cat-cow posture, and from a downward dog pose. Even if moving your body into these shapes is not available for you, you can choose to explore and receive the benefits of intentional breathing and pandicular movements while seated in a chair.

Script

Orienting and Centering

To begin, find a comfortable seat in a chair or on the floor. Notice your body sensations, your breath, and any emotions that are present for you in this moment. This will serve as a baseline and will allow you to notice subtle changes in how you feel throughout the practice.

Intentional Breathing

Take some time to notice if there is a particular area of your body where you are holding tension. For the next few minutes, I invite you to breathe into this area of your body. If needed, use your imagination to send your breath into this area, noticing any sensations that arise. What does this area of your body need? Would it be helpful to place a hand over this area of your body as you breathe? How does this part of your body want to move? Allow yourself to find any intuitive movements that honor your sensations. Continue to breathe into this area of your body. You might notice new sensations in another area of your body. Now you can send your breath here. You might notice emotions. If so, simply allow them to rise to the surface of your awareness, and exhale as you release any physical or emotional tension. Remember, you can take breaks from the practice as needed.

Cat and Cow

To continue this movement exploration, I invite you to move into a tabletop position on your yoga mat. Take some time to orient to this shape. If you would like, begin to move your spine with your breath. Inhale into cow pose by lifting your tailbone and head to the sky, which will lower your belly. Then exhale into cat pose, lifting your spine and arching your back as you curl your tailbone and head forward. Continue moving back and forth with your breath as it feels right to you. Feel free to pause in flexion or extension of your spine or to change how you are breathing in this shape. Notice how it feels to breathe into the sensations of your body from this shape.

C-Curve

Now, see how it feels to move your spine side to side, creating a C-curve shape as your tailbone and head move toward each other. You can pause on each side and get creative with this shape. If you would like, you can lift the opposite foot as you curl your spine to the side. Continue moving back and forth as it feels right to you.

Puppy Dog

From a tabletop shape, see how it feels to reach your hands forward. This will lower your chest to the ground as you keep your hips lifted. You might reach up onto your fingertips, press one hand forward and then the other, or walk your hands from side to side as you open each side of your body. Follow any intuitive movements that feel good to you.

Downward Facing Dog

Come back into tabletop position, and if you would like, come into a downward dog shape by lifting your knees off the floor and pushing your hips up. You can keep your knees bent for this movement exploration as you find length in your spine. Or maybe you begin to alternately bend and straighten each leg. Once again, allow yourself to be guided by your sensations in this shape.

Pandicular Movement

You might choose to return to tabletop shape or stay in downward facing dog for this next movement exploration. Begin to find any additional movements that feel intuitive to you. Perhaps you return your awareness to the original area of tension that you began with during this practice. Or maybe you notice that new sensations are at the forefront of your awareness. Imagine that you are your favorite animal just waking up from a nap. Allow yourself to reach and stretch. You might play with making your body small by curling inward and contracting toward your center and then reaching and expanding your shape. You can think of this as a full-body yawn.

Continue to move between contraction and expansion in a way that feels natural and intuitive to you. Honor your rhythms with breath and movement. Allow your movements to come from your innermost knowing. There is no "right" way for you to do this practice. If you notice an area of tension in your body, see what happens if you contract your body toward this area of tightness, and then expand and open with your breath. Is there a shape that feels just right? Is there a sound that matches the sensation? As if having a conversation with your body, listen to your sensations. What does your body want you to know?

Completion

Continue this movement journey for as long as you would like. When you feel complete, I invite you to take a few minutes of stillness, resting in a seated position or on your back. When you are ready, notice what you are aware of now in your body, mind, emotions, and level of energy. Take some time to write down any observations, knowing that you can return to this practice as often as you would like.

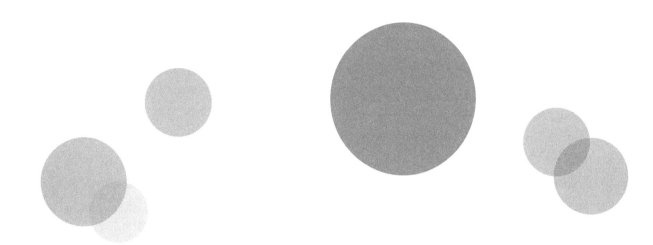

CHAPTER 5

Polyvagal Tools

Polyvagal Theory Basics

According to Dr. Stephen Porges's polyvagal theory (2011), the autonomic nervous system comprises a three-part hierarchical structure: the dorsal vagal system, the sympathetic nervous system, and the ventral vagal system. Dr. Porges describes how our nervous system develops phylogenically, in other words, we can observe evolutionary stages within our human brain and physiology. For example, the *dorsal vagal system* is a primitive and evolutionarily older defensive response set that is reflective of the way in which reptiles respond to threats by immobilizing. We also have our *sympathetic nervous system* which reflects how mammals respond to fear by running away or fighting in self-defense. Finally, the *ventral vagal system* is the most recently evolved portion of the nervous system. The social nervous system leads us to seek social connection to restore a sense of safety. It is the branch of the parasympathetic nervous system that helps you relax and connect to others when you feel safe. You know that your social engagement system is activated when you feel a warmth in your smile or a sparkle in your eyes.

The polyvagal theory system is hierarchical in that each branch of the nervous system is activated sequentially in response to the perceived safety of the environment. When we feel threatened, we initially attempt to reestablish a sense of safety and connection through the social engagement system. If this is unsuccessful, we typically engage the sympathetic nervous system, which prepares us to flee the dangerous situation or fight off the threat. However, if the situation feels overwhelming with no way out, then the dorsal vagal complex becomes activated, which engages a primitive expression of the parasympathetic nervous system and causes a "shut down" or immobilization response to occur.

Importantly, unresolved traumatic stress disrupts equilibrium in the autonomic nervous system, causing an imbalance between the sympathetic and parasympathetic functions. In particular, you might be caught in a chronic state of "fight or flight," which can lead to high levels of anxiety, stress, or panic. Alternatively, you might be stuck in chronic "shut down" mode, which can lead to feelings of fatigue, depression, fogginess, dizziness, or nausea. These imbalances can also disrupt physical health, as chronic activation of the sympathetic nervous system can lead to high blood pressure, blood sugar imbalances, increased cravings for salty or sugary snacks, obesity, sluggish digestion, and a suppressed immune system. Similarly, when the dorsal vagal complex is engaged for extended periods of time, it can lead to digestive disturbances (e.g., gastric reflux or irritable bowel syndrome), chronic pain (e.g., migraine headaches or fibromyalgia), and the development of autoimmune disorders.

The good news is that the practices provided in this section can help you to find balance in these systems. While your autonomic nervous system can function without you having to think about it consciously, you can learn tools that allow you to consciously influence your physiology.

Self-Awareness of Symptoms

Explore how traumatic stress shows up in your mind and body using the following self-assessment checklist of mental, emotional, and physiological symptoms.

This first group of symptoms indicates that your sympathetic nervous system may be stuck in defensive mode.

☐ I find myself thinking about the trauma at inconvenient times.

☐ I expect the worst to happen.

☐ I have difficulty relaxing or sleeping.

☐ I feel irritable or angry often.

☐ I sometimes cry uncontrollably or feel completely overwhelmed.

☐ I feel restless or jittery.

☐ I feel anxious or panicky.

☐ I have nightmares or wake up in a fright.

☐ I experience daytime "flashbacks."

☐ I feel "on guard" or hyperaware of people's body language or tone of voice.

☐ I experience shortness of breath or feel like I cannot get enough oxygen.

☐ I feel my heart beating rapidly or feel pains in my chest.

☐ I sweat profusely.

☐ I have frequent food cravings for sweet or salty foods.

☐ I have a hard time regulating my blood sugar.

☐ I get frequent colds.

☐ I grind my teeth or clench my jaw.

☐ I experience muscle tension in my arms and legs.

☐ I have difficulty focusing my mind at work or in school.

This second grouping of symptoms is related to your parasympathetic nervous system's more primitive dorsal vagal complex.

- ☐ I often feel tired or lethargic.
- ☐ I feel hopeless or depressed.
- ☐ I feel emotionally dull or numb.
- ☐ I feel ineffective or powerless.
- ☐ I feel shame or unworthiness.
- ☐ I feel foggy or dizzy.
- ☐ I feel disoriented.
- ☐ I have difficulty remembering things.
- ☐ I find it difficult to talk sometimes.
- ☐ I sometimes "go away."
- ☐ I have indigestion or acid reflux.
- ☐ I often feel nauseous.
- ☐ After eating, I have indigestion or diarrhea.
- ☐ I have been diagnosed with an autoimmune condition.

Perhaps you notice that you alternate between these two types of symptoms—for example, being keyed up sometimes and exhausted at other times. Take some time to write about your experiences here with an intention of increasing self-awareness of your symptoms.

_____

_____

_____

_____

_____

_____

_____

_____

Mobilization and Immobilization

One of the most debilitating symptoms of PTSD is dissociation. It is much more common than many people realize, in part because dissociation can present as a wide range of symptoms, including feeling foggy, tired, shut down, lightheaded, nauseous, or numb. In addition, dissociation can sometimes lead to lapses in memory, a feeling of "lost time," or having distinct, multiple parts of the self. Dissociation is especially common with complex PTSD, which occurs as a result of long-term exposure to traumatic stress, rather than in response to a single incident.

Dissociative symptoms are painful and tend to persist. If you relate to these symptoms, it is recommended that you and your therapist become comfortable talking about dissociation in a compassionate and caring manner. Such openness can greatly support healing from trauma. With the help of a therapist, you can increase your awareness of what triggers these symptoms, and you can learn strategies to regulate your nervous system that reduce the impact of these symptoms on your life. For some, mind-body therapies, such as yoga, meditation, and breathing exercises, become valuable, life-changing daily practices that can help them to stay grounded in a sense of safety for longer and longer periods of time.

The *Reclaiming Safety in Mind and Body* exercise (on the next page) is intended to increase your nervous system flexibility. Here you explore blending your social engagement system with your sympathetic and parasympathetic nervous systems. Tapping into your social engagement system when your sympathetic nervous system is activated allows you to mobilize the resources to play, exercise, or get creative. Conversely, tapping into your social engagement system when you feel shut down or fatigued can soften your defenses, which can help you form loving connections with others, relax, and achieve better sleep. This practice of alternating between safe mobilization and immobilization helps balance your mind and body by connecting you to the restorative side of your parasympathetic nervous system (Sullivan et al., 2018).

Reclaiming Safety in Mind and Body

Begin this practice by finding a place where you know you are safe. Find a comfortable position either standing, seated, or lying down. Look around your space and identify visual cues that indicate you are safe, here and now.

Now, take several long, deep breaths. Notice the sensations and the subtle movements created by your breath. Bring your awareness to the sound of your breath. Expand your sensory awareness to notice any other sensations in your body.

Next, begin to explore *mindful mobilization* by increasing the intensity of your breath while moving your body. Maybe you stand up into an active yoga posture. Perhaps you walk vigorously in place or around the room. You can even put on your favorite song and dance. Increase your heart rate just enough to notice that your breath quickens to support your movement. If you experience any anxiety or other distress, look around your space to remind yourself that you are safe now.

Finally, begin to explore *mindful immobilization* by returning to stillness either seated or lying down. You might even begin to explore how it feels to close your eyes. Allow your heart rate to slow down. Surrender your weight down toward the earth. Invite long, deep breaths by holding the out-breath longer than the in-breath to initiate a relaxation response. Choose to be still and soften any unnecessary tension in your muscles.

If you feel stuck, collapsed, or helpless at any point, this is a sign that you have dropped into a defensive immobilization response. If this is the case, open your eyes and return your awareness to your external space. Look around the room for cues that you are safe now. Once you are connected to an experience of safety, you might choose to close your eyes again and see if you can reconnect to the restorative side of your parasympathetic nervous system. Take some time to write about your experience.

_____

_____

_____

_____

_____

_____

Tools to Increase Vagal Tone

According to polyvagal theory, our neural circuits are constantly scanning the cues in our environment and categorizing them as safe, dangerous, or potentially life-threatening so we can determine how the nervous system should respond. This process is known as *neuroception*, and it occurs automatically and operates at an unconscious level, meaning that we are not aware of it happening (Porges, 2004). Through neuroception, our nervous system is constantly on high alert, searching for cues and signals that might indicate potential danger. This can include nonverbal cues such as body language, facial expressions, tone of voice, and even the overall energy of the environment. Our brain processes this information at an unconscious level and then guides our behavioral and physiological responses accordingly (Clarke, 2023).

Neuroception is a process that occurs within our bodies, specifically through our vagus nerve. The vagus nerve connects the brain to several key organs, including the heart, lungs, and digestive system, making it the longest cranial nerve in the body. For this reason, it is also known as the *wandering nerve*. One way to measure the health of your nervous system is by assessing your vagal tone, which reflects the extent to which your body can return to baseline after stress. People with *high vagal tone* are able to bounce back more quickly and return to a state of equilibrium. On the other hand, people with *low vagal tone* have an overactive stress response system, leading to chronic anxiety symptoms and difficulty managing stress (Porges, 2007). This handout contains strategies you can use to increase your vagal tone, which will help to reduce inflammation in the body and better regulate your stress response.

Massage

Research shows that light to moderate massages on areas of the body near the vagus nerve can increase vagal tone and slow heart rate. This includes massaging your feet as well as the right side of your throat (Lu et al., 2011).

Cold Exposure

Acute cold exposure has been shown to activate the neurons that are part of the vagal nerve pathway. Exposing yourself to cold on a regular basis can also lower your sympathetic nervous system's fight-or-flight response and increase parasympathetic activity through the vagus nerve (Jungmann et al., 2018). Here are some ideas to get you started:

- Take a cold shower. You can start off slow by finishing your next shower with at least 30 seconds of cold water and see how you feel. Work your way up to longer periods of time.

- Try a cold plunge in a bath of ice and water.

- Go outside in cold temperatures with minimal clothes.

- Submerge your face in ice-cold water.

Breathwork

Deep and slow breathing is another way to stimulate your vagus nerve. Practice slowing down your breath by taking about six breaths over the course of a minute. Make sure you breathe in deeply from your diaphragm. When you do this, your stomach should expand outward as you inhale and then fall back down as you take a long and slow exhale. This is key to stimulating the vagus nerve and reaching a state of relaxation (Gerritsen & Band, 2018).

Meditation

Meditation may sound intimidating if you've never tried it before, but it is one of the most effective healing techniques to stimulate the vagus nerve and increase vagal tone. You can start with just a few minutes a day. There are also apps like *Headspace* and *Calm* that can provide you with guided sessions if you would benefit from more structure.

Exercise

While it's no surprise that exercise is good for the mind and body, physical activity has also been shown to stimulate the vagus nerve. This may explain why exercise has such beneficial effects on the brain and overall mental health (Kai et al., 2016). You should aim for 30 to 60 minutes of exercise every day, whether it's walking, lifting weights, doing yoga or Pilates, going to a workout class, playing sports, or dancing.

Singing, Humming, Chanting, and Gargling

The vagus nerve is connected to the muscles in the back of your throat, so doing activities that engage the vocal cords—like singing, humming, chanting, and gargling—are all ways to activate your vagus nerve. One easy technique is to inhale deeply, and as you exhale, make a *hmmm* sound through closed lips, feeling the vibration travel down your throat.

Socializing and Laughing

Socializing and laughing can reduce your body's stress hormones, not only when *you* laugh but even when you hear laughter (Fujiwara & Okamura, 2018). Laughter sends a signal to your body to relax and stimulates the vagus nerve, so make it a point to hang out and laugh with your friends as much as possible.

Probiotics

It's becoming increasingly clear that the bacteria in your gut affect brain function via the vagus nerve. Because of this gut-brain connection, you can improve vagal tone by taking probiotics (Appleton, 2018). There are two specific strains that are directly related to the gut-brain connection as it relates to mood, anxiety, and depression: Lactobacillus and Bifidobacterium.

Straw Breath

One of the most efficient ways to improve vagal tone and create a calm body and mind is by changing how you breathe. Conscious breathing can help you cultivate nervous system flexibility so you can tolerate a range of different arousal states while responding effectively and efficiently. The following breath practice emphasizes a long, slow exhalation to produce a parasympathetic response in your body. In this breath, you will exhale through pursed lips shaped like a straw or an O. This action will help you lengthen the out-breath as compared to the in-breath. Engaging the muscles around the mouth also initiates a subtle stimulation of your vagus nerve. I encourage you to study the effect of this breath practice by noticing how you feel emotionally or by observing changes in your state of mind. The straw breath aims to help you engage your parasympathetic nervous system by lengthening your exhalation as compared to your inhalation.

To begin, find a comfortable seat in a chair or on the floor. Notice your body sensations, your breath, and any emotions that are present for you in this moment. This will serve as a baseline and will allow you to notice subtle changes in how you feel throughout the practice.

When you are ready, begin to create a straw shape with your lips. You can practice this breath with a physical straw, as well. To begin, inhale gently. Then purse your lips and exhale very slowly through your imagined straw for a count of eight. Then close your mouth and slowly exhale through your nose for a count of two as you engage the muscles in your abdomen and diaphragm to expel all of the air from your lungs. Allow your next inhalation to come naturally, and take three regular breaths. To counterbalance any overstimulation of the sympathetic nervous system, you can focus on diaphragmatic breathing as you inhale. If you would like, repeat this exercise two or three more times.

What are you aware of now as you notice your body, mind, emotions, and level of energy? Take some time to write down any observations, knowing that you can return to this practice as often as you would like.

Nourish Your Nervous System

Given the connection between the eyes and the vagus nerve, one way to achieve natural vagal stimulation is to practice stretching and engaging the eye muscles, which can ultimately help them relax. Your eyes have a direct connection to the suboccipital muscles that sit at the base of your skill, so by moving your eyes, you can release the muscles of your neck to increase blood flow to your vertebral artery, which supplies blood to the brainstem and vagus nerve (Rosenberg, 2017). I invite you to explore these movements for yourself with this practice, which will guide you through gentle eye movements and neck stretches to nourish your nervous system. If you have a history of glaucoma or other eye concerns, I recommended that you consult with a physician prior to engaging in the eye movements in this practice. I encourage you to move slowly with these eye movements and neck stretches, which will allow you to study the subtle effects of these practices.

Orienting and Centering

To begin, find a comfortable seat in a chair or on the floor. Notice your body sensations, your breath, and any emotions that are present for you in this moment. This will serve as a baseline and will allow you to notice subtle changes in how you feel throughout the practice.

Eye Movements

If you would like, begin to gently stretch and release the muscles of your eyes by focusing your eyes on a single point that is close in distance. One option is to place your palms in prayer pose about six inches in front of your eyes. Focus your eyes on your fingertips, and after about five to ten breaths, shift your gaze off into the distance, perhaps by looking out a window. Soften your eyes and allow yourself to receive the sights all around you by broadening your visual field of awareness in a panoramic manner. See if you can remain with a widened visual awareness for about five to ten breaths as you notice how you feel in your body.

There is no need to force these movements. Rather, allow your gaze to move between these points as if greeting a long-lost friend with a warm smile. When complete, take a moment to pause and sense your body and breath. If you would like, begin to explore how it feels to bring your eyes to the left and right without turning your head. If you find that you are straining your eyes as you move from side to side, reduce the intensity by finding a smaller range of movement. After about ten sets of eye movements, return your eyes to center. As you complete these movements, notice how you feel in body, mind, and breath.

Basic Exercise with Eye Movements

If it feels right for you, bring both hands behind your head for support. Gently rest the back of your head into your hands, allowing your hands to provide a little bit of support for your head. While in this position, explore how it feels to bring your gaze toward your right elbow. Stay here for several breaths and observe for subtle cues that your body is relaxing. There is no need to strain your eyes. You might notice an urge to yawn or sigh. Do not worry if you are not experiencing an obvious signal of relaxation. After about ten breaths, bring your gaze back to center. If you would like, rest your arms for a moment and then repeat the process, bringing your gaze toward your left elbow. Then return to center, release your hands, and pause to notice how you feel.

Forward and Back Neck Release with Eye Movements

Returning both hands to the back of your head for support, explore how it feels to gently stretch your chin upward as you open your elbows wide. If you would like, reach your eyes upward as if looking toward the center of your forehead. After a few breaths, release your hands in front of your face and allow your head to curl forward, cupping your palms over your eyes and supporting the weight of your head. If feels right, allow your eyes to close and rest. Notice how it feels to breathe into the sensations of your upper back, your neck, and the base of your skull. Take your time here, and when you feel ready, slowly lift your head and release your hands.

Side Neck Release with Eye Movements

This next movement can help release the muscles of the sides of your neck. Start by bringing your right ear toward your right shoulder. You can use your right fingertips to gently support your head while reaching your left hand in the opposite direction to amplify the stretch in the left side of your neck. While in this position, explore how it feels to bring your gaze to the right. Stay here for several breaths, and if you would like, notice how it feels to bring your gaze to the left. Take about thirty seconds to a minute here, and then switch sides to open the right side of your neck. To complete this practice, return your head to center and notice your experience.

Completion

What are you aware of now as you notice your body, mind, emotions, and level of energy? Take some time to write down any observations, knowing that you can return to this practice as often as you would like.

Build Neuroception and Discern Awareness

This exercise guides you in building neuroception and increasing awareness of your nervous system state, which can help you recognize when you are unnecessarily engaging in a defensive state.

- Would you be willing to explore a brief experiment aimed at increasing your awareness of your nervous system? I invite you to allow yourself to be curious about your experience and, as much as possible, to become aware of your experience without judgment.

- There are three levels of nervous system arousal, which include feeling: (1) safe and connected, (2) mobilized for fight or flight, and (3) immobilized and collapsed. There is nothing inherently wrong with any of these nervous system states. You might notice different emotions or memories connected to each. However, it can be valuable to notice changes that occur during our sessions.

- You can build self-awareness of cues that give you feedback about the state of your nervous system. Take a few moments to observe your body movements, posture, breath, heart rate, or level of energy that give you feedback about these three states.

- Does your breath feel short or quickened? Can you sense your heartbeat in your chest? Are you aware of tension in your belly, chest, or throat? Do you notice if you are holding yourself upright in a rigid manner, or does your posture feel collapsed? Do you feel calm, energetic, restless, or fatigued? What do these cues from your body tell you about your nervous system state?

- Our minds are constantly scanning for cues of threats. These cues might come from our external environment, our body, or our relationships. We engage our defenses when we perceive that we are not safe. If you notice that you are moving into a fight-or-flight response or are feeling immobilized and collapsed, see if you can notice what is leading you to feel unsafe.

- I invite you to share with me when you notice changes during sessions, as this will allow us to work together as a team to create a safe environment for trauma recovery.

- You can also enhance your awareness of your nervous system states between sessions. This will help give you feedback about how you are responding to your environment. It may also be helpful to ask yourself if you are responding accurately to a threat that is happening right now. Or perhaps you are reacting unnecessarily to a feeling that is connected to a memory from your past. Can you sense if your defensive response is necessary for the present circumstances?

Awaken Your Social Engagement System

This exercise enhances your social engagement system by inviting you to engage in small experiments in which you explore how subtle changes in somatic awareness can help you develop a felt sense of trust, connection, safety, and stabilization.

- Would you be willing to explore a brief experiment aimed at helping you connect to your social engagement system? Your social engagement system represents one branch of your vagus nerve, which passes through your face, throat, lungs, heart, and belly. Gentle movements and breaths through these areas of your body can help you feel safe and connected to yourself and others. I invite you to allow yourself to be curious about your experience and, as much as possible, to become aware of your experience without judgment.

- Let's begin by noticing your eyes. See if you can sense any tension or fatigue in this area of your face. Explore some movements in your eyes by widening them or squeezing them shut. Then begin to explore how it feels to soften your eyes into a gentle expression of warmth. If you'd like, think of someone you care about, and imagine sharing with them a loving smile from your eyes. Notice how the changes in how you express yourself through your eyes resonates in other areas of your body.

- Bring your attention to your mouth. Once again, see if you notice any tension in your jaw, lips, or cheeks. If you would like, find some movements to explore any sensations here by opening your mouth and closing it tightly. You might even fake a yawn until you induce a real yawn, as this can release tension in the jaw and soft palate in the back of your mouth. Then soften your jaw and allow your teeth to gently separate from one another. As with the eyes, you might imagine a loved one and engage a soft smile. As you release tension around your mouth, notice if you experience any corresponding release of tension in other areas of your face or body.

- Bring your attention to your throat. Notice if you are aware of any sensations or tension in this area of your body. Sense your breath as it moves through the back of your throat and encourages a deepening of your awareness into this area of your body. Perhaps explore any sighs or sounds that resonate with the sensations in your throat. If you would like, explore slowly dipping your head forward and lifting your head up. Notice the feeling of contraction in your throat and subsequent opening. Pause in stillness and notice any related sensations in other areas of your body.

- Bring your attention to your chest. If you notice any tension around your chest or shoulders, explore rolling your shoulders forward and back. Continue moving until you feel more connected to this area of your body. Now imagine your heart nestled into your lungs and how they are deeply interconnected. Your breath is a wonderful way to connect to your heart. Perhaps you would like to bring your hands over your heart and begin to sense the subtle movements of your breath in the lifting and lowering of your chest. With this quality of interconnection in mind, explore how it feels to reflect on a friend or a pet that enhances your sense of connection, gratitude, and love. As you breathe into this loving feeling, notice any related sensations in your body.

- Now bring awareness to your belly, and begin to notice any sensations, tension, or discomfort here. If you would like, bring your hands over your belly and begin to focus on breathing through your diaphragm, allowing your belly to rise with each inhale. See if you can release tension by softening your belly with each exhale. You might choose to close your eyes and settle into your chair. Notice how you feel as you let yourself be heavy or relax into support. See if you notice any subtle shifts in your digestion, such as a soft gurgling in your stomach or intestines, as a result of the deepening of your breath. Can you sense any other signs that your body is relaxing in response to your belly breathing?

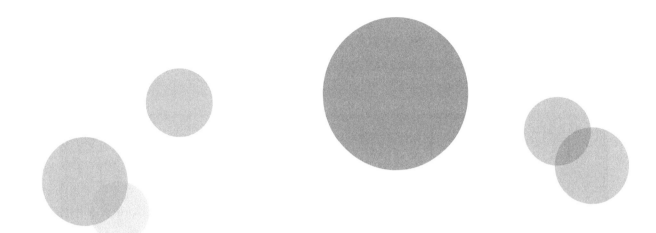

CHAPTER 6

Attachment Tools

Attachment Theory

Attachment theory explains how our early developmental experiences provide the basis for our sense of self. Our memories of these relational interactions are held deep within the implicit memory system. Children who grow up with caregivers who are predictable, consistent, attuned, and trustworthy will develop a *secure* attachment style. They can reach for connection yet also differentiate themselves from their primary caregiver. They feel supported in having boundaries and, thus, are able to develop an embodied sense of self. As adults, these individuals are able to move with relative ease between their needs for closeness and their needs for separateness.

In contrast, children who grow up with distant or disengaged caregivers might adapt by avoiding closeness, disconnecting emotionally, or becoming overly self-reliant. As adults, they may develop an *insecure-avoidant* attachment style, leading them to dismiss their own and other people's emotions or needs. Other children may grow up with caregivers who are both highly perceptive but can also be intrusive or invasive. This unpredictable parenting style can lead children to feel as though they cannot consistently depend upon their caregiver for connection. Consequently, they may develop an *insecure-ambivalent* attachment style that is characterized by uncertainty, anxiety, fears of abandonment, and a sense that relationships are unreliable.

In the most extreme situations of abuse, individuals may develop a *disorganized* attachment style. In these situations, children grow up with a parent whose behavior is a source of alarm or terror. Children are born with an innate, biological drive to attach with their primary caregiver and an equally strong drive to escape any source of threat. Since infants and young children are completely dependent upon their parents, those who grow up in an abusive environment must attach to the very person who is abusing them, and they must disconnect from the reality of the abuse in order to survive. This pattern often leads to dissociative symptoms in clients with C-PTSD.

Because we carry our relational experiences inside of us, these implicitly held memories can lead to relationship problems in adulthood that replay the painful dynamics of childhood. We engage in behaviors and interactional styles that are consistent with what we know and who we know ourselves to be. You can think of these early attachment relationships as teaching us a series of dance steps. We tend to look for others who dance in a similar manner, and if they don't, we hand them the instructions. For example, someone who was chronically rejected in childhood might continue to experience feelings of isolation or carry a belief that they are unlovable. They might feel overly dependent on others or unintentionally behave in a manner that leads someone to pull away from them. Conversely, they might carry a deep fear of intimacy that leads them to push others away when they get too close. Sometimes they might act aggressively or impulsively when intolerable emotions arise. As you can see, all of these relationship interactions can mimic abuse experienced during childhood. As a result, it is harder to navigate the typical challenges that arise when forming intimate relationships, parenting children, or developing meaningful friendships.

Adult Attachment Patterns

Use this worksheet to begin thinking about how your early developmental experiences shaped who you are today.

1. Describe your early family situation: where you were born, where you lived, whether you moved around much, what your caregivers did at various times for a living.

    _____

    _____

    _____

2. Describe your relationship with your parents as a young child. Begin as far back as you can remember.

    _____

    _____

    _____

3. Please choose five adjectives or words that reflect *your relationship with your mother* (or primary caregiver) starting from as far back as you can remember in early childhood—as early as you can go, but say, age 5 to 12 is fine.

    Mother (or primary caregiver):

    a. _____   b. _____   c. _____

    d. _____   e. _____

4. Think of an example for each word to illustrate a memory or experience that supports the word.

    _____

    _____

    _____

    _____

    _____

    _____

5. Please choose five adjectives or words that reflect *your relationship with your father* (or other caregiver) starting from as far back as you can remember in early childhood—as early as you can go, but say, age 5 to 12 is fine.

    Father (or primary caregiver):

    a. _____   b. _____   c. _____

    d. _____   e. _____

6. Think of an example for each word to illustrate a memory or experience that supports the word.

    _____

    _____

    _____

    _____

    _____

    _____

7. Which parent or caregiver did you feel closer to, and why?

    _____

    _____

    _____

8. As a child, when you got upset, what would you do?

    _____

    _____

    _____

9. What was it like the first time you were separated from your parents or other caregivers?

    _____

    _____

    _____

10. What was it like for you and for them during this separation?

_____

_____

_____

11. If you were sick, injured, or emotionally distressed, what would happen?

_____

_____

_____

12. Were you ever very afraid or terrified of your caregivers? If so, how often?

_____

_____

_____

13. How did your relationship with your caregivers change over time?

_____

_____

_____

14. As a child, did anyone close to you ever die or leave you? If so, who?

_____

_____

_____

15. How were those losses for you, and how did they impact you and your family?

_____

_____

_____

16. Are you close with your caregivers now? Why or why not?

_____

_____

_____

17. Why do you think your caregivers behaved the way they did while you were growing up?

_____

_____

_____

18. What are the main things you've learned about caring for a child from your caregivers?

_____

_____

_____

19. How do you feel all of these issues of your attachment history have affected your ability to be open, to attune, and to resonate with others in your personal or your professional life?

_____

_____

_____

20. Did you find this worksheet difficult? What was most difficult about it?

_____

_____

_____

Family Values

Your family of origin is the environment that initially shapes your understanding of "normal." However, just as attachment isn't necessarily love, "normal" isn't necessarily healthy. As an adult, it's important to examine those values that you introjected as a child. That is what this worksheet will help you do.

Circle the words and phrases that are most descriptive of the way your family system functioned while you were growing up.

Lenient/Permissive	Open	Closed
Unenforced rules	Reasonable rules	Strict rules
Spoiling	Nurturing	Punishing
Unstructured	Structured	Rigidly structured
Unsupervised	Supervised	Rigidly supervised
Disorganized	Flexible	Chaotic or rigid
Ungrounded thinking	Okay to think for self	Thinking is done for you
Ignore choices	Have choices	Choices are strictly limited
Lack direction	Appropriate guidance	Dictatorial
Overly tolerant	Tolerant	Intolerant
Ignore verbal abuse	Verbally respectful	Verbally abusive
Ignore tirades	Emotions are allowed	Emotions are punished
Abandoning	Healthy	Abusive
Lost	Freeing	Enslaving

Circle the spiritual values that you learned as a little kid.

We learned that God is . . .		
Unreliable	Consistent	Strictly rule-bound
Illogical	Balanced	Extreme
Best ignored	Safe	Demanding
Disinterested/unconcerned	Caring	Angry

Which of the description(s) in the previous tables best fits your family of origin experience?

_____

_____

_____

What role(s) best helped you live in your family of origin. Hero? Overachiever? Rebel? Scapegoat? Lost child? Target child (i.e., singled out for abuse)? Clown? Other? Give an example.

_____

_____

_____

Describe a typical scene (or two) that illustrates a day in the life of a child within your family of origin.

_____

_____

_____

If you are in a family now, circle the category that best describes your family system.

Lenient/Permissive   Open   Closed

Family Sociogram

This is an art project. Well, it's sort of an art project, but unlike most art projects, this one requires *zero talent* in the art department (seriously). You will be plotting your family constellation using a "sociogram," placing all the focus on the process rather than product. Developed by Jay Moreno (of psychodrama fame), a sociogram is a graphic representation of your interpersonal relationships.

To draw a sociogram of your family, list the members of your family by placing each name within its own circle on a piece of paper. Use a ray (i.e., a solid line with an arrow at the end) to represent any relationships in which one person feels a close attachment to the other. If the feeling is reciprocated, then draw a solid line with arrows at both ends. For any relationships in which the pair is not closely attached or is in conflict with one another, connect them with a broken line. When you're done, answer the following questions regarding your family sociogram.

What circles did you draw first? Why?

_____

_____

_____

_____

Did you need to change or erase anything? Why?

_____

_____

_____

_____

Look at the sizes of the circles. How do they compare with one another?

_____

_____

_____

_____

Where did you place the circles spatially in relation to one another (far away, close to, on top of, below, or next to one another)?

_____

_____

_____

_____

How complex or simple is the drawing?

_____

_____

_____

_____

Do you notice any patterns or textures that might be psychologically significant? If so, describe that here.

_____

_____

_____

_____

Was there anything surprising to you about your sociogram or the exercise in general? Why or why not?

_____

_____

_____

_____

Repairenting: Imagery for Disrupted Attachment

This imagery exercise is designed to facilitate the development and introjection of an emotionally attuned, mirroring, nurturing attachment figure—a competent inner parent providing unconditional positive regard—not unlike Winnicott's "good-enough mother."

To begin, allow yourself to be comfortable, either lying down or sitting up, with your back, neck, and spine fully supported. Knowing that you will not be interrupted for the next little while, begin by gently closing your eyes.

(Clinician should breathe audibly with the exhalation longer than the inhalation.)

Now bring your attention to the direct experience of your breath—however it is, and however it changes. Allow yourself to softly focus your awareness on the breath that is arising right now . . . the in-breath and the out-breath . . . the rising and the falling. If you can, try to follow one full cycle of the breath from the beginning of the in-breath through its entirety to the beginning of the out-breath through its entirety. Allow yourself the time and the space to be in direct contact with the breath throughout one entire cycle.

(Clinician should breathe audibly with the exhalation longer than the inhalation.)

As you continue to pay attention to the breath, you may notice distractions that arise. Just allow yourself to notice those distractions . . . any bodily sensations and any thoughts that may arise. If possible, allow yourself to become aware of the separateness of those bodily sensations. Notice how those sensations are separate—distinct from your thoughts, your ideas, and your words.

(Clinician should breathe audibly with the exhalation longer than the inhalation.)

Now, as you continue with this focused awareness, you will notice how often you lose contact with the breath . . . maybe you become caught in a thought or an idea or plan or maybe some other bodily sensation pulls your attention. When a distraction happens, simply notice that you have lost connection with the breath, and gently bring your awareness back to the breath.

(Clinician should breathe audibly with the exhalation longer than the inhalation.)

Gently bring your awareness to any sensations in your body. Notice any tension, pressure, tightness, warmth, coolness, pain, or other recognizable sensations. You may also notice that the thinking part of your brain wants to label these sensations. Allow it, and then gently return your awareness to the direct experience of the sensations themselves. If you'd like, begin to notice sensations in various parts of the body. You might begin with the feet, working your way up the body . . . noticing the ankles, shins, knees, thighs, buttocks, hips, lower back, upper back, shoulders, biceps, elbows, forearms, wrists, hands . . . now beginning again at the neck . . . jaw . . . behind and under the eyes, forehead, crown of the head, and finally the back of the head. If you'd like, you may consciously relax any overly tight muscles—noticing your choice to do so or not.

Maintain this awareness for the next little while.

(Wait 45 seconds.)

Now gently allow your attention and awareness to rest on any sensations in the abdomen or belly area. Notice any sensations—whether "comfort" or "discomfort." Without any effort to distract yourself from them or to change them, allow the sensations to just be there. If you do try to get rid of them or distract yourself from them, simply notice that you have done so, then gently return your awareness to the sensations.

Maintain this awareness for the next little while.

(Wait 45 seconds.)

Now, with a gentle breath, bring to mind a time when you were close to—that is, physically close to—somebody; somebody you could trust, fully and completely. It could be anybody: a parent or grandparent, sister or brother, or a family member; it could be a friend, a partner, or anybody else—anyone with whom you have had many experiences of complete trust.

If you are unable to conjure such a person, bring to mind a childhood pet to whom you felt connected and whom you trusted completely.

Bring to mind the image of this person or pet. Invite this person or animal to be here with you now. Take as much time as you need to feel this presence fully. Look deeply into the face of this person or pet, seeing as clearly as you can. While gazing into one another's eyes, take a few deep breaths—holding this experience of connection.

Now bring to mind a time in your early childhood when you felt happy—just comfortable, unworried, and at ease . . . it may be a time when you were with this trusted person or pet. With that image in your mind, gently bring your attention to your abdomen, noticing any sensations associated with this memory of contentment and happiness in childhood.

Looking deeply into the face of the person or pet, notice their reaction to your experience of this fond memory. Perhaps you see no reaction, and if that is the case, simply notice and then return to your attention to your own emotions and bodily sensations. If you see a reaction on the face of the person or pet, notice it . . . and then again notice your own emotions and bodily sensations and/or feelings about the other's reaction.

Maintain this awareness for the next little while.

(Wait 45 seconds.)

Now, bring to mind a time in your early childhood when you felt emotional discomfort—maybe a time when you felt threatened, frightened, frustrated, angry, helpless, or ashamed and humiliated.

Begin looking deeply into the face of the person or pet and notice their reaction to your experience of this unpleasant memory. Perhaps you see no reaction, and if that is the case, simply notice and then return your attention to your own emotions and bodily sensations. If you see a reaction on the face of the person or pet, notice it . . . and then again, notice your own emotions and bodily sensations and/or feelings about their reaction.

Try and stay with this experience of your mutual reactions for at least 15 seconds.

Now, letting go of that image, refocus your attention on your breath—the direct experience of the breath—however it is . . . and however it changes. Allow yourself to softly focus your awareness on the breath that is arising right now . . . the in-breath and the out-breath . . . the rising and the falling. If you can, try to follow one full cycle of the breath from the beginning of the in-breath through its entirety to the beginning of the out-breath through its entirety. Allow yourself the time and the space to be in direct contact with the breath throughout one entire cycle.

(Clinician should breathe audibly with the exhalation longer than the inhalation.)

Now, consider the possibility that you may presently have such a person or pet within your own mind. Allow yourself to conjure an image or concept of such a being . . . allow it to take any shape or form.

Give yourself a few moments to observe this being. Notice its qualities . . . Does it appear soothing? Receptive and attuned? Kind? Concerned? Understanding? Does it appear forgiving? Charitable? Patient and tolerant? Does it seem as capable and competent? Reliable and trustworthy? Nurturing and devoted as the person or pet with whom you interacted just a few minutes ago?

Now, make some gentle inquiries about this being, "Does this being appear to be disapproving and judgmental or loving and accepting? Does it appear to be kind and generous or mean-spirited and inconsiderate? Does this being appear to provide safety and security or does it appear dangerous? How do you feel about this entity? Do you trust this entity or not?"

With this new entity in mind, gently allow yourself to notice any sensations in your body . . . paying particular attention to your abdomen . . . noticing any feelings that come up around this being. Just for a moment, withholding any labels or judgments, allow the sensations and feelings to remain in your awareness.

(Wait 45 seconds.)

Now, keeping this being close, bring to mind a time in your early childhood when you felt happy—just comfortable, unworried, and at ease. With this image in your mind, gently bring your attention once again to your abdomen—noticing any sensations associated with this memory of contentment and happiness in childhood.

Now, looking deeply into the face of this being, notice the other's reaction to your experience of this fond memory. Perhaps you see no reaction, and if that is the case, simply notice and then return to your attention to your own emotions and bodily sensations. If you see a reaction on the face of this being, just notice it . . . and then once again, notice your own emotions and bodily sensations and/or feelings about the other's reaction.

(Wait 45 seconds.)

Again, keeping this being close, bring to mind a time in your early childhood when you felt emotionally uncomfortable—maybe a time when you felt threatened, frightened, frustrated, angry, helpless, or ashamed and humiliated.

Looking deeply into the face of this being, notice the other's reaction to your experience of this memory. Perhaps you see no reaction, and if that is the case, simply notice and then return to your attention to your own emotions and bodily sensations. If you see a reaction on the face of the being, notice it . . . and then again, notice your own emotions and bodily sensations and/or feelings about the other's reaction.

Now, with a gentle breath, begin to notice any appraisals, assessments, judgments, opinions, beliefs, interpretations, or any other ideas that occur as you continue to focus on your bodily sensations, feelings, and/or emotions as they relate to what you have experienced during this meditation.

(Wait 20 seconds.)

Now, letting go of that image, refocus your attention on your breath—the direct experience of the breath—however it is . . . and however it changes. Allow yourself to softly focus your awareness onto the breath that is arising right now . . . the in-breath and the out-breath . . . the rising and the falling. If you can, try to follow one full cycle of the breath from the beginning of the in-breath through its entirety to the beginning of the out-breath through its entirety. Allow yourself the time and the space to be in direct contact with the breath throughout one entire cycle.

(Clinician should breathe audibly with the exhalation longer than the inhalation.)

And when you are ready, begin to notice the chair or bed beneath you. Pay attention to the sensations in your feet. Now your hands . . . gently make a fist, then release it, stretching your fingers wide. Now, bring yourself back to this room by slowly counting up from one to five. When you reach the number five, your eyes will gently open. You will be awake and alert, and feeling only peace. One . . . two . . . three. Take a deep breath . . . four . . . and five.

Transference Exercise

Begin this exercise by conjuring up an image of your significant other, your spouse, or a close friend. Now bring to mind some aspect of their personality to which you have a strong reaction—positive or negative.

Write down your reaction here:

_____

_____

_____

Now describe in some detail that aspect (or those aspects) of their personality and your reaction to them. Write down the thoughts and feelings you have while experiencing that part of them. Write down how you behave in reaction to that part.

_____

_____

_____

_____

_____

_____

Next, conjure up an image of your parents or primary caregivers.

Is the personality characteristic of the person that you wrote about, along with your reaction to it, reminiscent of—or in some way similar to—your relationship with one (or both) of your parents /caregivers?

Note: Transference may be trickier than simply reacting to others the way you reacted to your parent(s). Here are several possibilities:

- You see the other in the same way as you believed your parent to have been (simple transference).

- You see the other as being like what you *wish* your parent *could* have been like.

- You see the *other as you* were as a child, and you act as your parent did.

- You see the other as you were as a child, and you act like you *wished* your parent could have acted.

Attachment Timeline

You may be surprised at how much information clients have forgotten about that emerges when you ask them to write down their painful patterns or moments on a timeline. This intervention helps clients see and understand issues that previously may have felt out of reach or hidden. It allows them to trace how unresolved trauma may have dogged their trail, how pain has been carried and repeated. It can also help them identify times when they did get the support they needed or break their silence, feel, and heal.

1. Provide the client with a copy of the *Attachment Timeline* worksheet (on the next page) or a blank sheet of paper and a writing utensil.

2. Ask the client to recall relational patterns or moments from their life and add these to their timeline. I recommend keeping your instructions vague so that they don't try to get it "right." You might say, "Jot down any moments in your life, relational dynamics, or events that felt impactful. This might include moments that hurt you, frightened you, felt traumatizing, or made you withdraw into yourself and shut down, as well as moments when you felt seen, heard, and understood. Take your time. There are no wrong answers; just add anything that comes to you."

3. When they are done, invite the client to share their timeline.

4. When done in a group format, you can move into focused role plays once clients are finished with their timelines. Invite the clients to talk to themselves at any point along their development, using an empty chair or a role player to represent them at that age. Some clients may wish to talk to a future self (whether a feared one or a desired one) or trace their timeline back into the past—even before they were born—to understand intergenerational trauma.

Attachment Timeline*

Next to the appropriate, approximate years, jot down anything in your life that felt impactful. This might include events, periods of time, or relational dynamics that felt deeply hurtful, frightening, or overwhelming, such as moments you felt frozen or became immobilized. It might also include moments when you felt seen, heard, and understood.

	80	
	75	
	70	
	65	
	60	
	55	
	50	
	45	
	40	
	35	
	30	
	25	
	20	
	15	
	10	
	5	
	0	

* Reprinted from *Relational Trauma Repair Therapist's Guide (revised edition)*, © 2014 Tian Dayton.

Developing a Nurturing Voice

Developing a nurturing inner voice is one way to counterbalance the critical parental messages that so many of us have introjected—the voice that keeps telling you that you're not good enough, that something is wrong with you, that you've always been a disappointment and will always be. Presently, that voice and its messages serve only to limit you and keep you stuck in the past, whereas creating a new one—a responsive, empathic voice to calm, soothe and encourage you—would be much more helpful in the present.

Exercise 1

Ask yourself these questions:

1. Do you know anybody who has this nurturing quality? They may be real or fictional—it really doesn't matter. Who is it?

2. When you've settled on one person, bring them to mind and allow them to truly come to life. Picture the person in their nurturing aspect. What does this person look like? What are they doing? Perhaps singing to a child, stroking their hair? Using a calming voice when a child is scared? Cooking a favorite meal? Reading a storybook? Whatever feels right.

3. Allow that scene of nurture to become as vivid as possible. Truly listen to the words being said and the tone of voice that nurturing figure is using.

4. Now, imagine being one of the people in the scene, either the child or the nurturing figure, whichever feels right for you. What would it feel like to be that child or nurturing figure? Try taking on that role. Truly embody it for a few minutes.

5. Now imagine a time when you were criticizing yourself. Hear the words you said and the feelings that those words brought up for you.

6. Now consciously switch out of the critical voice and into this more nurturing one—words and tone.

7. Notice what it feels like to be responded to with kindness and compassion instead of criticism.

8. Practice this imaginally a few more times.

9. The next time you find yourself using the critical voice, once again consciously switch out of the critical voice and into this more nurturing one, both words and tone.

10. Practice switching voices as often as you are able.

Exercise 2

1. Remember a time when someone said "thank you," and you knew that they truly meant it. How did it feel to be acknowledged, appreciated, or loved? Embody that feeling for a few moments.

2. Now remember a time when a loved one acknowledged something good that you did or said. How did it feel to be acknowledged, appreciated, or loved? Embody that feeling for a few moments.

3. Now remember a time when you felt appreciated or loved. How did it feel to be acknowledged, appreciated, or loved? Embody that feeling for a few moments.

4. What do you value most about yourself?

5. Of the people to whom you matter (and who matter to you), if asked, what would they say they value most in you? What qualities do they admire?

6. Now, think of your closest friend. If asked, what would they claim to value most in you? Are those things the same (i.e., do you value the same things in you that your friend does)?

7. What other things about you do you value, but others may not recognize? What are they?

Traumatic Attachment Patterns

Recognizing the signs of traumatic attachment can help you in adult relationships. Are you putting up with too much? Or are you not willing to put up with anything? Are you confusing your partner with your reactions to distance and closeness? Do you need to leave this relationship, or are you just triggered?

Check the signs of traumatic attachment that you recognize:

☐ Difficulty with not being listened to

☐ Difficulty when people don't understand you

☐ Worrying that they don't love you; feeling unlovable

☐ Fear of being abandoned

☐ Fear of being cheated on

☐ Not wanting to be touched

☐ Wanting to be held all the time; only feeling safe when someone is there

☐ Worrying you're not good enough

☐ Worrying the other person isn't good enough for you

☐ Wanting to leave bad relationships but you can't

☐ Wanting to run away when you get close to someone

☐ Can't bear being alone/apart

☐ Feeling suffocated

☐ Putting up with abusive behavior

☐ Not letting your partner in; unable to share feelings

☐ Feeling rage when feelings are hurt

☐ Unable to tolerate partner's anger or silence

☐ Unable to set boundaries or say, "This is not okay"

Remember that these patterns developed as a way to survive when you were very young. They were the best you could do in a bad situation.

The Four Steps to Freedom

Claudia Black's (1999) "Four Steps to Freedom" provides a simple tool for you to work your way to freedom from the past. Use this worksheet whenever you find yourself being triggered. With repeated practice, you will find yourself increasingly able to recognize that you have been triggered, to trust that there is a connection to the past, and to assume that you are still carrying some conscious or unconscious belief as a result of that experience. Once you become aware of how these old beliefs are constricting your life, it becomes easier and easier to challenge them.

1. Assume that the distress you are experiencing has been triggered and is related to the childhood past. Describe that distress (tears, hurt, anger, shame, hopelessness), and see what happens when you assume it is triggered and related to the past.

   _____

   _____

   _____

   _____

   _____

   _____

   _____

2. Connect that distress to its roots in the traumatic past by fast-forwarding through your childhood history for 20–30 seconds and noticing where the feelings and body sensations best fit. Describe in just 1–2 sentences where the distress fits. Try to acknowledge where it might fit rather than trying to be sure.

   _____

   _____

   _____

   _____

   _____

   _____

   _____

3. Identify the internalized old beliefs that developed as a result of that experience. Describe a belief or beliefs about yourself that resulted from how you were treated.

_____

_____

_____

_____

_____

_____

_____

4. Find a way to challenge that old belief so that you can begin to develop new beliefs that better fit your life today. Describe what happens when you label the belief as old. What would you like to believe now? What would you want a child in that situation to believe?

_____

_____

_____

_____

_____

_____

_____

Family Trifold

The family trifold is a great tool to help you identify what characteristics and values (both positive and negative) you learned from your parents. For example, you may like the ways in which your parents interacted with others, or you may feel the exact opposite and want to modify how you handle your own interactions. The empowering part of this intervention is that you get to choose! It helps create perspective because no person is all bad or all good, even though it may seem that way at times. Every person has some positives and some negatives. One may outweigh the other, but both sides exist. By thinking about the pros and cons of your parents, who were your first relationship models, you can begin to evaluate who you want to become. It can also help you break the cycle of any abusive behaviors that you want to be intentional about not repeating.

To begin this exercise, fold a piece of paper into thirds, creating a trifold. Then draw a horizontal line through the middle. On the first third of the paper, write "Mom" at the top, as well as a plus sign in the top half of the page for her positive traits and a minus sign in the bottom half for her negative traits. Do the same thing for the two remaining sections, except write "Me" and "Dad" in the top sections instead, respectively. Alternatively, you can use the blank *Family Trifold* at the end of this worksheet.

Once you're done, fold the paper into thirds so that only one person is visible at a time in order to increase focus and decrease distraction. Complete the "Mom" and "Dad" sections first, then move on to your own. Make sure to write down several examples in each category. If you are having a hard time coming up with examples, remember that no one is all good or all bad. Every person has pros and cons.

Once the trifold is completed, highlight all the similarities you share with your parents—both the pros and the cons. For example, in the sample *Family Trifold* template, the person may find validation in realizing that they are similar to their parents in terms of being kind and liking to help others. They may identify that they want to be more like their parents with regard to cooking or fixing things. That realization, in turn, may give them some positive goals that they can use to connect to their parents, whether they are still alive or have passed on.

Similarly, in realizing that they are distant and yell a lot, that same person may identify these as areas in which they want to change. These may be qualities that they did not appreciate about their parents and that they do not want to pass on to their own family. They may recognize that they will have to be vigilant about not becoming disorganized or always running late because these are the traits that were modeled for them. If they want to be different, then they will have to be intentional in doing these things a new way.

Completing this exercise can be a powerful experience, as you may realize that you have already become like your parents in many ways. This realization can be validating in terms of the positives, but also anxiety-provoking in terms of the negatives. Remember that anything that is learned can also be unlearned. You can change anything you want to because *you* are in control of who you become. Relational styles are learned behaviors that can be unlearned and relearned at any time. You can nurture the positive traits you want to keep and change the negative traits that you do not want to repeat. You have the power to change.

Mom	Me	Dad
+ Humble Likes to help others Good cook	+ Kind Achiever Like to help others	+ Good provider Kind Helps me fix things
— Always busy Disorganized Yells a lot	— Distant Yells a lot Risk taker	— Distant Always late Not compassionate

Family Trifold

Dad		
+		

Me		
+		

Mom		
+		

Worry and Connection

When you have experienced attachment trauma, it can lead you to fear that other significant relationships in your life will end as well. For example, if your parent passed away, you may become anxious about losing other close loved ones, such as a remaining parent, sibling, or spouse. Attachment trauma can also cause you to feel anxiety in relationships whenever a relationship rupture or disconnect happens. This can reinforce negative beliefs, such as the belief that you are unlovable or not good enough. This worksheet helps you identify patterns of connection and disconnection in your relationships and examine how anxiety impacts your relationships.

1. How have your last three relationships ended?

   _____

   _____

   _____

   _____

   _____

2. Is there a pattern to how your relationships have ended? Why or why not?

   _____

   _____

   _____

   _____

   _____

3. How does this impact how you feel about future relationships?

   _____

   _____

   _____

   _____

   _____

4. What could you do differently to control the outcome of the next relationship?

_____

_____

_____

_____

_____

5. What can you control about your relationships?

_____

_____

_____

_____

_____

6. What can you not control about your relationships?

_____

_____

_____

_____

_____

Sadness and Loss of Connection

Sometimes when a relationship ends, people are only able to see the things that they lost. This can lead them to spiral deeper into depression and to lose all motivation to keep moving forward. While the loss of a relationship is challenging, it can also make you stronger. This worksheet will help you identify the pros and cons of the relationship that you lost, bringing you into a more balanced mindset.

1. The things that I enjoyed most about this relationship were:

    _____

    _____

    _____

    _____

    _____

2. The things that I did not enjoy about this relationship were:

    _____

    _____

    _____

    _____

    _____

3. I feel sad that this relationship ended because:

    _____

    _____

    _____

    _____

    _____

4. I can express my sadness in these healthy ways:

    _____

    _____

    _____

    _____

    _____

5. I feel relieved that this relationship ended because:

    _____

    _____

    _____

    _____

    _____

6. If I am feeling overwhelmed, I can:

    _____

    _____

    _____

    _____

    _____

7. What I learned from this relationship:

    _____

    _____

    _____

    _____

    _____

CHAPTER 7

Brain-Based Neuroscience Tools

How Your Brain Remembers the Trauma

After a traumatic event or a traumatic life, survivors might have only a very fragmented narrative of what happened or no clear story at all. Many survivors say, "I don't remember anything," without realizing that when they suddenly startle, feel afraid, tighten up, pull back, feel shame or self-hatred, or start to tremble, they *are* remembering the past. Because trauma is remembered emotionally and somatically more than it is remembered in a narrative form that can be expressed verbally, survivors often feel confused, overwhelmed, or crazy. Without a memory in words or pictures, they do not recognize what they are feeling as memory.

What they also do not realize is that human beings do not just remember events. We remember in many different ways. Each brain area stores memory in a different way and form. With the thinking brain, we might remember the story of what happened but without a lot of emotion connected to it. With our sensory systems, we might spontaneously see the images or hear the sounds connected to the event. Our emotions might remember how something felt. Our bodies might remember the impulses and movements and the physical sensations (tightening, trembling, sinking feelings, fluttering, quivering) experienced at the time.

Write in what each part of your brain remembers. There is no need to write in all the details. Just a few words or sentences is fine—such as "I remember what happened" or "I don't remember my childhood" or "I can talk about it without any feelings" or "I only have overwhelming feelings and reactions."

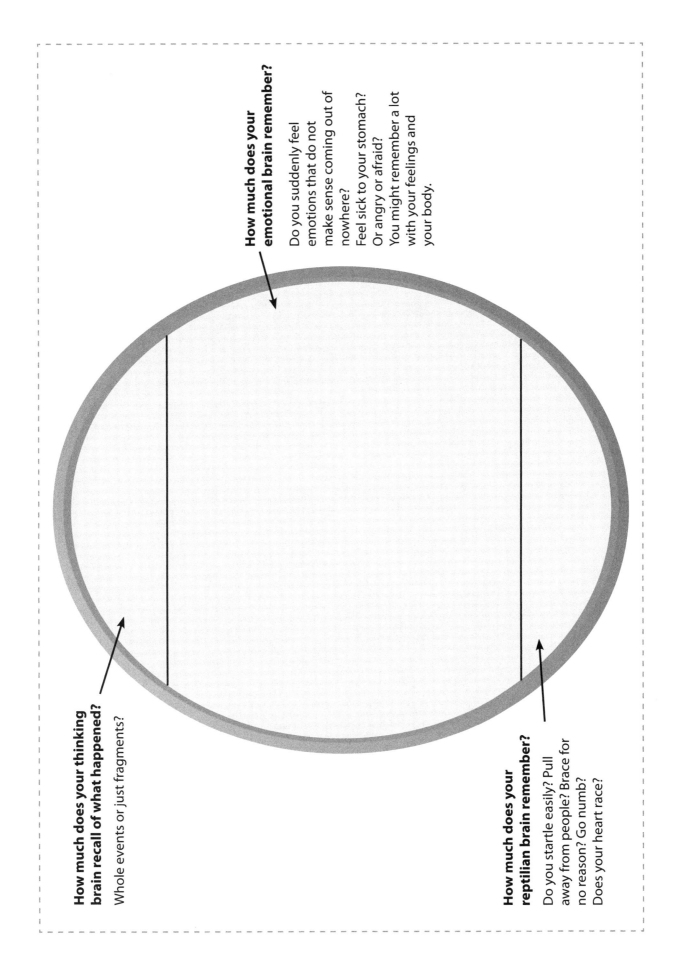

How much does your emotional brain remember?

Do you suddenly feel emotions that do not make sense coming out of nowhere?
Feel sick to your stomach?
Or angry or afraid?
You might remember a lot with your feelings and your body.

How much does your thinking brain recall of what happened?

Whole events or just fragments?

How much does your reptilian brain remember?

Do you startle easily? Pull away from people? Brace for no reason? Go numb? Does your heart race?

Recognizing Triggers and Triggering

Each time you think you might be triggered, write in your reaction (feelings, thoughts, physical responses), its intensity, what was happening just before, and how you coped. Did you try to ignore it or suppress it? Did you judge yourself or the trigger? Do not judge, just notice.

Date, time, situation	Feelings, thoughts, and physical sensations that got triggered	Intensity: 0–10	Trigger: *What was happening just before?*	Coping: *What did you do to cope?*

How Can You Tell You Are Triggered?

Recognizing the signs of being triggered helps you to know your reality: Are you triggered, or are you really in danger? Do you need to leave your job, or are you just experiencing being triggered? Recognizing that you are triggered does not mean your feelings are unimportant. It means that your feelings are remembering something far worse than what triggers them.

Check the signs of being triggered that you recognize:

☐ Shaking, quivering   ☐ Wanting to run away

☐ Overwhelming emotions   ☐ Teeth clenching

☐ Difficulty breathing   ☐ Feeling unbearable

☐ Body wanting to collapse   ☐ Feeling terrified, panicky

☐ Feeling "possessed"   ☐ Hating yourself

☐ Wanting to give up or die   ☐ Hating others

☐ Wanting to hurt myself   ☐ Feeling rage

☐ Wanting to drink or use drugs   ☐ Feeling overwhelming shame

☐ Knees knocking   ☐ Emotions do not fit the situation

☐ Going numb all over   ☐ Actions do not fit the situation

☐ Sudden intense physical or emotional reactions   ☐ Clenching or churning or pit in stomach

When you recognize the signs of being triggered, just keep reminding yourself that "it's just triggering—I am triggered—that's all that is happening."

How Our Nervous System Defends Us

When we are in danger, the sympathetic nervous system is immediately mobilized. Heart rate speeds up to increase oxygen flow to muscle tissue. We feel a surge of energy, and all nonessential systems in the body shut down, including the thinking brain, so that all our energy is focused on fighting, fleeing, ducking, or getting out of sight. Two conditions then activate the parasympathetic system. If defending ourselves is more dangerous than complying, or if we are trapped, then the parasympathetic nervous system acts as a brake on our defensive impulses, and we become passive and compliant. We "play dead." If we survive the danger and the threat is over, then the parasympathetic system helps us rest, lick our wounds, and repair. Perhaps you have sometimes wondered, "Why didn't I fight back?" The answer is that "you" did not make that decision. Your body and brain determined that it was not safe to fight. Your thinking brain turned off, and your body instinctively decided what to do next.

Use this worksheet to describe how your nervous system works. Whatever you notice will not only help you understand your actions and reactions now—it will also tell you more about how you survived.

When you get triggered, what does your sympathetic nervous system do? What are your fight-or-flight responses like? What does your parasympathetic system do? Which is more familiar?

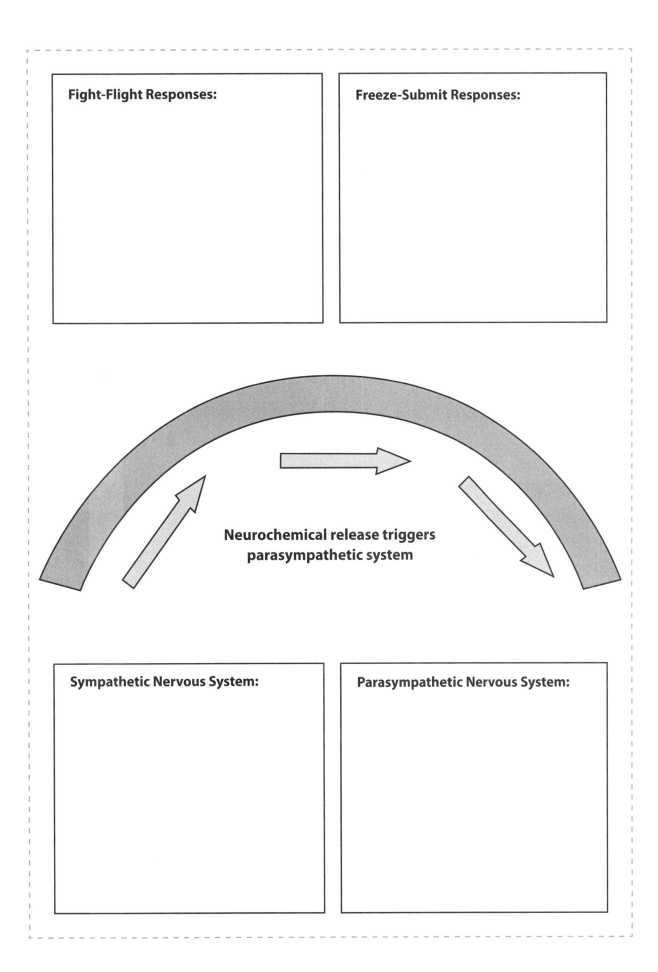

Fight-Flight Responses:

Freeze-Submit Responses:

Neurochemical release triggers parasympathetic system

Sympathetic Nervous System:

Parasympathetic Nervous System:

Window of Tolerance

The window of tolerance is a concept originally developed by Dr. Dan Siegel (1999) that describes the optimal zone of arousal in which a person can manage the stressors of everyday life. When you are operating within this zone—or "inside" the window of tolerance—your thoughts are clear and rational, and your emotions are regulated and controlled. If you are in this optimal arousal zone, you will:

- Feel present

- Feel safe

- Be resilient

- Be able to adapt to fit the situation

- Experience empathy

- Feel and think simultaneously

- Effectively communicate with others

- Feel open and curious (versus judgmental and defensive)

- Be able to regulate your emotions

- Have an awareness of boundaries (your own and others)

However, when you tip outside of your window of tolerance, the prefrontal cortex shuts down, affecting your ability to think rationally and manage difficult emotions. This can cause arousal levels to rapidly increase (*hyperarousal*) or decrease (*hypoarousal*), leading you to feel out of control and to become "stuck" outside of your window for quite some time. When this occurs, you can experience difficulty sleeping, lack of concentration, and an inability to manage emotions. Physically, your body may be tense and on the brink of an explosion, which can result in angry outbursts and hostility. Let us look at hyperarousal and hypoarousal in more detail.

Window of Tolerance

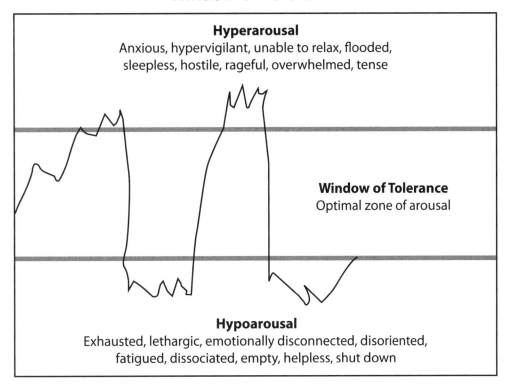

Hyperarousal
Anxious, hypervigilant, unable to relax, flooded, sleepless, hostile, rageful, overwhelmed, tense

Window of Tolerance
Optimal zone of arousal

Hypoarousal
Exhausted, lethargic, emotionally disconnected, disoriented, fatigued, dissociated, empty, helpless, shut down

Understanding Hyperarousal

When someone is *above* their window of tolerance, they are in a state of hyperarousal, which can manifest in physical symptoms such as rapid heart rate, shallow breathing, tense muscles, and sweating. Mentally, hyperarousal may lead to difficulty concentrating, racing thoughts, and irritability. It can occur quickly and can be hard to prevent or recover from. Some common symptoms that may occur in this state include:

- Angry outbursts or agitation
- Muscle tension or shaking
- Anxiety, fear, or panic
- An inability to rest
- Emotional overwhelm
- Racing thoughts
- Sleep issues
- Defensiveness
- Hypervigilance

- Intrusive images
- Difficulty being in busy or crowded environments
- Difficulty concentrating
- Chronic pain
- An elevated heart rate
- Hypertension
- Impulsivity
- Restlessness

You can get sent into a state of hyperarousal when you are stressed or encounter reminders of traumatic memories. It's important to recognize that hyperarousal is a natural response to perceived threats or overwhelming emotions. The body goes into "alarm" mode in an attempt to respond to the perceived danger and protect itself (Gill, 2017). If you have experienced trauma, though, this alarm mode becomes overactive—leading you to react to triggers that do not represent a true threat to your safety.

Understanding Hypoarousal

When someone is *below* their window of tolerance means, they are in state of hypoarousal, which can manifest as emotional numbness, physical lethargy, and a lack of desire to carry out tasks they normally enjoy. In this state, it's important to engage in activities that bring you joy and connection without pushing yourself too far beyond your window of tolerance (Gill, 2017). Common symptoms that someone may experience in this state may include:

- Depression
- Low energy
- Memory loss
- Slow cognitive processing ("I can't think")
- Feelings of shame
- Emptiness
- Feelings of disconnection

- Feelings of being shut down
- Helplessness
- Inability (or lack of desire) to speak
- Blank stare
- Dissociation
- Slow digestion
- Low blood pressure

Like hyperarousal, you can often be triggered into a state of hyperarousal when you feel threatened, recount traumatic memories, or experience emotions associated with a past trauma. Even a perceived threat can be enough to send someone into a state of shutdown or even dissociation. The instinct to freeze, shut down, and become emotionally withdrawn is an adaptive response in the face of a true life-threatening situation, but when it persists in the absence of danger, it can contribute to chronic anxiety.

Trauma and the Window of Tolerance

This worksheet can help you become aware of how your sympathetic and parasympathetic nervous systems still react after the trauma has passed, how they still affect your feelings and behavior, and how you may need a wider window of tolerance. Often, our sympathetic and parasympathetic responses occur predictably. Certain situations trigger one response or the other, and certain situations are positive triggers that help widen the window of tolerance. Include that information on this worksheet, too, to help yourself anticipate trauma-related triggers and seek out positive triggers.

On the next page, circle the signs of autonomic hyper- and hypoarousal that you notice in yourself, and add any other signs not listed. Write in the situations that seem to stimulate these different states. For example, are you more hyperaroused when alone or when around people? Are you more in the window of tolerance at work?

Signs of Chronic Hyperarousal:

Emotional overwhelm, panic, impulsivity, hypervigilance, defensiveness, feeling unsafe, reactive, angry, racing thoughts, AND:

_____

_____

_____

_____

When do I find myself hyperaroused?

_____

_____

_____

_____

Window of Tolerance:

My feelings and reactions are tolerable; I can think and feel simultaneously; My reactions adapt to fit the situation; AND:

_____

_____

_____

_____

When do I find myself in the window of tolerance?

_____

_____

_____

_____

Signs of Chronic Hypoarousal:

Numb, "dead," passive, no feelings, no energy, unable to think, disconnected, shut down, not present, ashamed, unable to say "no," AND:

_____

_____

_____

_____

When do I find myself hypoaroused?

_____

_____

_____

_____

Window of Tolerance Assessment

Use this worksheet to identify and recognize the symptoms of hyperarousal and hypoarousal within yourself. Becoming more self-aware of these symptoms will help you assess if you are currently above (hyperarousal), below (hypoarousal), or within your window of tolerance.

In the table on the next page, circle the symptoms you are feeling, and use this information to rate your level of hyperarousal or hypoarousal.

Symptoms

1 **Hyperarousal** *(more anxious)*	**Hyperarousal** • Increased arousal • Anxiety, anger, or loss of control • Impulse to fight or run away	• Anxiety • Impulsivity • Intense reactions • Lack of emotional safety • Hypervigilance • Intrusive thoughts • Fear • Shaking	• Rigidness • Defensiveness • Anger or rage • Physical and emotional aggression • Obsessive thoughts and behaviors • Emotional outbursts • Racing thoughts
5 **Window of Tolerance** *(calm and regulated)*	**Window of Tolerance** • Balance and calm • Stability and control • Ability to function effectively and handle the adversities that life throws at you	When you're in your window of tolerance, you feel like you can deal with whatever is happening in your life. You might feel stress or pressure, but it doesn't bother you too much. This is the ideal place to be. • Emotional regulation • Ability to self-soothe • Effective functioning	
10 **Hypoarousal** *(more depressed)*	**Hypoarousal** • Decreased arousal • Depression, emotional numbness, or exhaustion • Shutdowns or freezing	• Feeling of being on autopilot • Lack of energy • Inability to think or respond • Memory loss • Numbness • Feeling of zoning out	• Shutdowns • Reduced physical movement • Shame • Depression • Difficulty engaging in coping skills • Low levels of energy

My rating is: _____

What symptoms are the most severe?

_____

_____

_____

_____

_____

Widen Your Window of Tolerance

This exercise focuses on widening your window of tolerance by increasing your capacity to tolerate emotional or somatic distress.

- Would you be willing to explore a brief experiment aimed at helping you stay present with distressing sensations and emotions? This practice can help you widen your window of tolerance and ultimately prepare you for trauma reprocessing.

- Take a few breaths, and begin to notice if there is any distressing emotion or body sensation that is present for you in this moment. Rather than trying to make this distressing feeling go away, this practice invites you to notice what happens when you allow yourself to focus your awareness on this emotion or sensation. You have a choice during this process, and you can take your attention away from the distressing feeling at any point.

- You might notice an urge to judge your experience as bad or scary. Instead, see if you can describe the sensations or emotions you are having. As you bring your awareness to the distressing emotion or body sensation, see if you can notice whether it has a temperature. Is it hot or cold? Does it have a texture? Is it dull or sharp, dense or dispersed, radiating or prickly? Is there a weight to the sensation, such as feeling floaty or heavy? Is there a color or shape to it?

- You might notice that you have an urge to tell a story about this emotion or sensation. For now, see if you can return to your intention to stay with the feeling, and observe any subtle changes as you bring your awareness to your experience.

- Perhaps you notice a negative thought or belief that interferes with your ability to stay present with this emotion or body sensation. For example, you might believe you are weak if you feel sad, or you might fear something bad will happen as a result of the sensation in your body. See if you can return to an intention to observe your experience.

- Now that you have brought your attention to your distressing emotion or body sensation, take some time to notice if the feeling has changed in anyway. Were you able to stay with your experience just a little bit longer? Has the sensation lessened in intensity, or has it perhaps increased? Either way, I invite you to take a moment to appreciate yourself for bringing your awareness to your distress. In time, this practice builds your capacity to heal from trauma.

Do You Fight, Flee, or Freeze?

Through the stress response, the amygdala is communicating to us that we should fight, flee, or freeze. Read through the following lists, and check off the statements that apply to you. Then compare the number of check marks you placed in each category to see which approach your amygdala most frequently encourages you to take.

Fighting

☐ When I am stressed, I find myself wanting to hit something or someone.

☐ When someone offends me, I feel like fighting with them.

☐ I often snap at others when they frustrate me.

☐ I throw or kick things when I am angry.

☐ When someone says something rude to me, I don't let them get away with it.

☐ I have a hard time sitting still or keeping my mouth shut in tense situations.

☐ If someone startles me, I am at risk of striking them.

☐ Sometimes I physically hurt myself rather than hurting someone else.

Fleeing

☐ I typically avoid situations that stress me out.

☐ Whenever things start to go wrong, I just want to leave.

☐ When things don't go smoothly, I have no interest in them.

☐ I have a tendency to put off things that I need to do.

☐ I will pretend I don't know about something in order to avoid addressing it.

☐ I frequently cancel activities that I planned to participate in.

☐ I often wish I could just run away from it all.

☐ I can come up with a million excuses not to do something.

Freezing

☐ I frequently find myself at a loss for words when I am stressed.

☐ When I panic, I have a hard time doing anything constructive.

☐ In difficult situations, I stay quiet and hope no one notices me.

☐ When I'm stressed, I frequently find myself unable to take action.

☐ When something is frightening, my muscles become tense and stiff.

☐ If someone startles me, I freeze and don't move.

☐ I'm slow to react or recover in a stressful situation.

☐ I shut down and feel paralyzed when someone is angry.

☐ I have high expectations for myself.

☐ When I set a goal for myself, I can be very hard on myself.

☐ I tend to be harder on myself than on other people.

☐ I hate it when I feel like I've let someone down.

☐ It is difficult for me to tell someone no.

☐ I often suspect that others are disappointed with me.

☐ If someone wants something, it's easy for them to guilt me into doing it for them.

☐ I feel ashamed about who I have become.

Client Exercise

Regulating the Dysregulated Autonomic Nervous System

The following exercises are effective for activating the parasympathetic nervous system and reducing the stress response.

Yawning

Here's an extremely contagious method for activating the parasympathetic nervous system: yawning. If you haven't voluntarily or involuntarily initiated a yawn yet, it's a safe bet that you will while reading the next few sentences. Yawning is a natural respiratory reflex that improves circulation to the face, relaxes the eyes, and counteracts the shallow, rapid breathing that is generally associated with stress. Yawning requires a deep, slow inhalation, followed by a full exhalation. Because yawning triggers the relaxation response, you should repeat it as often as you like. It's also cheap, portable, and effective.

1. To begin, sit or stand comfortably.

2. Shrug, rotate, then shake out your shoulders for a few seconds.

3. Locate your jaw joints by putting your fingers on both jaws. Add a slight bit of pressure as you begin to open and close your mouth, as you feel the joints with your fingertips.

4. Once you've located the joints, begin to lightly massage those muscles. (The jaw muscles can exert the strongest force; consequently, they tend to be the tensest muscles in the body.)

5. As you continue to massage any tight spots, begin to open your mouth, and slowly begin to inhale.

6. Open your mouth a bit wider . . . wider . . . wider.

7. Open the back of your throat. Allow the air to rush through your breathing passages.

8. At the end of the inhalation, complete the yawn by exhaling loudly with a "huff" or a sigh.

9. Allow your breath to return to normal.

10. Take a few deeper breaths.

11. Remain sitting or standing comfortably.

12. This time, in addition to stretching your face muscles as you begin the open-mouthed inhale, without straining, stretch your arms out wide to the sides, then stretch them up as far up as comfortably possible.

13. Pay attention to the muscles as they stretch.

14. After you have deeply inhaled and fully stretched, complete the yawn by exhaling loudly with a "huff" or a sigh, while dropping your arms to your sides.

The Mammalian Diving Reflex

As far as we know, every mammal has an automated response system for diving in cold water (less than about 21°C). This mammalian diving reflex allows dive times to be extended by maximizing oxygen expenditure efficiency while submerged. Briefly, this reflex allows the body to enter a state of hibernation in which oxygen depletion is less detrimental to the brain, which increases the odds of survival in cold water drownings.

The following parasympathetic nervous system responses are typical (and in this order):

1. The heart rate slows.

2. The blood flow to extremities becomes constricted.

3. The blood and water are allowed to pass through organs and circulatory walls into chest cavity.

The first two items begin to happen immediately (i.e., as soon as the face hits cold water). The slowing heart rate is almost instantaneous, while the constricted blood flow happens more gradually.

1. The slowed heart rate serves to conserve oxygen (preventing depletion), thereby increasing the amount of available time underwater without dramatically impairing performance.

2. The decreased blood flow provides more of a long-term (minutes to hours) survival benefit, but seriously impairs performance.

3. The third response is a bit scarier because the body *intentionally allows fluid to fill the lungs and chest cavity* (to prevent organs from being crushed from extreme pressure). For surface-dwelling mammals, it serves a survival function and therefore only kicks in as depths become extreme.

Interesting. But what does it have to do with trauma-informed interventions?

Well, when you are in a state of extreme emotional arousal, information processing suffers dramatically. In order to recover this crucial function, the nervous system essentially needs to be reset or rebooted. The activation of the mammalian diving reflex is an effective method of doing just that. The reflex can be voluntarily activated by submerging your head in a bowl of ice water (not freezing) or splashing your face (just below the eyes and above the cheekbones) with icy cold water. Here are the steps:

1. Fill a bowl with icy cold water.

2. Bend/lean over.

3. Hold your breath.

4. Put face in icy cold water for 30 seconds.

5. Make sure that most sensitive part of the face (area underneath eyes/above cheekbones) feels the icy water.

Additional methods for activating the diving reflex include placing an ice-cold gel pack or mask over/around the eye area or holding your breath for 30 seconds while bending forward.

Who Shouldn't Do This

- Anyone with bradycardia (heart rate < 60 beats per minute)

- Anyone with known cardiac problems

- Anyone with an eating disorder (particularly anorexia nervosa)

Hand Warming

When we are stressed, blood is shunted away from our hands and feet and directed to vital organs and the large muscles of our shoulders, hips, and thighs, enabling us to react physically to danger (i.e., fight or flee). But as you well know, most times the stress response is inappropriate for present situation (i.e., we are not in grave danger—being neither chased nor attacked).

The more stressed a person is, the lower the temperature in the hands; the lower the stress level, the higher the temperature should be in the hands. (Research has shown that stress causes at least one or two degree Fahrenheit decrease over a five-minute period.)

A biofeedback technique, aptly named *hand warming*, is designed to counteract the stress response via increasing parasympathetic activation. By simultaneously focusing your attention on your hands, while mentally conjuring images of warmth (e.g., holding a cup of hot chocolate, sitting by a fireplace, caressing someone's warm skin, or sitting in a sauna or hot tub), you can actually increase the temperature of your hands, consequently inducing a general sense of calm in your body and mind.

1. To begin, allow yourself to be comfortable . . . either lying down or sitting up with your back, neck, and spine fully supported. Knowing that you will not be interrupted for the next little while, begin by gently closing your eyes.

2. Now begin to bring your attention to your breath—the direct experience of your breath—however it is . . . and however it changes. Allow yourself to softly focus your awareness onto the breath that is arising right now. . . the in-breath and the out-breath . . . the rising and the falling. If you can, try to follow one full cycle of the breath from the beginning of the in-breath and through its entirety to the beginning of the out-breath and through its entirety. Allow yourself the time and the space to be in direct contact with the breath throughout one entire cycle.

3. As you continue to pay attention to the breath, gently guide your awareness to your hands, noticing any sensations, energy, and the temperature in your hands. Bring to mind an image of warmth. Perhaps you are sitting by a fire, or warm and cozy under some blankets, possibly cuddled up with a loved one or pet, or lying on the beach under the blazing sun. Whatever brings with it the sense of warmth . . . heat.

4. Once you have the image, allow it to become as vivid as possible.

5. Now, feeling the warmth, begin to notice your breath again . . . coming slowly and easily. Deepening with each inhalation . . . exhale fully and completely. Feel the warmth on your skin . . . completely comfortable . . . completely relaxed.

6. As the next breath arises, pay attention to this deep and comforting relaxation. Breathe here for a moment. . . .

7. And when you are ready, gently bring yourself back to this room by counting up from one to five. When you reach the number five, your eyes will gently open. You will be awake and alert, feeling only peace. One . . . two . . . three. Take a deep breath . . . four . . . and five.

Learning to warm your hands via your thoughts requires no biofeedback instruments, just a little bit of relaxation training. However, in order to measure and track changes in temperature, you may wish to get a monitor. Alternatively, a much cheaper option would be to purchase a stress control biofeedback card. Several options are available online.

Mental Grounding Tools

These mental grounding tools are designed for you to use during episodes of panic or emotional overwhelm to help you cope with the experience as it is happening. When you're triggered, let these exercises do the thinking for you. Simply pick an exercise, follow the instructions, and continue until you feel calm. You may even want to write these exercises down on individual cards and carry them around with you for when panic strikes.

Categories

It is easy to let your mind get caught up in panic, but that just makes things worse. Instead, do something that requires enough brainpower to keep you grounded.

- Pick a category (e.g., sports teams, sitcoms, state capitals, top hits, historical figures).
- Name as many things as you can think of in that category.

Go Backward

Doing things that fully engage your brain can help pull you away from an experience of panic, thus lessening its intensity. To do this, simply do something backward:

- Spell your full name backward, then continue with names of loved ones.
- Read text from a book or article backward.

Sing Along

It may sound silly, but singing a song you love is great way to distract yourself mid-panic. You can put a familiar song on and sing along or just belt something out that you know by heart. If you are uncomfortable singing aloud, try to remember the lyrics of a favorite song. Either recite them in your mind or write them down.

Physical Grounding Tools

These physical grounding tools are designed for you to use during episodes of panic or emotional overwhelm to help you cope with the experience as it is happening. When you're triggered, let these exercises do the thinking for you. Simply pick an exercise, follow the instructions, and continue until you feel calm. You may even want to write these exercises down on individual cards and carry them around with you for when panic strikes.

Water or Ice

Because panic is such a physical experience, it can be helpful to distract your body from the physical sensations of hyperarousal. Do something to shock your brain and body:

- Hold an ice cube.

- Splash cold water on your face.

Self-Massage

When you are panicking, you can use physical touch to both soothe yourself and as a form of distraction from the uncomfortable sensations. Give yourself a quick massage:

- Use your thumb to massage the palm of your other hand and/or forearm.

- Place both hands on the back of your neck and use your fingers to massage in a circular motion.

Drink a Glass of Water

When available to you, simply having a drink of water can calm down your nervous system and shift your focus mid-panic. Just grab the nearest cup, fill it with water, and take a sip (or more). Focus your attention on the sensation of relief as the water enters your throat. If you were experiencing dry mouth, continue taking sips until that sensation subsides.

Client Exercise

Distraction Tools

These distraction tools are designed for you to use during episodes of panic or emotional overwhelm to help you cope with the experience as it is happening. When you're triggered, let these exercises do the thinking for you. Simply pick an exercise, follow the instructions, and continue until you feel calm. You may even want to write these exercises down on individual cards and carry them around with you for when panic strikes.

Shock

Sometimes the panic experience feels so uncomfortable that you feel like you need immediate relief. In these moments, do something to shock yourself:

- Clap loudly near your ear.

- Snap a rubber band on your wrist.

This will help shift your attention quickly away from panic thoughts and sensations. Once you have a little bit of your attention back, use it to visualize a calming scene or continue to another distraction exercise.

Distraction Rainbow

Distract your brain away from the panic sensations using the colors of the rainbow as your guide:

R: Think of something red.

O: Think of something orange.

Y: Think of something yellow.

G: Think of something green.

B: Think of something blue.

I: Think of something indigo.

V: Think of something violet.

Repeat until you feel more control.

Change

Doing something to change your situation, surroundings, or sensations is another tool you can use to distract your brain and body from being entirely consumed by the panic experience.

- Change the temperature by going outside or taking clothing on or off.

- Change the scenery by going outside or inside (depending on where you are) or by switching rooms.

CHAPTER 8

Tapping and Self-Havening Tools

Self-Havening Touch

Mindful touch is a form of psychosensory therapy, which means that sensory input (rather than language or chemicals) is used to change people's moods, sensations, thinking, and behavior. One powerful mindful touch technique is *self-havening*, which incorporates soothing touch to four locations that have been found to exhibit the strongest response to tactile stimulation: the brow, cheek, shoulders, and hands (Harper, 2012).

The havening touch works by decreasing the impact of pain and stress on the mind and body while enhancing feelings of well-being. It does so by changing the electrochemical state of your brain (Sumich et al., 2022). When you use self-havening, you're giving your brain a wonderful, calming bath of feel-good experiences and ultimately giving your amygdala a safe haven in which she is able to heal. (That's where the name *havening* came from.)

Let's go through the mechanics of how the practice works:

1. The first touch involves the simple motion of gently rubbing the palms of your hands together as if you are washing them.

2. The second touch involves giving yourself a nice, soothing hug. To do so, start with your arms crossed, with your hands at your shoulders, and then move them down slowly and repeatedly over your upper arms to your elbows.

3. The third touch is a motion similar to what you might do when you are wiping away a tear or receiving a facial massage. Start with your hands together over your nose and glide them over your cheeks from the middle outward with your fingers, always smoothly and gently.

4. The fourth touch is similar to the third, but it involves moving your hands over your forehead, just above your eyebrows, with that same inward-to-outward motion.

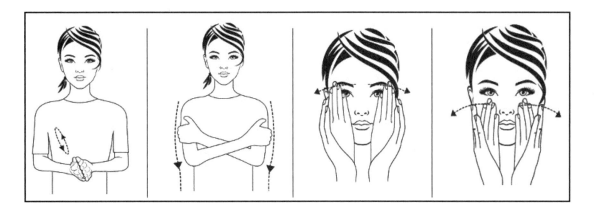

If your motions seem a little disjointed, try doing it backward from the order I explained with five repetitions of each touch—first with the forehead five times, then move down to your cheeks, then go to your shoulders, and then end with your hands. Then go back to the top and start again. Sometimes people will notice they have a "sweet spot"—a type of self-havening touch that feels best for their mind and body. For others, their preferred type of touch may vary across situations. For example, after a particularly long day, I find that the forehead touch brings the greatest calm, but when I'm having fitful sleep, arm havening is my natural go-to.

As you're practicing these motions, this is a wonderful opportunity to practice interoception—deepening your relationship with your body. Turn your attention inward and notice what forms of touch you like. You can even let your natural responses to stress or anxiety guide you. For example, if you have a tendency to wring your hands or pick your nails, you might find that palm havening is a delightful alternative. Or if you tend to experience forehead or jaw tension, you might find that face havening is just what you need to soothe away the tension. The most important part of the self-havening touch experience is to lovingly connect and attend to *you*. After all, this whole journey is about you.

Learning from Difficult Moments

1. Begin to apply the self-havening touch. Given that you're building muscle memory with self-havening, I invite you to apply the touch in the following sequence: first rubbing your hands together, then crossing your hands over your chest and moving them down your arms to your elbows in a sweeping motion, then moving your fingers across your cheeks, and finally moving them across your forehead. Of course, if you already know your "sweet spot" or you find it during this exercise, feel free to focus on that location. The most important piece is to continue applying self-havening touch throughout this exercise.

2. As you continue the self-havening touch, welcome your breath into the experience:

   a. Take a deep breath in through your nose, counting 1, 2, 3, 4.

   b. Hold 1, 2.

   c. Gently exhale through your mouth, counting 1, 2, 3, 4, 5, 6.

   d. Hold 1, 2.

   e. Repeat this breathing exercise one more time.

3. Now think back across recent days and find a moment that brought up some difficult feelings or emotions. Once you have found that moment, invite it to become the center of your attention.

4. Turn your focus to the feelings connected to this difficult moment. Try not to indulge the story of that experience because that story belongs to your narrative thinking brain. Instead, tap into your survival brain by focusing on the feelings and sensations elicited by that difficult event. If you notice any thoughts intruding into your experience, turn those thoughts into clouds and invite them to float away. Then return your focus to the feelings associated with this difficult moment.

5. As you begin to welcome the feelings of this moment, take three deep breaths, gently inhaling through your nose and exhaling through your mouth. Remember to continue using the self-havening touch.

6. Now identify the strongest feeling you experienced in that moment. Invite this feeling to become the new center of your awareness. Imagine that this feeling is an

old friend, showing up in your world to give you a message. You might even greet this feeling—"Hello, old friend. Thank you for letting me know you're here."

7. Still applying the soothing and loving self-havening touch, now turn your attention to your thoughts about this feeling. What is your mind up to? Is there a particular narrative that your mind starts to spin when this feeling is present? If so, welcome that story. It's teaching you about your past, and that story is born out of your survivorship, which means it's a story about your resilience.

8. Welcome in three more deep and gentle breaths, inhaling through your nose and exhaling through your mouth, and invite your mind to explore the possibility of having a different relationship with this story. What if sadness and loss were opportunities for connection and growth? What if anxiety and stress were opportunities for confidence and strength? Whatever the feeling or its narrative, ask yourself if what you're experiencing now is too much to handle. Whatever the answer, now notice this: You *are* handling it! You are here, sitting with this feeling, which takes strong work!

9. Now return to your breath and notice that even with this feeling, you continue to breathe, because this feeling too shall pass. Your intention today is to simply notice this feeling and its story.

10. Describe this feeling and the old narrative associated with it.

    _____

    _____

    _____

11. Now let's begin to create your new, resilient narrative. What would you like to think the next time this feeling state shows up? For example, if you were previously feeling anxious and telling yourself, "I can't do it," then you might tell yourself, "It's okay to try" instead. How might you have felt differently in that experience if you had these other thoughts present?

    _____

    _____

    _____

12. Take a moment to express your gratitude for the incredible power of self-healing that your mind and body carry within: *Thank you, brain. Thank you, body.*

Sculpting Your Brain for Success

You just spent some time with a difficult feeling state. Now we will practice a resilience-building exercise where you will focus on cultivating a desired emotional state.

1. Find a comfortable seated position and gently bring your awareness to your breath. Right now, you're not trying to change anything—you're just noticing the current state of beingness as it is here and now.

2. Begin applying the soothing self-havening touch—touching your hands, arms, and face in any order—and continue applying this touch throughout this practice.

3. As you settle in, take a moment to offer intentional gratitude for your body. For your lungs that expand and contract as you gently breathe. For your muscles that move you in this world. For the microscopic cells that use oxygen to fuel, heal, and renew you. For the state of being awake and alive. Notice where you feel gratitude in your body, including the color of gratitude, its energy, and its loving presence.

4. Now create an intentional healing breath:

    a. Gently inhale through your nose, counting 1, 2, 3, 4. Hold 1, 2.

    b. Gently exhale through your mouth, counting 1, 2, 3, 4, 5, 6. Hold 1, 2.

5. Allow your breath to return to its normal cadence. Notice how your soothing self-havening touches create a calm state that is ideal for setting an intention for your mind and body.

6. Now find an emotion or state of being that you would like more of in your life. Perhaps it is a feeling of calm or peacefulness, or an ability to be more focused. Or perhaps it is the desire to feel more energized. As you explore these possibilities, notice if you can remember a time when you have embodied this state before.

7. Once you've identified your preferred state, invite it to become the center of your attention. Notice if it has a color or an energy associated with it. Invite your mind to explore this possibility. Perhaps it is a vibrant blue or a soft, glowing white. Perhaps it even has movement to it, like bubbles or a shimmer.

8. Imagine gently breathing in that color or energy, welcoming it into your mind and body. And as you are present with this energy, ask yourself, "What if I were _____?" Quietly complete the question with your chosen state. Ponder again, "What if I were _____?" Envision navigating this new day with its challenges and opportunities, carrying your chosen state with you along with its color or energy, continuing to ponder in your mind, "What if I were _____?"

9. As you're setting your intention with this chosen state, notice if there is an item or a symbol that represents this state of being, such as a waterfall or a sunrise. With a gentle breath in, invite that symbol and its beautifully colored energy to connect into your mind and body. Imagine it expanding within you as you slowly exhale.

10. Take another slow, easy breath in and then gently release it. Notice the new possibility of embodying this experience. With another gentle breath in, thank this energy, this state of being, for its presence, and know that at any time you can cultivate this desired state of mind.

11. Welcome another gentle breath in:

    a. Inhale through your nose, counting 1, 2, 3, 4. Hold 1, 2.

    b. Gently exhale through your mouth, counting 1, 2, 3, 4, 5, 6. Hold 1, 2.

12. Then allow your breath to return to its normal loving cadence and gently invite your awareness back into your space, this moment, here and now.

After completing this sequence of self-havening practices, revisit the journaling you completed as part of the *Learning from Difficult Moments* exercise, and reflect on that difficult moment again. What do you notice? Has anything shifted or changed? You might feel less anxious when recalling the moment or even find that your anxiety has been replaced by your preferred feeling state. Could this new feeling state play a role in further supporting you to shift the narrative of that previous experience? Take a moment to do some additional journaling about any shifts you experienced.

_____

_____

_____

_____

_____

_____

CPR for the Amygdala

CPR for the Amygdala is designed to help you regain physical and emotional balance when you find yourself on those neural freeways of stress. It uses the mindful touch from self-havening in combination with "brain games" that redirect your thoughts away from the emotionally activating experience. Brain games are essentially any form of cognitive distraction that occupies your working memory resources. Humans can only hold about seven pieces of data in their working memory at one time (Miller, 1956), so if you can give your working memory something different to do, while calming your amygdala through mindful touch, you can stop the stress reaction (de Voogd & Hermans, 2022).

Let's do a quick distraction exercise so you can see how powerful your working memory can be in occupying your attention:

1. Imagine that you are holding a basketball in your hands. Notice the weight, texture, size, and even smell of the ball.

2. Now imagine dribbling your basketball five times and then shooting a basket. With each dribble, count in your mind as the ball bounces—1, 2, 3, 4, 5—and then shoot the basketball.

3. Now repeat the same exercise but with the other hand. Dribble the basketball five times, counting in your mind with each dribble, and then shoot the basketball.

By connecting to the sensory experience of dribbling and shooting a basketball, you're using your working memory resources to conjure up that experience in your mind's eye. The more sensory components and concrete structure a distraction has to it, the more effective it will be. Your primary goal is to make sure that you're using up all your working memory resources so you can reverse engineer your amygdala's stress reaction. Once your amygdala is calm enough, your thinking brain can come back online, allowing you to evaluate the present moment and make logical choices.

To integrate *CPR for the Amygdala* into your routine, use the acronym SNAP, as though you're going to snap your amygdala out of a stress reaction:

1. **S**ense into the experience of emotional activation, distress, or disturbance.
2. **N**otice the intensity of the experience and rank it on the scale of 0–10.
3. **A**pply the self-havening touch.
4. **P**reoccupy your brain with brain games to redirect your attention and focus.

CPR for the Amygdala: Introductory Practice

1. **Sense:** Begin by checking in with yourself. What's happening in your mind and body right now? Let your awareness drift from the top of your head to the tips of your toes. If you feel completely calm right now (good for you!), perhaps imagine that you're experiencing a stressful situation. For me, as soon as I imagine I'm running late for a meeting, my stress level spikes.

2. **Notice:** What is your level of emotional activation right now? On a scale of 1–10 (where 1 = *calm and relaxed*, and 10 = *out of control*), where would you rate yourself right now? Write down the number here: _____.

3. **Apply:** Begin self-havening by applying gentle and mindful touch to your palms, upper arms, and face, alternating between them in any order that feels good to you. You will continue self-havening throughout step 4.

4. **Preoccupy:** As you continue self-havening, you're going to use a simple breath and counting exercise to guide your attention and preoccupy your mind. If possible, practice inhaling through your nose and exhaling through your mouth while going through this exercise. Please note that the breath counts provided here are simply suggestions, and you may increase or decrease them in length to suit your comfort. Ideally, though, you should aim to have a longer exhalation compared to the inhalation.

    a. Take a gentle breath in:

        i. Inhale, counting 1, 2, 3.

        ii. Hold 1, 2.

        iii. Gently exhale, counting 1, 2, 3, 4, 5.

    b. Take another gentle breath in:

        i. Inhale, counting 1, 2, 3, 4.

        ii. Hold 1, 2.

        iii. Gently exhale, counting 1, 2, 3, 4, 5, 6.

    c. Take one final gentle breath in, still applying the self-havening touch:

        i. Inhale, counting 1, 2, 3.

       ii. Hold 1, 2.

      iii. Gently exhale, counting 1, 2, 3, 4, 5.

5. Once you've completed step 4, stop applying the self-havening touch and check in with yourself again. Do you notice any shifts? Rate your level of emotional activation again, from 0 to 10: _____. Has this number changed from earlier? What else do you notice?

Building Your Personalized CPR Program

In the *CPR for the Amygdala* introductory exercise, you used self-havening with a simple breath distraction to practice what it feels like to be in a mindful, resilient interaction with yourself. However, creating your own *personalized* CPR program is vital to build resilience, soothe a reactive brain, and deepen your relationship with yourself.

There are four primary types of brain games to choose from in order to preoccupy your working memory resources and interrupt the stress response: (1) movement exercises, (2) category or narrative activities, (3) numbers tasks, and (4) songs or word games. Of course, choosing distraction techniques that work for you is the most important point. If songs and word games aren't your thing, not a problem! Skip that category. It is also important to choose brain games that are interesting to you but that aren't too difficult, as you don't want to stress yourself out even more. For example, if you have math anxiety, it might cause your amygdala more distress if you try to multiply big numbers, so you might choose simple counting instead.

To build your own personalized inventory of brain games, look through the following list of distractions and identify any that you'd like to try out. You can also add your own ideas. Then, return to *CPR for the Amygdala: Introductory Practice* and practice step 4 using three of the brain games you've identified in this exercise.

For the movement exercises, aim to engage in a count of approximately 20 elements for each movement. For the remaining categories, it is ideal to say the distractions aloud, as that further engages your working memory resources.

Movement Exercises

- Dribble a basketball
- Pick up seashells on the beach
- Skip rocks
- Play fetch with your dog
- Do sun salutations
- Lift weights

- Kick a ball in a net

- Hit golf balls

- Climb up and down a flight of stairs

Category or Narrative Activities

- Play alphabet games (e.g., list from A to Z as many first names, living things, artists, authors, musicians, places, cities, countries, cars, fruits, or vegetables as you can)

- Name the ingredients to your favorite recipe

- Describe the steps to an enjoyable task (e.g., going fishing, tacking up a horse, taking a photo)

- Name as many colors as you can (e.g., azure, crimson, peridot)

Numbers Tasks

- Count forward or backward (by 2s, 3s, 4s, 5s, and so on)

- Do multiplication tables

- Count something in your environment (e.g., cars passing by, books on a shelf, wags of your dog's tail)

- Calculate the number of days remaining before a special date (e.g., your birthday, a holiday)

Songs or Word Games

- Sing or hum your favorite songs

- Recite nursery rhymes

- Spell words forward and backward

- List 10 onomatopoeias (words that imitate the sound they represent, like *zap* or *sizzle*)

- Pick a starting word, then list as many rhyming words as you can

- Form as many words as you can using only the letters in your full name

CPR for the Amygdala: Soothing After an Unpleasant Event

1. **Sense** into a past experience of emotional activation, distress, or disturbance. This will be known as your "target" for the exercise. Given that you are just learning and developing mastery with this practice, I recommend that you begin working with an event that elicits no more than a 5 on a 0–10 scale.

2. **Notice** the intensity of the experience and rank it on the scale of 0–10: _____.

3. **Apply** the self-havening touch to your hands, arms, and face in any order that feels good to you.

4. **Preoccupy** your mind by starting with a gentle breathing exercise, inhaling to a count of 4 and slowly exhaling to a count of 6. Then, as you continue applying the mindful self-touch, complete one brain game from your personal distractions inventory. Repeat this process two more times, each time using a different brain game from your inventory.

5. Once you've completed step 4, stop applying the self-havening touch and check in with yourself again. Reassess your level of emotional activation in relation to the target (0–10): _____.

6. If you are still above a score of 2, continue the SNAP sequence until you are at or below a 2. Once you're at a 2 or below, reflect back on your identified target. Has it shifted or changed? What do you notice now?

_____

_____

_____

_____

_____

_____

_____

_____

Creating Possibilities Protocol

This protocol is a powerful self-care exercise that will repeatedly guide your brain to link into the resilient neural networks you want to increase your access to.

1. Find a comfortable, seated position. As you do so, notice the weight of your body and your feet on the ground. Begin by gently inhaling for a count of 4 and then exhaling for a count of 6. If you would like, begin incorporating self-havening touch to help strengthen the neuroplasticity experience. If you prefer, you might also simply place your hands gently on your lap or place a hand over your heart.

2. Now let's begin to move into relationship with your body by doing a slow body scan. Start by focusing your attention on the very top of your head, noticing any sensations, pressure, or tension that might be present for you. Then travel through the rest of your body—moving your attention down to your neck, shoulders, chest, arms, thighs, and legs, all the way to the tips of your toes—greeting the different parts of your body all along the way.

   Note: Doing a body scan for the first time can be difficult for some people. If this is the case for you, this exercise is particularly important. Pause the self-havening touch and use your hands to gently touch each body part as you move through the scan, creating a physical guide to help your brain tune into your body.

3. Once the body scan is complete, continue self-havening as you turn your attention back to your breath. Begin to contemplate a felt sense of what you would like to experience more of in this moment. It might be the opportunity to be calm and relaxed, or perhaps excited and curious.

4. As you think of this desired state that you would like to experience more of, assess the possibility of the statement "I am _____" on a scale from 0 (not possible) to 100 (completely possible).

5. If it feels 95 to 100 percent possible, skip to step 12. If it feels less than 95 percent possible, continue connecting your breath and your body as you hold on to this internal reflection, noticing how your mind and body exist in relationship with each other. Deepen your breath, expanding your diaphragm each time you inhale, and slowly releasing air each time you exhale.

6. As you continue to notice your chosen state, gently breathe in the possibility: "What if I were _____?"

7. Does this desired state have a color in your mind or perhaps a scent? Inhale the color or scent that represents the energy of this emotion, breathing in for a count of 4 and out for a count of 6. Can you recall a time in the past when you've felt this state? If so, bring those experiences to the center of your attention and again ask, "What if I were _____?" while welcoming and enhancing the possibility you have created. Repeat this "what if" question at least five times or until this target emotional state begins to feel more present.

8. Perhaps your mind is telling you that this "what if" question is now a real possibility. If so, ask yourself, "Can I be _____?" while continuing to breathe and applying the gentle self-havening touch. Notice the possibility of perhaps even starting to embody that state.

9. If that feels possible for you, move into "I can be." If there's a felt sense of "I can be," continue to gently state that in your mind, completing that sentence "I can be _____" at least five times with your chosen state. Continue to gently focus on the sensory experience, the felt sense of this energetic state.

10. It may take some people longer to plant the seeds that get them to the "I can be" stage. If this is the case for you, and the phrase does not feel authentic to you, then return to step 6 and repeat "What if I were _____?" in a loving and kind way. You will get there.

11. Once you are at the point where you feel like "I can be" is a possibility, you may be ready to move to the next stage of "I will be." If it feels authentic, repeat the phrase "I will be _____" five times or more. If not, go back to "What if I were _____?" or "I can be _____," whichever feels most authentic for you in this moment.

12. Eventually, your mind may jump forward to the realization that "Wow! This feeling state feels real! It's here!" If so, reevaluate the truth of the "I am" statement. If it feels 95 to 100 percent true, then move into ownership of this state by repeating "I am _____" five times. There is power and wonder in that "I am" experience—a place where you can move into owning the state. If it feels less than 95 percent true, return to the previous "What if" or "I can" statement, and end your healing session with another five repetitions of this statement.

13. Wherever you end up in relation to your chosen state, deepen your felt sense of this state—breathing in its color, scent, and energy—carrying an awareness of this state and floating it through your day and into future moments.

14. Notice the energy of being in this space. Notice what it feels like to be in a deep relationship with this experience. Reflect on this, and write down any observations. Know that at any time, you can choose to return to this felt sense and choose to wake up these neural networks and embody this state again. The "what if," "I can be," "I will be," and "I am" statements are representative of growth happening in your mind. These seeds can come in very handy in times when you become emotionally activated.

_____

_____

_____

_____

_____

_____

_____

_____

_____

_____

_____

_____

_____

_____

_____

_____

_____

_____

_____

_____

_____

Holding Neurovascular Points

Neurovascular points are specific spots on the head that activate blood flow to the area. The area of interest is the prefrontal cortex—the part of the brain responsible for, among other things, regulating the amygdala's response to stress, planning, decision making, and executive function.

Holding the neurovascular points while thinking about a stressor seems to suspend the stress response by preventing the blood from leaving the forebrain, in other words, keeping the prefrontal cortex engaged in top-down regulation of the amygdala. By interrupting a key component of the fight-or-flight response, the *neurovascular hold* allows you to think more clearly while contending with difficulties.

1. Locate the two points with your fingertips. They are midway between your hairline and your eyebrows, directly over the midpoint of each eyebrow.

2. Using the fingertips of both hands, apply light pressure while stretching the skin taut, eliminating any slack.

3. Continue holding the pressure as you inhale to the count of four. Pause. Exhale to the count of four.

4. Bring to mind a stressful situation—past, present, or future.

5. Keeping the stressor in mind, continue holding the pressure as you inhale again to the count of four. Pause. Exhale to the count of five.

6. Continue holding the pressure as you inhale again to the count of four. Pause. Exhale to the count of six.

7. Continue holding the pressure as you inhale again to the count of four. Pause. Exhale to the count of seven.

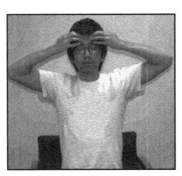

8. Continue holding the pressure as you inhale again to the count of four. Pause. Exhale to the count of eight.

9. Repeat often.

Acupressure Points

Both Western and Eastern medicine agree that there is a need to keep the electromagnetic circuits of the body (described as meridians in the Chinese system of acupuncture) flowing freely. During periods of increased stress, levels of both adrenaline and cortisol rise, consequently lowering the electrical potential across neuronal membranes in preparation for the short-term defensive actions of fight or flight. In this survival state, the body directs electrical energy away from the neocortex (the thinking part of the brain) and toward subcortical area—specifically, the sympathetic branch of the autonomic system. In an actual emergency, this response is adaptive and life-saving; however, oftentimes in traumatized people, no danger is actually present, just a reminder of a past trauma. That reminder keeps inappropriately alerting the brain and body to continue dumping the stress hormones into the bloodstream.

The following exercises are designed to counter the *misguided* activation of the sympathetic nervous system by stimulating the parasympathetic nervous system. This stimulation decreases the release of adrenalin and cortisol and increases the electrical potential across neuronal membrane, thus allowing the prefrontal cortex (i.e., the thinking part of the brain) to reengage. In addition to the decrease in stress hormones, the semicircular canals of the inner ear are also stimulated by the electrical activity that occurs during the movements. These canals activate a part of the brainstem called the reticular formation (whose job it is to screen out distracting stimuli), which in turn creates a more awake, alert, and focused attention in the thinking part of the brain.

Holding K-27 Points

The purpose of holding these points is to activate certain brain areas to improve communication between the right brain hemisphere and the left side of the body (and vice versa), increase blood supply to the brain, increase oxygen intake, and increase flow of electromagnetic energy. The K-27 points are located just below the collarbone. To find them, place your fingertips on the U-shaped notch at the top of the sternum. Move your fingers down one inch, then out toward each shoulder.

1. First locate the K-27 points and massage both sides.

2. Now, spread the fingers on your right hand and place it with the palm side down over your breastbone and heart (covering both K-27 points).

3. Now, spread the fingers on your left hand and place it with the palm side down over your navel.

4. With a bit of pressure, begin to hold these points.

5. Continue holding the pressure, as you inhale to the count of four. Pause. Exhale to the count of four.

6. Continue holding the pressure, as you inhale to the count of four. Pause. Exhale to the count of five.

7. Continue holding the pressure, as you inhale again to the count of four. Pause. Exhale to the count of six.

8. Continue holding the pressure, as you inhale again to the count of four. Pause. Exhale to the count of seven.

9. Continue holding the pressure, as you inhale again to the count of four. Pause. Exhale to the count of eight.

10. Repeat often.

Three Thumps

The following three exercises only work if you vigorously thump the respective acupressure points, so this is the only instance in this book in which you will not be asked to be gentle with yourself. (Obvious contraindications, such as injuries to the area and medical implants, apply.)

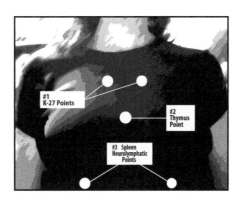

1. **Thump K-27:** The K-27 points are located just below the collarbone. To find them, see the previous *Holding K-27 Points* exercise.

    a. Move your fingers down one inch, then out toward each shoulder.

    b. Bring your fingers together as shown.

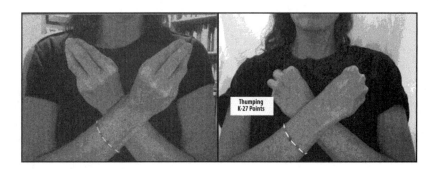

    c. Cross your hands so that the left hand thumps the right point, and the right hand thumps the left point.

    d. Breathing deeply in and out through your nose, begin thumping the K-27 points.

    e. After three deep breaths, allow your arms to return to your sides and relax.

2. **Thump the Thymus Gland:** The thymus gland, which plays a vital role in the body's immune system, is located in the center of the chest, on the upper part of the sternum, just between your nipples. For this thumping, you will choose an affirmation from the following list, or if none of those fit, conjure your own. You will repeat it to yourself (silently or aloud), as you vigorously thump the thymus gland. The key to benefiting from affirmations is to feel the feelings depicted in the words you are saying, so pick one that works for you.

- I am calm.
- I am peaceful.
- I am loved.
- I am centered.
- I choose to see the good in the people.
- I will make time to breathe.
- I can make a difference

- I have been blessed over and over again.
- I can control my reactions to today's challenges.
- I live my life with gratitude.
- I am whole and perfect just as I am
- I give thanks continually as I move through each day.

a. Once you've settled on an affirmation, begin by breathing deeply in and out through your nose.

b. Bring your fingers together as shown, and begin thumping the point in the center of the chest, as you speak your affirmation.

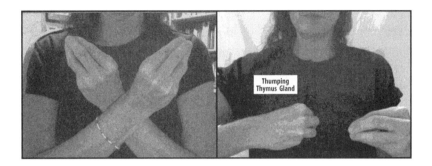

c. After three deep breaths, allow your arms to return to your sides and relax.

3. **Thump the Spleen Neurolymphatic Points:** The spleen neurolymphatic points are the depression between the seventh and eighth ribs, just below the level of the sternum. To locate these points, begin at about three or four inches under your armpit and continue along this line (around the bra line if you wear one) to the point directly under the nipples.

a. Begin by breathing deeply in and out through your nose.

b. Bring your fingers together as shown.

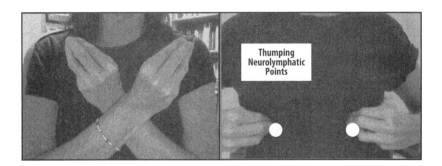

c. Breathing deeply in and out through your nose, begin thumping the neurolymphatic points. The spleen neurolymphatic points are generally sore, so you may want to begin by rubbing them, and as the soreness diminishes, switch over to thumping.

d. After three deep breaths, allow your arms to return to your sides and relax.

Tapping Points

There are at least 19 tapping points* used in tapping therapies, each of which is associated with an energy meridian. Here are the common tapping points with their related meridians:

- Top of head (TOH): governing vessel 20

- Back of head (BOH): governing vessel 17

- Forehead (FH): governing vessel 24.5 (third eye point)

- Eyebrow (EB): bladder 2

- Side of eye (SE): gallbladder 1

- Under eye (UE): stomach 1

- Under nose (UN): governing vessel 27

- Under bottom lip (UL): central vessel 24

- Under collarbone (UCB): kidney 27

- Under arm (UA): spleen 21

- Under breast (UB): liver 14

- Center of chest (CH): central vessel 20 (thymus gland)

- Little fingernail (LF): heart 9

- Middle fingernail (MF): pericardium 9

- Index fingernail (IF): large intestine 1

- Thumbnail (TH): lung 11

- Side of hand (SH): small intestine 3

- Back of hand (BH): triple-warmer-3 (gamut spot)

- Inside wrist (IW): meeting points of meridians on the fingers

- Sore spot (SS): a neurolymphatic reflex point on the left side of the chest above the breast; it is rubbed in a circular motion rather than tapped

---

* There are many more acupoints other than those listed here. If you are interested in learning more, I suggest that you review a book on acupuncture.

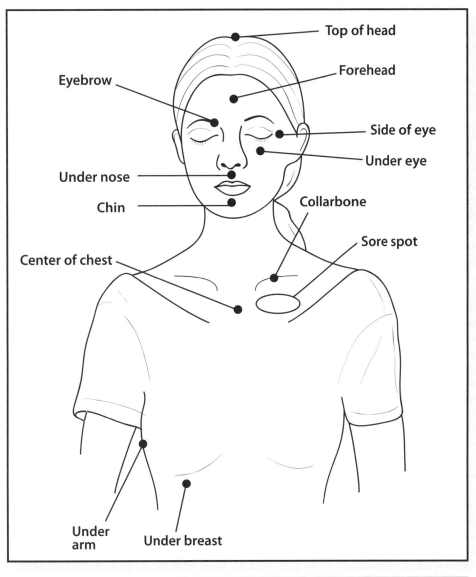

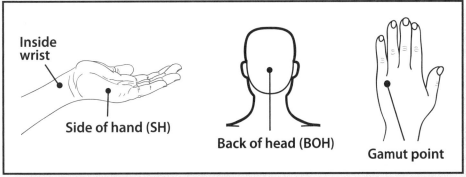

Thought Field Therapy

The granddaddy of the tapping therapies is thought field therapy (TFT), developed by Roger Callahan (1985). Here are the steps involved in a comprehensive TFT recipe:

1. Think about the problem, get in touch with the feeling involved, and rate your SUD level.

2. Treat for psychological reversal.* Tap on the little-finger side of the hand (SH) or rub the sore spot (SS) while saying three times, "Even though I [*state the problem*], I accept myself."

3. Next, tap on each of the following treatment points five to seven times:

    a. Eyebrow (EB)

    b. Under eye (UE)

    c. Under arm (UA)

    d. Under collarbone (UCB)

    e. Little fingernail (LF)

    f. Index fingernail (IF)

    g. Under collarbone (UCB)

4. If your SUD rating decreases by at least two points, tap repeatedly at the back of the hand (BH) while doing the following: close your eyes, open your eyes, look down and to the left, look down and to the right, rotate your eyes clockwise, rotate your eyes counterclockwise, hum a tune, count to five, and then hum again. This is known as the 9 Gamut Treatment (9G).

5. Check the SUD rating, and repeat the sequence starting at step 3. You should repeat the sequence even if the SUD rating is not lower after the 9G, and then check the SUD rating again.

---

* Psychological reversal occurs when your actions or motivation are in the opposite direction of your desired goal. It's like walking backward when you intend to go forward. For example, a healthy choice might be to quit smoking, yet a person who is reversed will continue to smoke in spite of their insistence that they want to quit.

6. If at any point the SUD lowering stalls, repeat the correction for psychological reversal indicated at step 2 with the following variation: "Even though I *still have some* [*state the problem*], I accept myself."

7. Continue altering between the series of tapping points and the 9G treatments until the SUD rating is within the 0–2 range. Note that other aspects of the problem may emerge during treatment and should be treated accordingly.

8. Do floor-to-ceiling eye roll (ER) or elaborated eye roll (EER) until the SUD rating is a 1 or 0 (preferably a 0). The ER involves looking down toward the floor without moving your head and then slowly raising your eyes up toward the ceiling while tapping on the gamut spot. The EER involves tapping on the gamut spot and taking a deep breath once your eyes are pointed at the ceiling, extending your gaze up into your forehead, then closing your eyes as you exhale and relax.

9. Challenge the results by trying to get the distress level back. If the SUD rating does not increase, you're done for now. If it does increase and you get back some level of distress, continue with the treatment.

Emotional Freedom Techniques

Emotional freedom techniques (EFT) is a comprehensive tapping sequence or algorithm developed in the 1990s by Gary Craig, who studied with Roger Callahan. The basic protocol is as follows:

1. Think about the problem, get in touch with the feeling involved, and rate your SUD level.

2. Tap on the little-finger side of the hand (SH) or rub the sore spot (SS) while repeating the setup statement three times. For example, "Even though I [*state the problem*], I accept myself."

3. Next, tap each of the following treatment points five to seven times while using a reminder phrase, such as "this problem":

    a. Eyebrow (EB)

    b. Side of eye (SE)

    c. Under eye (UE)

    d. Under nose (UN)

    e. Under bottom lip (UL)

    f. Under collarbone (UCB)

    g. Under arm (UA)

    h. Inside wrist (IW)

    i. Top of head (TOH)

4. Continue with this sequence of tapping points, each time checking the SUD level and any related issues that may come up after a tapping sequence. For example, there may be different scenes involved in a trauma, or different thoughts and emotions involved with some other problem being treated, each being a different aspect to tap on. At such times, the setup and reminder phrases may be altered accordingly.

5. Challenge the results by trying to get the distress level back. If the SUD rating does not increase, you're done for now. If it does increase and you get back some level of distress, continue with the treatment.

Find Emotional Freedom with Self-Tapping

The emotional freedom technique (EFT) is a therapeutic modality based on Chinese medicine that involves self-tapping on traditional acupressure points on the face and upper body. For this self-tapping exercise, you'll state a psychological concern aloud with an intention of unconditional self-acceptance.

- Would you be open to exploring a self-tapping practice to help reduce emotional distress? This practice invites you to tap on traditional acupuncture meridian points.

- To begin, I would like you to choose one area of concern or distress that you are experiencing right now. Notice your emotions and sensations, and identify a level of distress from 0 to 10, with 10 being the "worst distress possible" and 0 being "no distress at all."

- Once you have chosen a focus for the practice, I invite you to repeat the following "setup" phrase three times with me while tapping with one hand on the side of your opposite hand: "Even though I have . . . [*name the client's area of concern*], I deeply and completely accept myself."

- Now name just the area of concern while you tap each of the following points five times. Usually, you choose just one side of your body.

  - The inside edge of your eyebrow
  - The outside of your eye
  - Under your eye
  - Under your nose
  - Under your lips in the crease of your chin
  - Under your collarbones (you can use both hands to tap both sides)
  - Under your arm near your ribcage

- Now observe how you are feeling. Take a moment to reflect on your area of concern, and rate your level of distress on a scale of 0 to 10, with 10 being the "worst distress possible" and 0 being "no distress at all."

- Notice if the sensation has changed or if a new area of concern has come to the surface. If so, repeat the steps with this new area of concern. Continue until the level of distress is reduced to a tolerable level or gone.

Internal Family Systems Tools

Introduction to Parts Work

We bring parts work into therapy by helping clients recognize that we all have different states of mind, emotion, and physiological arousal. This handout provides psychoeducation you can use to help clients understand parts work and invites them to be curious about their own parts.

- All of us have parts of ourselves. For example, you might recall times when you have felt young, small, or helpless. Other times, you might have felt self-critical or controlling of others. Or there may be times when you feel disconnected from yourself.

- Some parts may be easier for you to like or may feel more familiar. You may have other parts that you would rather push away. For example, some people feel capable or confident when they go to work but lonely or sad when they come home at the end of the day. It is common to experience conflicts between parts. Additionally, there may be a part of you that wants to heal and part that is afraid of feeling your emotions.

- Even if you do want to make room for your emotions, you may feel blocked by a part who criticizes, rejects, or blames the part of you who is vulnerable. Or you might feel the need to manage your distress by seeking a sense of control, by needing to be perfect, or by staying excessively busy. While it might seem counterintuitive, you can think of this critical or controlling part as a protector who has been working hard to shield you from feeling your pain. When it is left unaddressed, you are more likely to feel stuck in your life or unable to meet your goals.

- Parts work addresses this internal conflict by helping you gain access to the vulnerable exiled parts of yourself that are often hidden underneath your protective defenses. These exiled parts hold the painful emotions, sensations, and memories related to the traumatic events from your past. In time, you can help these exiled parts release their burdens.

- You can release these burdens by connecting to an inner source of wisdom that you carry within you—known as your adult, presented-centered Self—which is always available to support your healing journey. You know that you are connected to your center when you feel calm, clearheaded, and courageous. Once you are connected to your wise Self, you are able to tap into your intuition and your intellect. This allows your adult Self to turn toward all parts of yourself with curiosity and compassion, which is a process that allows you to attend to and heal the wounds from your past.

All Parts Are Welcome

In Internal Family Systems (IFS), our credo is: All parts are welcome! Here is an exercise to help you welcome all of your parts.

Turn your attention inside and begin with this offer:

"I want to help anyone who needs help. To do that, I need to know all of you."

Then provide this information:

"If you overwhelm me, I can't be there to help you."

And make this request:

"Please be here with me rather than taking me over and, when you're ready, let me know who you are. I will write this down."

Write down the parts (thoughts, feelings or sensations) that you hear, see or sense inside (use extra paper if needed):

_____

_____

_____

_____

_____

_____

_____

_____

_____

_____

Going Inside to Identify Parts

This exercise will help you go inside, notice, and be available to your parts. Each person experiences their parts differently, usually through one of the senses. Parts can show you a thought, feeling, or sensation. Some people hear their parts, some see their parts, and others feel their parts emotionally or physically. To identify your own parts, follow the prompts below and adjust as needed. You may want to write down or record what you notice.

1. Settle into a comfortable position.

2. Notice your back against the chair, your feet on the floor, and your contact with the ground.

3. Close your eyes and take a couple deep breaths if that feels comfortable. Notice.

4. Focus your attention inside and notice any thoughts, feelings, or sensations that show up.

    a. You may notice physical sensations—some may be pleasant, others may be unpleasant.

    b. You may notice one feeling or many feelings.

    c. You may hear one thought or many thoughts competing with each other.

    d. You may notice blankness or fogginess inside. That's okay.

5. You may also notice your mind wanting to distract you and shift your focus away from that sensation, feeling or thought.

6. Be curious about whatever you notice.

    a. What does this part of you want you to know?

    b. What is it holding for you?

7. If you can, send it gratitude for showing up, even if what you have noticed is negative.

8. Notice how the part responds to your gratitude.

9. When you feel ready, come back to the room.

Notice how your energy shifts when you focus your attention internally for a few minutes. Are you calmer, more peaceful, or perhaps more agitated?

The 6Fs

IFS treatment begins by walking through the 6Fs with protective parts. The following six steps can help protective parts differentiate from the Self. The first three steps (find, focus, flesh out) involve helping parts to unblend.

1. **FIND** the part in, on, or around the body.

    a. Ask the client, "Who needs your attention right now?"

    b. "Where do you notice it?"

2. **FOCUS** on it.

    a. Ask the client to turn their attention inside.

3. **FLESH** it out.

    a. Ask the client, "Can you see it? If so, how does it look?"

    b. "If not, how do you experience it? What is that like?"

    c. "How close are you to it?"

4. How do you **FEEL** toward the part?

    a. This question is your Geiger counter for the client's Self-energy. Any answer that is not in the ballpark of the 8 Cs (the qualities of Self-energy: calm, curiosity, confidence, courageousness, clarity, connectedness, compassion, creativity) means that a second part is influencing the client's thoughts. If so, you ask this second part if it is willing to relax so you can talk to the target part. If it is not willing to relax, you ask it what it needs you to know. This process may lead you to a second (or third, or fourth...) target part.

    b. Reactive parts often need to feel heard and validated. You stay with them until they are willing to let you get to know the target part.

    c. Once they agree, you ask the client, "How do you feel toward the (target) part now?"

5. Be**FRIEND** the part by finding out more about it.

    a. The fifth step involves learning about the target part and developing a friendly relationship. This builds relationships internally (Self to part) and externally (part to therapist).

    b. Ask the client, "How did it get this job?" "How effective is the job?" "If it didn't have to do this job, what would it rather do?" "How old is it?" "How old does it think you are?" and "What else does it want you to know?"

6. What does this part **FEAR**?

    a. Ask the client, "What does it want for you?" "What would happen if it stopped doing this job**?"**

    b. This key question will reveal any lurking polarization (e.g., "If I stop feeling anxious, I'm afraid the suicidal part will take over") or it will reveal the exile it protects (e.g., "If I stop feeling anxious, I'm afraid Jane will feel all alone and worthless").

Get to Know a Part

This meditation is designed to help you get to know a little bit about a part that you want to help or change your relationship with.

If it feels good, go ahead and take a deep breath and think of a part who you'd like get to know a little better.

Go ahead and focus on that part wherever you find it, in, on or around your body. If you can't focus on it, that's okay. Either way, notice how you feel toward it.

If you feel anything other than curiosity or acceptance, ask the reactive part if it would be willing to separate from you and not interfere just so you can learn more about your target part. We're not going to let it take over, we're just going to get to know it.

And keep doing that with reactive parts until you feel curious about the original part.

You may find that you don't get there, that other parts won't separate, which is okay. You can just spend the time listening to their fears about separating. But if they do let you feel at least curious about the original one, then it's safe to listen.

What does that original part want you to know about itself? What has the part been trying to do for you? To you? What might it need from you?

I'll stop talking for a little while now and let you get to know it and then come back with time to return.

(*Pause*)

Okay, in the next few minutes we'll begin to come back.

Thank the part for letting you know about it. And let it know this doesn't have to be its only chance to talk to you. If it wants, you can come back to it another time.

Before you come back to this room, make sure you thank all the other parts for letting you get to know this one or letting you know that they were afraid if they didn't. And when all that feels complete, you can, if it feels right, begin to take some deep breaths again and shift your focus back to the outside.

Assess Self-Energy: Feel Toward

In IFS, the overall goal is for all parts—the target part and any reactive secondary parts—to differentiate and make room for the client's Self to heal the wounded part. This exercise contributes to this goal by helping you check on the client's level of access to the Self. For the sake of clarity, the target part in this exercise will be a chronically anxious part, but you can write in whatever part you hear about internally.

Ask: "How do you feel toward the _____ [*anxious*] part?"

- If the client is significantly differentiated from reactive parts and says something along the lines of "I'm curious" or "I care," then proceed and be curious: "What does this part want to tell you about itself?"

- But if the client has a negative reaction (like "I hate it!") or the client expresses agreement along the lines of "Of course I feel anxious," then . . .

Ask: "Does this _____ [*hating or agreeing*] part need your attention first, or would it be willing to relax and let you be curious about the _____ [*anxious*] part?"

- If the reactive part is willing to relax, repeat the original question: "How do you feel toward the _____ [*anxious*] part now?"

- If, however, the client goes on agreeing with the anxious part, guide the client to inquire whether the anxious part is blended. To do this, simply ask, "Is the _____ [*anxious*] part blended with you right now?"

  ○ If yes, then ask, "Would it be willing to separate and meet you?" (meaning the client's Self).

  ○ If no, then you explore more to find out who is agreeing: "Okay, somebody else agrees, and maybe that part wants to say something. Let's ask all the parts who agree on this issue to meet with you in a group. Would they be willing to do that? Invite them all to join you at a big conference table and see who shows up."

After choosing a target part, the goal is to persuade reactive parts to unblend (differentiate), which will allow the client's Self to be present and befriend the target part. When a part reacts negatively (or positively) to the target part and will not unblend, you move on to the method called *direct access*.

Direct Access

Direct access is a two-way conversation in which the Self of the therapist speaks directly with the client's target part, periodically asking if the client's Self can be brought in on the conversation. In direct access, the therapist speaks to the part.

You can use direct access with clients or, for practice, you can conduct a role-play with a colleague or embody one of your client's protective parts by going back and forth between the therapist and the client, either changing chairs or shifting a bit to one side and then the other on a couch. Try this exercise with a protector.

1. "I want to talk to this protective part directly. Are you there?"

   _____

   _____

   _____

2. "What do you do for _____ [*client's name*]?"

   _____

   _____

   _____

3. "How long have you had this job?"

   _____

   _____

   _____

4. "How's it going?"

   _____

   _____

   _____

5. "What are you concerned would happen if you stopped?"

_____

_____

_____

6. "If we could help that part (the one who would take over and do something problematic if this part were to stop), would you still need to do this job?"

_____

_____

_____

7. "Have you met the _____ [*client's name*] who's not a part?"

_____

_____

_____

8. "Would you like to meet [*client's name*]? They can help you and the parts you're worried about."

_____

_____

_____

9. "Will you give _____ [*client's name*] permission to help the part you're worried about if it agrees not to take over?"

_____

_____

_____

Dialogue with Your Child

This exercise will allow you to get in touch with an inner child part. You'll need a pen or a pencil, or if you are so inclined, you may want to use several colored markers or crayons. You will be writing questions for your inner child in the left-hand column and answering these questions in the right-hand column.

1. Begin a conversation with your child part by writing down questions for this child part in the *left-hand column of the table*, using your *dominant hand* (the one with which you write). You might begin with simple introductory questions (e.g., "How are you?" or "How are you feeling?"). Ask whatever questions feel right for you, keeping in mind that the dialogue is with a child.

2. In the *right-hand column*, respond to each question from the point of view of your child part. To do so, after you have the question written, switch your pen or pencil to your *nondominant hand*, or switch to using a marker or crayon (again, holding it with your nondominant hand).

3. Read the question and, without forcing anything, wait and see what comes up. Just allow an answer to surface. The answer typically feels as if it is coming from another part of you. Because the dialogue is with the younger part of you, it shouldn't be surprising if the response sounds childlike.

4. When an answer does arise, write it down in the right-hand column.

5. It's not uncommon for there to be no response. After all, it's probably been a while since you've connected to this part. You may have to ask several times (and maybe on several occasions) before there is enough trust developed between you and the child part that they feel safe enough to be exposed.

6. When the child part does surface, they may reveal that they are angry with or scared of you. To which you would further inquire as to why that is, and what you can do to help them to begin to trust you.

7. Like every other new relationship, its development is a process rather than a one-time exercise. The ultimate goal is to not only access the child part, but to become a nurturing figure to this part.

Adult Question (Dominant Hand)	Child's Response (Nondominant Hand)

Create a Meeting Place for Your Parts

One way to identify parts is to create a meeting place for all of your parts, either in your mind or on a piece of paper. You can invite parts of all ages, parts that represent different emotions, or parts that represent strengths or challenging aspects of your personality.

- Sometimes it is helpful to create a meeting place where you can invite all of your parts to be in one place. For example, you might imagine or draw a conference table, campfire, or any other meeting place that you would like. Would you be interested in creating a meeting place for your parts?

- What kind of meeting place would you like to create? Would you like to draw your meeting place or simply imagine it?

- What parts of yourself would you like to bring to this meeting place? These parts might be different ages, such as a baby, inner child, teenager, or adult. Or you might explore parts that represent different emotions, such as a shameful, fearful, angry, joyful, courageous, or loving part. Parts might also represent different aspects of your personality, such as a creative, hard-working, critical, perfectionistic, or self-sabotaging part.

- Once you have identified your parts, take some time to place each part in your meeting place by either drawing them or simply imagining them. What parts might you place close to one another? Which parts would you separate further apart from one another? How would you describe the relationships between different parts of yourself? Are there any conflicts between parts? Are there any parts who nurture or protect other parts?

Connect to Your Adult Self

This exercise will guide you in connecting to your adult Self so you can access the 8 Cs of the Self: compassion, clarity, confidence, creativity, courage, calmness, connectedness, and curiosity.

- To begin, I'd like you to imagine that you are connected to your center. This is a place within you that can serve as a source of clarity, curiosity, and compassion.

- Take a few breaths and notice how you feel in your body. See if you can fine-tune your posture so you feel connected to your core. You might explore how it feels to lengthen your spine as you take a deep breath. Or notice how it feels to stand up tall. Continue to explore your posture until you find a stance that helps you feel strong, courageous, and calm.

- Feel yourself in the body of your adult Self. Take a look at your hands and notice that these are the hands of an adult. If you are able, stand up and recognize that you are in an adult body by reaching up to the top of a door frame. Remind yourself that you are an adult now and that you are safe.

- Orient to the time and date by looking at a clock or calendar. Notice the current date and time as a way to reinforce that you are an adult and not a child.

- Think of activities that you can do in your life now that were not possible when you were a child. For example, you can drive a car, go to work, take care of your own children, and vote.

- Explore bringing a warm, gentle smile to your face. Relax your face and slightly lift the corners of your lips. Invite a soft smile to your eyes. As you engage in this smile, allow a relaxed feeling to spread across your face, head, and shoulders. Notice if you can connect to a feeling of peace.

- Bring your attention to your heart by taking several deep breaths into your chest. Perhaps place one or both of your hands over your heart to enhance your connection to this area of your body. As you connect to your physical heart, I also invite you to notice the qualities your heart represents: warmth, generosity, and love. Notice how it feels to know that these qualities are always there inside of you.

- Now take several deep breaths into your belly. Again, you can place one or both hands over this area of your body to enhance your awareness. The area in your lower abdomen, about two inches below your navel, has been called the Dan Tian in the Qigong tradition and is considered a center of inner strength. As you focus your attention here, imagine being connected to a source of stability that can help you from being pulled out of balance by people or situations in your life.

- Now that you are connected to your adult Self, take some time to notice your thoughts, emotions, and body sensations. Perhaps you notice that you feel more grounded, are more connected to your center, or have an increased sense of clarity. If so, allow yourself to savor and enjoy this positive experience. You can reconnect here as often as needed by returning to these practices.

Differentiate from a Part

Once the client is connected to their adult Self, you can invite them to differentiate from any parts with which they are overidentified. Ideally, this helps the client to have greater clarity about the functions of protective parts and to have compassion for wounds carried by exiled parts. Signs that a client is blended with a protective part include self-criticism, perfectionism, a tendency to be judgmental toward others, or aggressive behavior. Signs that a client is blended with an exiled part include overwhelming emotions of sadness, hopelessness, helplessness, or shame.

This exercise asks questions and offers suggestions to help the client unblend from a critical protective part and, when needed, to differentiate from a young exiled part. Ultimately, this will help the client gain access to the vulnerable emotions held by the exiled part so resolution and healing can be achieved. Importantly, it is common to move between the previous exercises in this section as you explore this practice:

- Now that you are connected to your adult Self, I invite you to turn toward the part of you who feels . . . [*e.g., young, anxious, sad, not enough, worthless, lonely*]. Notice how you feel toward this part of yourself. What is it like to witness this part of you? From the perspective of your adult Self, what do you believe about this part of you?

If the client appears blended with a critical or rejecting part—limiting the client's ability to explore their younger, more vulnerable part—then explore the following questions and statements.

- I notice that you are feeling critical toward the part of you who is feeling . . . [*e.g., young, anxious, sad, not enough, worthless, lonely*]. I understand that this criticism once served to protect you. Is the critical part willing to step back and allow you to be present with this vulnerable part of you?

- We are not trying to get rid of this critical part but are asking it to step back for the time being. Rather than casting off this part, I invite you to reflect upon the ways that this part has functioned to protect you.

- Perhaps you might offer appreciation to this part for its job. If you weren't able to be vulnerable when you were a child, this part may have helped you maintain a sense of control. Now ask yourself whether it is still necessary to protect yourself in this way. Might it be safe to soften your defenses?

If the client appears overidentified with a young part, then explore the following questions and statements.

- You seem to be feeling very little or young right now. Can you take a moment to reorient to your adult Self? Now that you feel more connected to your center and your strength, is there anything that this young or vulnerable part wants you to know? Invite your adult Self to give the young part a tour of your life now. Show the young part where you live and where you work. Share the ways that your present-day life is different from the experiences you had in childhood.

Invite a Dialogue with an Inner Critic

This is an additional intervention that is beneficial for clients who struggle with an unrelenting self-critical part. In this case, you invite the client to explore a dialogue between their inner critic and the part of themselves who is being criticized. This is accomplished through an empty chair dialogue between the critic and the young or exiled part. As with all therapeutic interventions, it is important that the client express their willingness to participate with this experiment, so begin by inviting the client's consent. In setting up the dialogue, you will ask the client to identify whether they are more connected to the critical voice or the part who feels criticized. You will then invite them to begin the dialogue by giving voice to the part who they are more identified with. As a result, you will need to tailor the order of the suggested prompts offered here to reflect your understanding of the client's unique presentation and internalized parts.

- I notice that you are . . . [*e.g., feeling self-critical, calling yourself worthless, feeling like you need to be perfect, dismissing your emotions*]. When you have a strong inner critic, it can be helpful to explore an empty chair dialogue with this part of yourself. This process also invites the part who is being . . . [*e.g., criticized, put down, controlled, dismissed*] to have a voice. Would you be willing to explore a dialogue between your inner critic and the part of you being criticized?

- It is important to know that this dialogue is not real and does not require that you speak these words to your . . . [*e.g., mom, dad, abuser*] in real life. We are working with your internalization of their presence and voice as it lives inside of you. This dialogue is to help you find resolution within yourself as you express what you were never able to say in the relationship.

- Let's set up the room so you have an empty chair in front of you. Take a moment and check in with yourself. Do you feel more connected to the part of you who is critical or to the part who feels criticized?

- When giving voice to your inner critic, give yourself permission to really exaggerate this part of you! Notice your tone of voice and posture. Do you notice any familiarity in your body language or in the message communicated by this critical part of you? Does this voice remind you of anyone from your past? When giving voice to the part of you who feels criticized, notice how you feel when you are being criticized and judged. What thoughts and emotions arise? From this seat, look at the chair of your inner critic. Give yourself permission to express how it feels to be criticized. You might say, "I feel insignificant when you talk to me like that," "You have unrealistic expectations of me," or "I can never get it right!" Notice your posture and tone of voice as you sit in this chair. Are you aware of times from the past when you felt this way?

- Often, self-criticism and self-aggression are manifestations of anger turned inward. Ask yourself what would have happened had you expressed anger toward . . . [*e.g., mom, dad, abuser*] when you were a child. Instead of attacking yourself, can you give yourself permission to be angry at . . . [*e.g., mom, dad, abuser*] now?

- Now cultivate a dialogue by going back and forth between the chair of your inner critic and the part of you who feels criticized. Take your time until both parts have had an opportunity to be heard. Continue to explore any memories or associations that arise related to each part. See if you can understand what motivates the critical part. Is it an attempt to protect you from feeling vulnerable? Is it a remnant of unfinished business of your . . . [*e.g., mom, dad, abuser*] that had nothing to do with you? Begin to explore the needs of the part of you who feels criticized. Does this part need kindness, nurturance, or protection?

- Since this dialogue is in your imagination, you get to decide how it ends. You are allowed to seek resolution and create a new outcome. What might it be like for the critic to soften and meet the needs of the part who feels criticized? Perhaps, you can imagine that your . . . [*e.g., mom, dad, abuser*] offers an apology that never happened in real life. This is your internal world, so how do you want to bring this dialogue to completion?

Identify Allies for a Young Part

This healing practice helps you identify supportive people or imagined allies for a young or exiled part. This practice can be especially helpful if you feel resentment, hatred, or disgust toward the young part. In this case, you might not be capable of offering compassion from your adult Self toward the young part.

- All children deserve to be nurtured, protected, and wisely guided by caring parents or caregivers. If you did not receive this support in childhood, you might have a hard time feeling compassion for a young part of yourself now. In this case, it can be helpful to identify other people or to imagine allies who can offer nurturance, protection, and wise guidance for this young part. Would you be willing to identify some supportive resources for this part?

- You might have had people at various stages of your life who met these needs, such as a caring relative, neighbor, or teacher. Or you might have people in your life now who support you. Can you identify a supportive person or people who could help you as you work through difficult memories from your past? Is there someone in your life who has supported you, believed in you, stood up for you, or guided you during difficult moments in your life?

- Even if you did not or do not have these people in your life, you can imagine the presence of allies who represent these positive qualities. An ally can be an animal, ancestor, spiritual presence, or fictional character from a movie or book. I'd like you to identify a few imagined allies who could help you as you work through difficult memories from your past. What allies might offer care, warmth, or nurturance? You might also want to imagine allies with a strong presence and fearless capacity to protect you.

- Now bring to mind this young part, and take a few moments to identify the needs of this part of you. Imagine these supportive people and allies providing care, protection, or wise counsel for this young part of yourself. What emotions or sensations arise as you imagine having these supportive people and allies with this part of you?

Facilitate Repair Scenarios

Once the client has unblended from their parts, you can invite them to explore creating a repair scenario to facilitate a resolution of the wounds from the past. The interventions on this handout offer examples of how to identify the needs of a younger, vulnerable part and repair these wounds. As with other healing practices, you might notice that the client has difficulty maintaining compassion for this part. If the client begins to blend with a critical part of themselves, it may be necessary to help them connect to their adult Self or to invite them to bring in allies by revisiting the previous exercises in this section.

- I invite you to turn toward the part of you who feels . . . [*e.g., young, anxious, not enough, worthless, critical*]. Often, these parts of ourselves carry unmet needs, such as the need to be nurtured, supported, accepted, seen, heard, understood, respected, protected, rescued, or removed from an unsafe situation. Once we identify an unmet need, we can explore creating an imagined repair for that part of yourself.

- Take a moment to recall a memory of a time in your life that is connected to this part. Where were you? How old were you? Were you alone or with others? What made this time so difficult? What emotions were you feeling then?

- Now, from the perspective of your adult Self, can you imagine what you might have needed in that time?

If the client has difficulty connecting to the need, you can share what you imagine the need might have been. For example, you can say:

- If I were there with you then, here is what I imagine you would have needed. [*Name what you imagine was the missing experience for the client.*] Does that feel accurate to you?

- Imagine your present-day self walking into that scene and nurturing your younger self. Can you imagine gazing at this younger you in a loving and compassionate manner?

- What emotions do you see on the face of your younger part of yourself? How does it feel to know that these emotions are now understood and seen? Is there anything that you would like to say to this younger part? Is there anything else you might do to offer a sense of comfort, support, or acceptance for that younger you? Take your time with this process until you feel a sense of completion. What do you notice now as you offer this nurturance to this part of yourself?

- Can you imagine your adult Self standing up for this young part? You will not let anyone hurt this part of you! You are allowed to have boundaries. Notice if there is a need to rescue or remove your younger part from an unsafe situation. If so, imagine taking this part of yourself away from danger. Now imagine bringing this young part of yourself to a safe place. Take your time until you have created a sense of safety for this part. Now what do you notice as you offer protection and safety to this part of yourself?

- If you find it difficult to imagine your adult Self being a resource for this young part, you can explore bringing in an ally into this scene from your past. In what ways might this person nurture or protect you? Maybe you would like to imagine them helping this part of you stand up against an abuser, or perhaps they help remove this part of you from an unsafe situation. Are there any other allies you would like to bring into this scene? Take your time with this process until you feel a sense of completion. Notice how you feel in your body and any emotions you are feeling.

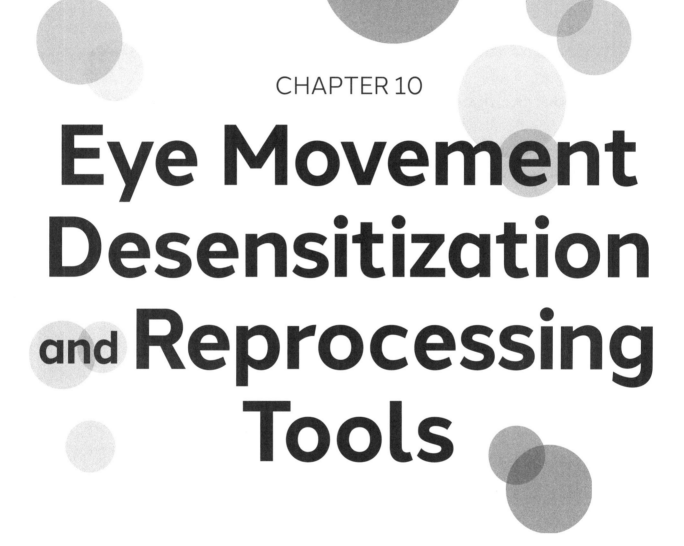

CHAPTER 10

Eye Movement Desensitization and Reprocessing Tools

The EMDR Process

Eye movement desensitization and reprocessing (EMDR) is made up of eight phases:

1. **History taking and treatment planning:** To begin, we will gather information about your history, trauma, and current symptoms. We'll then develop a treatment plan and goals.

2. **Preparation:** During this phase, we will continue working to establish trust, and you will be educated on the EMDR process. You will learn about bilateral stimulation and begin incorporating it with resourcing and coping techniques.

3. **Assessment:** Here, we'll pick a specific target to focus on. This can be a memory, experience, or image that is causing you distress. We will also identify any beliefs, emotions, and sensations related to this target.

4. **Desensitization:** At this point, we will begin using bilateral stimulation (through eye movements, tapping, audio, or other methods) as we focus on the selected target. This phase aims to reduce the emotional charge of the target identified in phase 3.

5. **Installation:** Once the emotional charge is reduced, you will focus on installing, or strengthening, the positive belief that you identified during phase 3. This will help to replace your negative beliefs related to the traumatic memory.

6. **Body scan:** Here, you will check for any physical tension or sensations related to the trauma that may still be present, or you may simply notice the physical relief that you are experiencing.

7. **Closure:** At the end of each reprocessing session, we'll discuss all the progress you've made during that session. We can revisit any resourcing or relaxation techniques, if needed, to assist you in feeling grounded and safe.

8. **Re-evaluation:** At the next session, we'll discuss and assess your progress since the last session and address any remaining issues that you would like to focus on next.

Phases 1 and 2 can take several sessions to complete. Phases 3 through 7 are done in one session, and these phases will be repeated until you feel that you have addressed all the targets that you want to heal and work through.

Each phase includes a lot of steps within, but rest assured that I will guide you through these steps in a more simplistic way as we go.

Timeline of Events and Resiliency Factors

Let's explore some of the events in your life that may be causing you symptoms of distress. We are going to start by creating a timeline of events using the *Timeline of Events and Resiliency Factors* template. We can take our time with this exercise, as this may feel overwhelming, so be gentle with yourself as we walk through this process. We can take as much time as needed. Some people find it helpful to just start with a certain period of time and build upon this in upcoming sessions.

As we construct your timeline, we will also identify your own personal resiliency factors. These are things that helped you to cope during these difficult times in your life.

In the column labeled *Negative Life Experiences*, identify difficult life experiences that you have faced. These can be things that you directly experienced, learned about, were told happened, or witnessed.

In the column labeled *Positive Life Experiences*, identify any of the positive things that you enjoyed, experienced, or leaned on during these years that gave you a sense of hope or helped you endure. These can be accomplishments you are proud of, new skills or hobbies you developed, friends you made, positive or favorite memories, people who encouraged or supported you, or favorite sports, musicians, books, movies, or characters that inspired hope, creativity, or freedom.

Timeline of Events and Resiliency Factors

Negative Life Experiences	Age	Positive Life Experiences
	0	
	5	
	10	
	15	
	20	
	25	
	30	
	35	
	40	
	45	
	50	
	55	
	60	
	65	
	70	
	75+	

Containment Imagery Script

The container is an imaginal resource used in EMDR that addresses the need to compartmentalize distressing material so clients can be present in the here and now and attend to their needs. Be clear: This script is not a repression or suppression of memories, thoughts, affect, or emotion. It is a technique to allow clients to attend to what they need to attend to until they have the necessary resources to attend to those distressing or disturbing memories, thoughts, affects, or emotions. (Remember: Time is a resource.)

Script

Allow yourself to be comfortable . . . either lying down or sitting up with your back, neck, and spine fully supported. Knowing that you will not be interrupted for the next little while, begin by gently closing your eyes.

(Clinician should breathe audibly with the exhalation longer than the inhalation.)

Now begin to bring your attention to your breath—the direct experience of your breath—however it is . . . and however it changes. Allow yourself to softly focus your awareness on to the breath that is arising right now—the in-breath and the out-breath, the rising and the falling. If you can, try to follow one full cycle of the breath from the beginning of the in-breath through its entirety and then to the beginning of the out-breath through its entirety. Allow yourself the time and the space to be in direct contact with the breath throughout one entire cycle.

(Clinician should breathe audibly with the exhalation longer than the inhalation.)

As you continue to pay attention to the breath, you may notice distractions that arise. Just allow yourself to notice those distractions . . . any bodily sensations or any thoughts that may arise. If possible, allow yourself to become aware of the separateness of those bodily sensations—notice how those sensations are separate and distinct from your thoughts, your ideas, and your words.

(Clinician should breathe audibly with the exhalation longer than the inhalation.)

Now, as you continue with this focused awareness, you will notice how often you lose contact with the breath . . . maybe you become caught in a thought or an idea or plan, or maybe some other bodily sensation pulls your attention. When a distraction happens, simply notice that you have lost connection with the breath, and gently bring your awareness back.

(Clinician should breathe with the exhalation longer than the inhalation.)

We'll begin now with a deep breath in through your nose . . . inhaling slowly and deeply. Exhale through pursed lips until all the air has been released.

(Clinician should breathe audibly with the exhalation longer than the inhalation.)

Now we are going to be creating a container. It doesn't matter what kind of container it is, as long as it can "hold" any and all disturbing material. If you were going to develop such a container, what would it look like? Some people have used boxes, safes, trunks, or chests; others have used bookbags, knapsacks, or other pieces of luggage. It can be anything really, a tank, a submarine, an underground well—anything that suits you.

(Clinician should breathe audibly with the exhalation longer than the inhalation.)

Can you bring to mind an image of something like that—something that would be able to contain any and all disturbing material? When you have one in mind, take a good look at it. What material is it made out of? How is it held together? How big is it? What color is it? Are there any markings on it? If there are markings, notice them; if not, that's fine. But I'd like you to add something to this container. I'd like you to add in some way— whether it be a note or a sign or an inscription of sort—a notation to indicate that this container will remain tightly sealed. It will remain tightly sealed until you wish to open it and retrieve something from it. Otherwise, it will remain sealed. It can be opened—but only by you—and it should be opened only in the service of your healing.

(Clinician should breathe audibly with the exhalation longer than the inhalation.)

So once again, look at your container. Does it already have that message on it? If not, place it on there now.

(Pause.)

Now, how does this container open? Are you able to open it by yourself, or do you need help? Is there a lock on it? If not, feel free to put one or several on it now.

(Pause.)

(Clinician should breathe audibly with the exhalation longer than the inhalation.)

Once the locks are in place, we'll experiment with opening and closing them, locking and unlocking them. As you do that, notice how much, or how little, effort it takes to open and close the container.

(Clinician should breathe audibly with the exhalation longer than the inhalation.)

When you feel comfortable handling it, I'd like you to think of something that you might put into the container—just for practice. Do whatever is necessary to open it up, and then place something in there. When I say "something," I mean anything, really, that may be distressing or disturbing to you right now. It could be thoughts or worries, bad feelings or bad memories . . . it could be something that you have to do but not right this minute. Or it could be something that keeps you from being present with this exercise. It could be self-judgment, doubt, or pain. Whatever it is, you're going to put it into the container . . . whatever you need to do to get it in there, do that now.

(Pause.)

(Clinician should breathe audibly with the exhalation longer than the inhalation.)

Once the disturbing material is in, close it up and lock the container.

(Pause.)

Now, breathe deeply as you look at the locked container, securely holding anything that you need or want it to hold.

(Breathe audibly with the exhalation longer than the inhalation.)

Notice how you feel in your body having set aside whatever distressing thing you put in your container. Can you sense that it is fully contained? Is there something that keeps it from feeling fully contained? If so, can we try opening your container and putting that in there as well? Remember that this container is yours and will hold anything and everything you need it to hold for as long as you need it to.

(Clinician should breathe audibly with the exhalation longer than the inhalation.)

Now imagine walking away from your container so that it is no longer in your sight. Notice the feeling in your body now that you are no longer burdened by what you put in the container. Notice your breath—your in-breath and your out-breath—and any sensations of relief you feel in your body. Maybe your shoulders have dropped a bit, or some of the tension in your neck has subsided. Whatever feelings of relief you notice, breathe deeply and just notice.

Whatever you put in the container is now securely locked inside. It is for you to open whenever you wish to put things in or take them out.

So now, just for practice, let's go back to your container. Once you have it in sight, look closely. See if you can read what is written on the outside.

(Pause.)

Continue focusing on your breath as you continue to approach the container. When you are within reach, unlock it and open it up. As you open it notice that what you put in there is still there, separate from you. You might want to put something else in, or maybe even a few things. Or you may just wish to lock it back up. Whatever feels right and safe to you, do that now.

(Pause.)

(Clinician should breathe audibly with the exhalation longer than the inhalation.)

And once you're finished practicing putting things in your container and securely locking it back up, you can walk away from the container. As you walk away, begin to bring yourself and your awareness back to this room. Know that this resource—this secure container—is available to you at any time. Know that you can use it to hold any and all disturbing things. Know that all the things that you have chosen—or anything that you choose to contain in the future—will be secure and will remain secure. You can access the material whenever you feel ready to do so. But for now, you may leave it, knowing it is safely and securely contained.

(Clinician should breathe audibly with the exhalation longer than the inhalation.)

And now, whenever you are ready, gently bring yourself back to the room by counting up from one to five. When you reach the number five, your eyes will gently open. You will be awake and alert, and feeling only peace. One . . . two . . . three. Take a deep breath . . . four . . . and five.

Your Restoration Team

For this exercise, we'll work together to create a support system for you, known as your *restoration team*. Your restoration team can include anything that you find helpful—be creative! You might include fictional characters from books or movies, musicians, animals, objects, symbols, people in your life (dead or alive), imaginary people or anything else that resonates with you. Let's begin:

1. We will start with some bilateral stimulation as I prompt you to think of certain categories of people you can include on your restoration team. These are just suggested categories that may or may not resonate with you.

2. First, think of a someone or something that would represent acceptance or unconditional love to you.

3. Next, think of someone or something that would represent protection or strength.

4. Continue by thinking of someone or something that would represent wisdom or insight.

5. Now, think of someone or something that would represent inspiration.

6. Finally, think of yourself at your best—the person you are striving to become.

7. Take a deep breath in and out as we stop the bilateral stimulation. What did you notice?

8. We are going to have you notice all of these figures, people, or objects once more as we add some bilateral stimulation.

9. Bring all of these figures, people, or objects to mind once more. As you do, just notice what they would want to remind you of. What message would they want to leave you with or encourage you with? Who would they tell you to remember that you are?

10. Take a deep breath in and out as we stop your bilateral stimulation.

> **Therapist Note:** Encourage the client to select figures, objects, or resources that have not harmed them or caused any type of trauma. If it is difficult for some clients to think of certain categories can also use qualities that the client already embodies. These categories can be used or developed at any time and are interchangeable. Encourage the client to use these in and outside of session when they need support.

Visualize Your Peaceful Place

This healing practice invites you to visualize a real or imagined place where you feel safe, relaxed, peaceful, and calm. It also includes a self-tapping practice called the *butterfly hug*, which draws on EMDR's use of bilateral stimulation to calm the nervous system. If your client's feeling state shifts in a negative direction while engaging in self-tapping, stop and explore with them whether any intrusive thoughts or imagery is interfering with the peaceful place visualization.

- I invite you to take some time to visualize a calm or peaceful place to give your mind and body a chance to feel comfortable and relaxed. This practice is important because we often do not release the impact of traumatic events until we feel safe.

- Is it okay with you if we identify an image of a place that feels peaceful and calm to you? This place can be real or imaginary. Maybe you can think of a place or time when you felt safe or relaxed in your life. Perhaps you would like to choose a place from a movie or book, or you can create a place from your imagination.

- Use your senses to enhance your imagery. What do you see? What do you hear? Are there any smells that you associate with this place?

- This is *your* imagined place, so you can be creative. You are in charge of this place. You can decide if you want to bring another person or an animal into this place. As you think about your place, are there any changes that you would like to make?

- Let me know if any negative thoughts or intrusive images interfere with your ability to feel safe and relaxed while imagining your peaceful place. If so, continue to take your time to make changes to the imagery until you feel relaxed. For example, you can place a fence or wall around your peaceful place to add a layer of protection.

- If you'd like, we can do a self-tapping practice called the butterfly hug, which can feel calming. Cross your arms over your chest so your palms are resting on your sternum, with your fingers extending toward opposite shoulders, and interlock your thumbs to create the image of a butterfly. Begin alternately tapping your hands for 15 to 20 seconds, as if they were the wings of a butterfly. As long as this feels positive, we can explore another round of self-tapping while you visualize your calm and peaceful place. If at any point you feel uncomfortable, simply stop the self-tapping.

Anchoring

This is another resourcing skill that can help you manage triggers and stressors. This exercise will require you to think of one of your most cherished or favorite memories or experiences in life. Let's begin:

1. Describe the experience you are thinking of—including your age, what was taking place, all the sensory details, and any specific body sensations, emotions, and thoughts.

2. Now let's strengthen this memory by adding bilateral stimulation as you bring it to mind. You're turning the volume up on this memory or making it brighter and more vivid in your mind. Pull the memory closer to you, noticing all you felt during this time that made it feel special. [*Bilateral stimulation should be very rapid, lasting approximately 20 to 30 seconds.*]

3. Take a deep breath in and out as we stop the bilateral stimulation. Can you share with me what you noticed?

4. Let's enhance the positive sensations of this memory once more. Take another deep breath in and out, starting the bilateral stimulation again as you notice the positive memory. [*Bilateral stimulation should be very rapid, lasting approximately 20 to 30 seconds.*]

5. Stopping the bilateral stimulation and taking a deep breath in and out, choose an anchor word that represents this memory or the feeling you get from this experience. For example, you might choose something like *strong*, *unstoppable*, or *accomplished*. What word is coming up for you?

6. Beginning bilateral stimulation again, think of this memory as vividly as you can. You will now state your anchor word out loud three times. Then we will stop bilateral stimulation.

7. Now let's use this anchor word to help you shift your feelings or thoughts. Bring up something that has been causing you distress.

8. Starting bilateral stimulation, focus on this stressor for a moment. Now, state your anchor word out loud three times again and then stop the bilateral stimulation.

9. What shifted from the distressing memory? Some people find that they are unable to think of the stressor or that it doesn't feel as upsetting anymore. You can use this as way to shift your focus if you need to outside of session.

    Note: If the client did not notice a change in their feeling state, it may help to change the anchor word to something that fits more appropriately.

Negative and Positive Cognitions

As you consider the issue we are targeting for treatment, what is the negative belief you have about yourself because of this event? Circle any of the beliefs that stand out to you from the negative cognition list.

What do you wish you could believe about yourself instead? Circle anything you wish to believe from the positive cognition list on the next page. How true does this positive belief feel to you on a scale of 1 to 7, with 1 being "completely false" and 7 being "completely true"?

Negative Cognitions	Positive Cognitions
I don't deserve love.	I deserve love.
I am a bad person.	I am a good/loving person.
I am terrible.	I am fine as I am.
I am worthless or inadequate.	I am worthy or worthwhile.
I am shameful.	I am honorable.
I am not good enough.	I am enough.
I deserve only bad things.	I am deserving.
I am permanently damaged.	I am okay.
I am ugly.	I am beautiful the way I am.
I should have known better.	I did the best I could at the time.
I am stupid.	I am intelligent (or able to learn).
I am insignificant or unimportant.	I am significant (or important).
I am disappointment.	I am okay just the way I am.
I deserve to die.	I deserve to live.
I deserve to be miserable.	I deserve to be happy.
I am not in control.	I am now in control.
I am powerless or helpless.	I am capable.
I am weak.	I am strong.
I cannot get what I want.	I can get what I want.
I will fail.	I can succeed.
I have to be perfect.	I can make mistakes.
I cannot stand it.	I can handle it.
I cannot trust anyone.	I can choose whom to trust.
I cannot be trusted or cannot trust myself.	I can (learn to) trust myself.
I cannot protect myself.	I can take care of myself.
I am in danger.	It's over; I am safe now.
It's not okay to feel or show my emotions.	I can safely feel my emotions.
I cannot stand up for myself.	I can stand up for myself.
I cannot let it out.	I can choose to let it out.
I am different or don't belong.	I can be myself.

Identifying Emotions, Body Sensations, and Intensity

We are now at the final part of the protocol before we start adding bilateral stimulation. Let's identify the emotions and physical sensations you are experiencing, as well as how intense these emotions and sensations feel:

1. As you think of this issue that we are focusing on, what emotions or feelings come up for you?

   _____

   _____

   _____

2. Where do you notice these feelings and emotions in your body? Describe where in your body you notice these feelings as well as what it feels like.

   _____

   _____

   _____

3. As you notice the emotions and sensations that this issue brings up, how much does this issue or memory bother you on a scale of 0 to 10, with 0 being "not at all bothersome" and 10 being "the most something could bother you"?

   _____

   _____

   _____

Reprocess a Traumatic Memory

The purpose of reprocessing a traumatic memory is to review an event and to reduce the amount of emotional or somatic distress clients experience when reflecting on that experience. This intervention is intended to help clients achieve this level of reprocessing and desensitization. You do so by helping clients stay oriented to their present experience of safety while they recall the traumatic event. You begin this process by working with clients to identify a focus for the session. Often, it is beneficial to start by talking about any current distress they are experiencing, as this will allow the focus of the session to be most relevant to their current needs.

- Let's take some time to identify a focus for our session. Check in with your body and mind, and begin to notice anything that is bothering you or any current distress that you are experiencing.

- Once you have identified a current stressor, begin to notice any beliefs about yourself that arise. What emotions or body sensations are you experiencing?

- Sometimes our current distress is related to memories from the past. Do you recall other times when you have felt this way? If there are many events that come to mind, I will write these down, and we can choose whether you would like to work with the current disturbing event or one of these memories from your past.

- Now that we have chosen a focus for the session, go ahead and return your awareness to your emotions and body sensations. Begin to notice if there are any images that arise in relationship to this event. Are you aware of any related negative beliefs about yourself? [*If needed, you can review the list of common negative cognitions from the* Negative and Positive Cognitions *worksheet in this chapter.*]

- I'd like you to take a moment to imagine how you will feel once this disturbing event or experience is resolved. What emotions do you imagine you might feel when you achieve some sort of emotional resolution? What new beliefs would you like to have about yourself? [*If needed, you can review the list of common positive cognitions from the* Negative and Positive Cognitions *worksheet in this chapter.*]

- Now bring your attention back to the event you have chosen as a focus for this session and the belief that . . . [*restate the negative belief that the client previously identified*]. On a scale of 0 to 10—with 10 being the "worst distress possible" and 0 being "no distress at all"—how much distress are you aware of right now?

- As you reflect on the event you have chosen as your focus for our session, I would like you to observe your emotions and body sensations. Remember, you are in charge of the pace. You can stop or pause this process at any point either by letting me know verbally or by simply lifting your hand.

- If it feels alright to you, I'll suggest that you keep your focus on this event for about 30 more seconds. I'll let you know when the time is over. If this feels too short or too long, let me know.

- Now go ahead and return your sensory awareness to the room. What are you noticing? Describe any thoughts, images, or sensations that are present for you now.

- When you are ready, once again return your attention to the event for about 30 seconds. [*Continue guiding the client into short periods of mindful reflection on the event with intermittent check-ins about their experience.*]

- If you'd like, let's explore adding bilateral movements while you pay attention to the event you have chosen as a focus for the session. [*You can use the butterfly tap from the* Visualize Your Peaceful Place *exercise in this chapter, or if you are trained in EMDR, you might also introduce bilateral eye movements, tactile pulsers, or alternating sounds in headphones. Continue short sets of focusing on the traumatic event with added bilateral stimulation.*]

If the client reports associations to other events, trust their process, but periodically return their awareness to the original focus as a way to observe any changes in their level of distress. If a client describes intrusive negative thoughts or beliefs during reprocessing, then reintroduce the cognitive reappraisal questions from the *Invite Cognitive Reappraisal* worksheet in chapter 1. If a client is working with a memory related to a young part, return to the IFS practices from chapter 9. If the client reports thoughts or images, but has little connection to their emotions or sensations, work with them to develop greater embodied self-awareness with the tools in chapter 2. If the client reports feeling stuck in their somatic sensations, integrate movement interventions from chapter 3 to facilitate a sense of release or resolution through the body. If you observe cues that the client is dissociating during the exercise, or if the client reports any feelings of being flooded or overwhelmed, then ask them to place the disturbing memory into a container. For example:

- I notice that you are leaving your window of tolerance. Let's go ahead and put the disturbing event into your container and bring your full awareness to the room. Look around the room and observe that you are safe right here and now. The event that we are speaking about is over. If you would like, you can engage in bilateral movements while you focus on the here and now, and see if this helps you feel more connected to a sense of safety. Once again, you can use the butterfly tap exercise. When you feel safe and connected to yourself, we can slowly explore returning your attention to the disturbing event.

Continue reprocessing the memory until the client describes feeling a sense of resolution or a SUDS of 0. At this point, ask them to reflect on any positive changes they have noticed during the session. If the client has difficulty noticing any positive change, you might reflect back to them any positive change or insight that you observed during the course of the session.

- I am aware that we are coming to the end of our session time today. As we prepare to complete our work for today, take a few moments to notice any positive change or insight that you would like to take with you. Notice how you feel in your body as you reflect on this positive change. What beliefs about yourself do you notice now? How do you imagine that you could bring this new awareness into your life? Take some time to explore this new awareness.

If the client continues to exhibit a high level of distress toward the end of a session, invite them to place the event (and any related images, thoughts, emotions, and body sensations) into their container.

- Take a few moments before leaving here to today to place any remaining disturbing images, thoughts, emotions, or body sensations into an imagined container that can hold these experiences until you return to therapy. Remember, you have a choice about when to think about any distressing memories from your past.

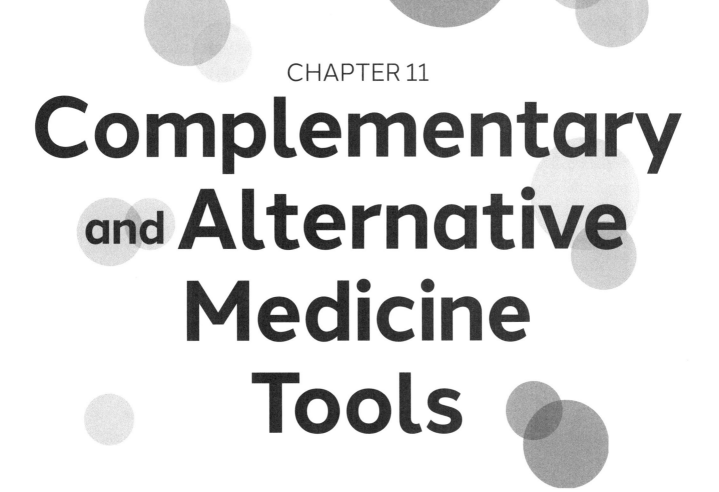

CHAPTER 11

Complementary and Alternative Medicine Tools

Explore Physical Health and Identify Healthcare Goals

It is often necessary to focus on basic healthcare needs to facilitate stabilization when working with clients with trauma. Here, you can explore with clients whether they are getting enough sleep, eating at regular intervals, staying hydrated, and sufficiently digesting their food. As needed, you can then prioritize interventions to address these basic needs by ensuring that clients have access to food, set reminders to drink water, or learn sleep hygiene strategies to assist with debilitating insomnia. For example, you can encourage clients to reduce caffeine use during the day or manage computer or phone screen exposure after dark by wearing blue light–blocking glasses. Given that insomnia can lead to irritability, anxiety, poor concentration, confusion, and depression, you can also partner with other medical professionals to help clients access pharmaceutical medications, natural supplements, herbal medicines, bodywork, or acupuncture to assist with sleep.

- I would like to know a little about your physical health. Let's start with some basics. Do you have difficulty sleeping at night and, if so, how does this impact your life? Do you eat regular meals and have access to food that is nutritious? Do you drink enough water throughout the day? How is your digestion? [*If the client shares that they are struggling with any of these areas, begin to explore ways to support these basic needs prior to exploring other aspects of their health history.*]

- It can also be helpful to know more about your physical health history. Have you had or do you currently have any physical health challenges, such as digestive challenges, heart disease, headaches, skin conditions, allergies, thyroid imbalances, or autoimmune conditions? Do you experience any areas of chronic pain? Do you have any current health concerns for which you have not received any diagnosis?

- Let's take a look at the care that you have already received for your physical health concerns. What treatments have you had or are you currently using for your condition? Were or are these treatments helpful or successful? As a result of any illness or pain, have you had any invasive or traumatic medical procedures? Do you find yourself fearful of or avoiding medical care? Do you feel understood and respected by healthcare providers?

- In addition to traditional or conventional medical care, have you explored any complementary or alternative healthcare modalities, such as acupuncture, massage therapy, or bodywork? Have these helped reduce your symptoms?

- Have you ever worked with a nutritionist? Are you aware of any food sensitivities, intolerances, or allergies?

- Do you currently have an exercise routine? Does this help reduce your symptoms, or do you notice any symptoms that worsen after exercise?

- Do you currently engage in any mindfulness or relaxation practices, such as meditation, yoga, Tai Chi, or Qigong? If so, do you find these practices helpful in reducing your symptoms? Do you notice any exacerbation of symptoms during relaxation practices?

- Are there any lifestyle changes that you would like to create or goals that you would like to set for your physical health? These goals might include integrating an exercise routine into your life, creating more time for meditation or yoga, committing to writing in a journal, or focusing on dietary changes. Let's write down a list of these goals together.

Overcome Barriers to Healthcare Goals

Some clients might desire to integrate lifestyle changes, such as exercise, nutritional changes, or meditation, but have difficulty sustaining these health-promoting behaviors. It is common for a vicious cycle of shame to ensue in which clients feel powerless to meet their healthcare goals. For example, clients might know that they need to change their diet, exercise more, or set up a visit with a doctor to address a medical problem. However, they might also believe that nothing they do will make a difference, that they don't deserve to be healthy, or that change is impossible. Or they might not feel safe with or trusting of medical professionals, or they might fear that they will lose access to financial or emotional resources if they get better. As a result, they avoid doing the very activities that would promote their health. If left unaddressed, these factors can lead to the worsening of physical health problems.

Use this handout to help clients identify beliefs that interfere with their healing, such as the notion that nothing they do will make a difference or that they don't deserve to be healthy. You can also help clients identify and compassionately work with any feelings of shame, helplessness, fear, or distrust that impact their recovery. If you and the client identify a pattern of self-sabotage, you can return to the IFS practices from chapter 9. Or you and the client might identify a blocking belief or emotion that is connected to a traumatic event from the client's past. In this case, you can use the somatic repatterning practices from chapter 3 or the cognitive reappraisal exercises from chapter 1. It is also important to consider that some physical health problems will not go away. In this case, it may be necessary to help clients work toward grieving and accepting their chronic illness or autoimmune conditions as unresolvable. This process can allow clients to more successfully focus on the aspects of their healthcare that are under their control. As with the other interventions in this book, tailor the intervention to meet the needs of your client.

- **Identify blocking beliefs:** Sometimes we carry beliefs about ourselves or the world that interfere with our ability to get better or meet our healthcare goals. Would you be willing to take a look at the following list of blocking beliefs and explore if there are any you identify with?

    ○ I can never get better.

- I do not have the strength to heal or recover.

- I do not deserve to get better.

- I deserve to be sick.

- Nothing I do will make a difference in my health.

- If I get better, I will lose a part of who I really am.

- I am afraid of what this change will bring.

- I am permanently damaged.

- I am powerless or helpless to change my situation.

- People will only care for me if I am sick.

- **Identify blocking emotions:** Sometimes difficult emotions arise that sabotage your efforts toward healing. You might notice feelings of shame come up because you have put on weight or have had difficulty exercising. Or you might feel helpless to change your situation. Perhaps you feel distrusting of medical providers, which leads you to avoid getting necessary care. If left unattended, these emotions can interfere with your ability to meet your healthcare goals. Take a few moments to notice if there are any emotions that arise when you think about your healthcare goal to . . . [*e.g., stop eating sugar, see the doctor, begin exercising, stop smoking*]. Are you aware of any emotions that prevent you from following through with this goal?

  - Sometimes these emotions might be difficult to identify, but you might notice uncomfortable feelings in your body that lead you to avoid creating positive change. Can your turn toward these emotions and sensations with acceptance and compassion? You might try saying to yourself, "All of my feelings are welcome here" or "I fully accept myself even though I am having difficult feelings about creating change in my life."

- **Explore sabotaging parts:** You might notice a conflict between a part of you who wants to . . . [*e.g., stop eating sugar, see the doctor, begin exercising, stop smoking*] and a part of you who . . . [*e.g., is afraid of change, feels helpless, doesn't believe healing is possible*]. I invite you to turn toward the belief that . . . [*e.g., you can never get better, you do not deserve to get better, you are powerless to change your situation*] or the feeling of [*e.g., shame, anger, sadness, helplessness, confusion, fear*]. Do you recall other times in your life when you felt this way? Do you have any memories connected to this belief or these feelings? How old does this part feel? Notice how you feel toward this part of yourself. Is there anything that this part needs from you?

- **Build acceptance and compassion:** I invite you to turn toward the belief that . . . [*e.g., you can never get better, you do not deserve to get better, you are powerless to change your situation*] or the feeling of . . . [*e.g., shame, anger, sadness, helplessness, confusion, fear*]. What would it feel like to fully accept yourself, just as you are, with these thoughts and feelings? You might say to yourself, "I am okay just as I am" or "I am willing to accept myself even if I cannot completely recover." Notice how it feels to be with your experience without needing to change, control, or fix yourself.

- **Engage with change:** Take a moment to review your healthcare goals. Now that you have identified some of the barriers that interfere with your ability to reach these goals, you are ready to focus your attention on new beliefs and behaviors that will enhance your health. I'd like for you to choose one action that you would like to take during the week to support your health. This might involve making a dietary change, choosing an exercise goal, committing to a mindfulness practice, or engaging in a reflective activity, such as journaling or a creative project. Explore the kinds of support that you need to help you to be most successful with this new behavior. Take a moment to identify the best time in your day or week to engage in this activity. Where is the best location that will help you to be successful? Allow yourself to imagine completing the new behavior successfully. If you notice any blocking beliefs or feelings, explore if there is anything else that you need to navigate around or remove this barrier.

Food-Mood Diary

Research shows that what we eat affects our mood. If you do not pay enough attention to this food-mood connection, you can fall into eating habits that contribute to depression, anxiety, insomnia, addictions, and other issues. Observing your current diet, your emotions, and your physical responses will reveal the patterns in your self-nourishment. You can then use this information to make changes in your diet that can alleviate your physical symptoms, stabilize your energy level, and boost your mood. Defining, exploring, and meeting your own needs for nourishment is an essential form of self-care and self-agency.

To begin attending to your own food-mood connection, use this log to write down everything you eat and drink for three days, including all meals, snacks, and beverages (even water). Include approximate amounts and the time you consumed each item. Describe any digestive responses you experienced. Also indicate if your energy level and mood increased (↑), decreased (↓), or stayed the same (=) after consuming the item. Make as many copies of this template as needed (at least three for each day).

Food-Mood Diary

Date: _____

Time of waking: _____

Type of Meal, Snack, or Beverage	Amount	Time	Digestive Response	Energy Level (↑, ↓, or =)	Mood (☺, ☹, etc.)

Energy-Mood Clock

To better understand how your mood and energy levels fluctuate throughout the day, complete this worksheet on the same days that you complete the *Food-Mood Diary*. Record your energy level (1 = very little energy, 5 = very energetic) and your mood (happy/sad faces) for each hour of the day. Make as many copies of this template as needed (at least three for each day).

Date: _____

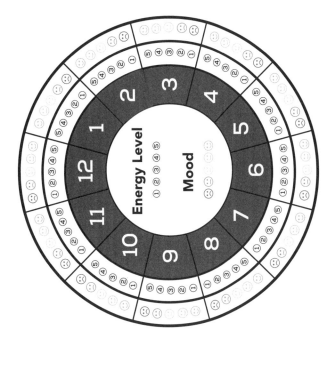

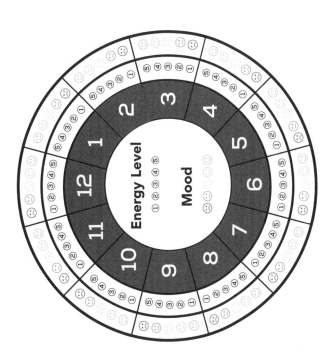

Understanding Your Circadian Rhythm

The degree to which you are attuned to the rhythms of the natural world affects your health and well-being. In particular, your circadian rhythm—how your body responds to the cycle of sunlight and darkness—has a large impact on your physical and mental health. Understanding your personal circadian rhythm is a good first step to recover from depression, PTSD, and more. This worksheet will help you find your optimal circadian rhythm, which is an important part of your overall health.

For the next 7–14 days, use the template that follows to keep track of your circadian rhythm. In the first row, record your current wake time and bedtime. Make sure to also record your energy level (1 = very little energy, 5 = very energetic) and mood (1 = feeling low, 5 = feeling great) when you wake up and go to sleep. In the notes section, write down how you feel overall, and any changes that you wish to see in your mood and energy levels.

Next, identify any adjustments you would like to make to your sleep schedule. For example, if you feel that you're not getting enough rest, you might set a goal of going to bed earlier so you can get more hours of sleep. For most people, restful sleep occurs when they go to sleep before midnight, between 9:30 and 11:30 p.m., and wake up 7–9 hours later. Changes to your bedtime should be made slowly, in increments of 10 minutes per day.

As you make these small adjustments each day, continue to keep track of your mood, energy levels, and any other effects on your body and mind.

Tracking Your Circadian Rhythm

Record your current wake time and bedtime in the first row, along with your associated mood and energy level. In the remaining rows, continue tracking this information each day to see how the changes you are making to your sleep schedule are affecting you.

Date	Wake Time	Mood (1–5)	Energy Level (1–5)	Bedtime	Mood (1–5)	Energy Level (1–5)	Notes

Grounding, Barefoot Walking, and Forest Bathing

Variations on the advice to "get outdoors" have long been offered as a solution for mental discomfort. In this activity, you'll explore the many ways you can engage with the earth, trees, and sky to feel better.

Grounding, barefoot walking, and forest bathing are activities that people have done for millennia to facilitate their well-being. *Grounding* refers to making physical contact with the ground—by standing on it with bare feet or by sleeping on the ground—and absorbing the earth's electrons. *Barefoot walking* is a form of grounding in which the soles of your feet are the grounding points, soaking up the dewy, ionized moisture of the morning. *Forest bathing* is the English translation of the Japanese term *shinrin-yoku*. Shinrin-yoku emerged in the 1980s as part of Japan's approach to preventive medicine. It is the practice of spending meditative time in a natural setting, using the five senses to enrich your connection with that setting.

Grounding reduces inflammation, pain, and stress, and it improves blood flow, energy, and sleep (Menigoz et al., 2020). It also improves the overall modulation of the vagal response (Sokal & Sokal, 2011), an important pathway of self-regulation. You can ground yourself simply by walking barefoot in the morning dew, whether that's on a sandy beach, on the forest floor, or in your backyard. Finding a few minutes every day to touch the ground can have powerful therapeutic effects.

Instructions

Identify an outdoor space near to where you live or work where it is safe to do grounding in the early morning for three to five minutes every day. Part of the exercise involves sitting or lying down, so bring a cloth blanket if needed but avoid rubber yoga mats.

Make sure it is safe to take off your shoes and socks—check for broken glass or anything else that could harm you. Then stand with your feet flat on the earth, hip-width apart. Lean back gently so your heels press into the earth. Then lean forward slightly so the balls of your feet press into the earth. Lift, then lower, your toes. Experiment with scrunching the earth with your toes as you focus on whole-body sensations. How does the earth feel beneath your feet?

Then walk a short distance in your green space with your shoes still off. When you are satisfied, brush off your feet and put your shoes and socks back on. Sit or lie down on the earth with your closed eyes. Can you feel the earth, including the dirt, leaves, or sticks on the ground? Feel the energy of the ground and where your body is contacting the earth.

Breathe in and out. If you are lying down, allow your belly to rise and fall with the energy of the earth. Allow yourself to become one with the earth. What can you hear? Can you listen to what is above you? To the sides of you? Can you hear anything beneath you that is on, in, or under the ground?

When you are ready to open your eyes, what do you see above you? What appears in your entire visual field? Can you integrate the discoveries of sight and sound? Can you find the chirping bird, the crashing wave, the tree branch blowing in the wind, the rapids interrupting the stream?

Take a deep inhale through your nose. In the short time since you have arrived, how has your sensory awareness expanded? What has changed about your mental clarity? Your mood?

Alternate Activities

The previous grounding exercise may not work well for everyone—maybe you're surrounded by concrete. Or maybe you'd like to add variety to your usual grounding routine. Here are some additional ideas to consider:

- Plan a trip to a nearby park, or perhaps even a day away in the country or at a cabin.

- Plan a trip to an ocean, lake, or stream and dip your feet in.

- Gather sand from the beach (where allowed) to use for a healing sand bath:

  ◦ Fill an old pillowcase with 2–3 pounds of sand from the beach or lakeshore. The sand should not have been sterilized or sold commercially.

  ◦ Pour the sand onto a cookie sheet and place in the oven at 325 degrees for 15 minutes. Then pour it back into the pillowcase.

  ◦ Apply topical arnica salve to any body part that is injured, tense, or sore. (If you have it available, a 1:1 ratio of CBD to THC cannabis salve works well too). Then apply the sand bag by resting it on the body part. It should be hot, but not hot enough to burn. The sand heals by its warmth, leading to improved lymphatic flow and relaxation.

Terpenes

Many of nature's fragrances emanate from plant chemicals called *terpenes*. Terpenes are the class of phytochemicals primarily responsible for the piney scents of the forest. They are released into the air by coniferous trees (pines, firs, spruce) along with rosemary, eucalyptus, and other plants. Terpenes have well-established anti-inflammatory effects when inhaled, making them useful for addressing pain, asthma, dermatitis, arthritis, and traumatic brain injury (Kim et al., 2020). You can integrate terpenes into your life to enhance mood and well-being.

The following are all terpenes; you will likely recognize many of them.

Name	Description	Healing Properties
Bisabolol	Gives chamomile its soothing smell	Has anti-inflammatory, analgesic, and antimicrobial properties
Borneol	Is found in many plants, including cannabis, sunflower, and teak tree; its odor is a mixture of mint and damp earth	Has anti-inflammatory and analgesic properties
Camphene	Largely responsible for the earthy, musky smell most people associate with cannabis	Has antioxidant and antibacterial properties
Caryophyllene	Gives cloves and black pepper their warm, spicy scent and flavor	Has anti-inflammatory, antifungal, and antibacterial properties; good for digestion
Delta 3 carene	Derived from cannabis; its scent is sweet and woodsy	Has anti-inflammatory properties
Eucalyptol	Derived from eucalyptus oil	Has antibacterial and antifungal properties; the oil is often used in bronchial steams

Name	Description	Healing Properties
Geraniol	Found in many flowering species, like citronella, rose, and geranium	May act as an antioxidant; may be a neuroprotective agent
Humulene	Gives hops their spicy, bitter taste and smell	Has antibacterial, anti-inflammatory, antinociceptive, and anti-tumorigenic properties
Limonene	Particularly abundant in cannabis strains; also found in many fruit peels and peppermint	Has mood-boosting effects, aids digestion, and may soothe heartburn
Linalool	Responsible for lavender's famously relaxing properties	Has antianxiety, antipsychotic, antiepileptic, and analgesic properties
Myrcene	Found in mangoes, lemongrass, and thyme	Has anti-inflammatory, muscle-relaxing, and even sedating effects
Pinene	Named for the pine species to which it lends its intense aroma; also found in aromatic kitchen herbs	Aids memory; contributes to alert wellbeing
Phytol	Provides the famously nostalgic scent of freshly cut grass; also found in green tea	Has anti-insomnia, antioxidant, and immunosuppressant properties
Terpinolene	This herbaceous scent is in tea tree oil, rosemary, and sage	Is a mood booster with antibacterial, antifungal, anti-insomnia, and antiseptic properties
Trans-nerolidol	Its sweet, spicy scent is what makes jasmine flowers so enjoyable	Is an antioxidant, antiparasitic, antimicrobial, and anticancer agent
Valencene	Named for its source, Valencia oranges	Is a very effective repellent against mosquitoes, ticks, and fleas; has antiallergic and anti-inflammatory properties

Plan to visit a green space that is accessible to you—the more natural, the better. You might visit a park, nature preserve, or campground where you can immerse yourself in the outdoors. If you don't have access to this type of space, simply find the greenest spot you can, or you can bring nature to you by purchasing terpenes (in the form of plants, foods, or essential oils) to use in this exercise.

Once you are in your green space, find a spot where you will have some privacy. Now explore your environment:

- Use a plant identifier app, such as PictureThis or LeafSnap, to identify some of the trees, bushes, grasses, flowers, and other plants in the area.

- With your eyes closed or open, inhale deeply through the nose. What do you smell?

- Inhale again. Can you identify which smells come from which plants?

- Can you name a terpene you are smelling?

- If there is a body of water in this area, are any smells coming from it?

- Can you smell the wind?

- Can you smell the dirt?

- Continue to explore this green space. Familiarize yourself with the flora and fauna, including learning about toxic plants or venomous insects, so you know what to stay clear of as well as what you can touch, sniff, and taste (if allowed).

- If you have access to conifers, rosemary bushes, or eucalyptus trees, try crunching a handful of their needles and inhaling the scent. How does it make you feel?

- Stay in your green space for as long as you can. Play in this space, exploring the natural world in new ways.

While in your green space, or after you return home, take a few minutes to reflect on your experience. How did you feel before your time in nature? During the exercise? How do you feel now?

Addressing Inflammation, Pain, and Depression

It is important to be able to differentiate between an inflammation process that is normal, localized, and even beneficial, and chronic inflammation, which underlies numerous disease processes, including depression. Improving digestion by eating anti-inflammatory foods is a vitally important method for reducing inflammatory diseases. This handout will help you better understand what inflammation is and how to address it.

Acute vs. Chronic Inflammation

Also called localized inflammation, acute inflammation describes the symptoms of an activated immune system. It may occur from a paper cut, a broken arm, a cold, a stubbed toe—any sudden body damage. Symptoms include puffiness, redness, soreness, heat, pain, stiffness, congestion, and itching. These symptoms indicate a well-functioning immune system, where the white blood cells rush to the scene of injury and infection to repair damaged skin barrier and kill any pathogenic invaders.

Chronic inflammation, in contrast, is a low-grade inflammatory response that persists for months to years. As the immune system works overtime, inflammation slowly damages the body. This inflammation may result from continued exposure to relatively low levels of an allergen or toxins like mold in the home. Food additives, processed and packaged foods, refined sugars, and carbohydrates—which are staples of the standard American diet (SAD)—all contribute to inflammation. The body reacts to this influx of not-so-good substances by sending chemicals to the skin, the sinuses, the gut, and the brain. Over time, these chemicals break down healthy cells and tissues.

Did you know that depression reflects a chronic inflammation process? Histamine is one of the chemicals that immune cells release when the body is chronically inflamed. A recent study showed that histamine inhibits the release of serotonin, the "happy" chemical in the brain (Hersey et al., 2021). Selective serotonin reuptake inhibitors (SSRIs) have long been the go-to pharmaceutical treatment for depression. Treating the inflammation by reducing exposure to histamine-triggering substances can help to treat the depression symptoms as well.

A simple way to help alleviate pain and depression is to incorporate turmeric into your diet. Turmeric, which can be purchased in both root and powdered form, contains curcumin, which is a potent antidepressant and anti-inflammatory. Turmeric is the main ingredient in curry and works well in a variety of recipes—just be sure to combine it with freshly ground black pepper, which is necessary for the absorption of the curcumin. Drinking a turmeric latte daily is a delicious way to ease pain and lift your mood.

SAD: Standard American Diet

Food additives, processed and packaged foods, refined sugars, refined carbohydrates, vegetable oils and fake fats

HAPPY: Food That Elevates Mood

Proteins (animal, plant, legume), healthy fats (olive oil, butter, fresh lard, coconut), vegetables, fruits, raw seeds and nuts, whole grains (for some people)

Hydrotherapeutic Methods for Mental Health at Home

In this worksheet, you will learn methods and principles to use water, hot and cold elements, and various natural aids to enhance your mood and health. Hydrotherapy practices can be an aid for relaxing into sleep, altering mood, and decreasing pain and dissociation. Use these methods daily for self-care and more intensively during any detoxification process.

To create your hydrotherapy space, find an area of your home that can serve as your quiet space, where you will assemble your self-care items. Some useful home spa items are listed here; mark any that you will need or would like, and gather them in your space.

- ❏ Air purifier
- ❏ Apple cider vinegar (can be added to a bath for fatigue)
- ❏ Blackout or blockout curtains
- ❏ Breathing tools (like Komuso)
- ❏ Chamomile tea (soothing and anti-inflammatory; the tea bags can be applied to the eyes)
- ❏ Coconut oil (to soothe and moisturize the body)
- ❏ Epsom salts
- ❏ Essential oils of choice
- ❏ Eye pad or mask
- ❏ Hot-water bottle, heatable rice bag, or body pads
- ❏ Incense or beeswax candles (paraffin or perfumed candles are often toxic)
- ❏ Jade roller (an instrument used in Chinese medicine to cool the body, enhance chi [energy], and aid relaxation; use the smaller end over smaller areas like the eyes and the larger end across the cheeks and forehead)
- ❏ Magnet pads (which use pulsed electromagnetic fields [PEMF] to balance our electromagnetic energy and are a good treatment for arthritis)
- ❏ Scalp massager (can be used dry or wet; is energizing and grounding)
- ❏ Skin brush (also called a dry brush)
- ❏ Soft towels and washcloths, or a robe

Feel free to add anything else that you find meaningful and nurturing. You might create an altar or area with unique items such as fresh flowers or plants, crystals, synchronicity tools (e.g., affirmation cards, Celtic runes, soul collage cards), or photos of loved ones.

You will also need a "wet" room, like a bathroom, where you can carry out water-based activities, or you can use plastic protective equipment in another space.

Hydrotherapy Activities

The following are some hydrotherapy techniques you can do at home. When choosing which ones to use, consider these principles of hot and cold techniques:

- Hot: Relaxing; reduces chronic pain

- Cold: Stimulating; boosts mood; reduces acute pain

- Hot and cold (alternating): Enhances circulation and immune function; balances mood

Applying Heat

When feeling anxious or in pain, apply a hot-water bottle or a rice-filled heating pad to your belly or the painful area. (Avoid electric heating pads because of exposure to electrical currents.)

Applying Cold

When feeling tired or in a low mood, jump into a shower that is lukewarm and slowly make the water colder until it is as cold as you can tolerate. Let the water flow directly on your spine for 5 minutes.

Alternatively, add 1 cup of apple cider vinegar to a bathtub of cool water and soak in it for 20 minutes when you are feeling fatigued or anxious.

Applying Hot and Cold

Mix ½ cup coarse sea salt and ½ cup baking soda. Mix in enough water so it becomes a thick paste. Add a few drops of your favorite essential oil. Jump in the shower with your skin brush, get wet, turn the water off, and begin scrubbing, starting at your toes and working up your whole body, from front to back. Turn the water back on and rinse off with warm water. Then make the water as hot as is comfortable, and finish with a minute of cold water. Towel dry and drink 6 ounces of water.

Constitutional Hot and Cold Hydrotherapy

Soak a large cotton T-shirt or tank top in the sink so it is sopping wet; wring out excess water and place it flat in the freezer. Spread two wool blankets lengthwise on a bed, and place a cotton or flannel sheet over them.

Take a shower using water that is hot, but not burning or uncomfortable. Let the water fall all over you for 5 minutes. Immediately after the shower, dry quickly, get the cold shirt from the freezer, and put it on. Use no clothing under or above this shirt. Lie down on top of the sheet, then roll yourself tightly into the sheet and blankets, wrapping yourself up from neck to toes, mummy-style. (You may want to ask someone else to help you wrap up tightly.)

Remain wrapped until your shirt is warm to the touch. During this time, sleep, rest, or listen to calming music. Then slowly come out of your cocoon, dress, and stay warm. Relax for the rest of the day, perhaps taking a walk in the fresh air.

Epsom Salt Bath

This bath is relaxing and detoxifying. Add 2 cups of Epsom salts (magnesium sulfate) and ½ cup of baking soda to a warm (not hot) bath. You may also add some essential oil, such as lavender. Soak for 20 minutes. The magnesium and sulfate will be absorbed, relaxing your muscles and helping you sleep. The bath can be slippery, so use a mat.

Skin Brushing

Skin brushing is a simple yet powerful approach for anxiety, depression, and dissociation. When tapering off medications, use the brush as often as necessary, or if you feel the urge to self-harm, use the skin brush instead—it will bring you back into your body, reduce anxiety, and stimulate endorphins.

Using a firm, bristled brush, brush one to two times a day on dry skin before a shower or bath for 3–5 minutes. Brush in the direction of the heart. Begin at the feet, then slowly work up the front and back of the body. Brush the legs, buttocks, abdomen, back, and arms. Pay particular attention to the armpits and chest (but avoid the nipples). Continue to the neck. At first, the brush may feel harsh; however, after a few sessions of brushing it should feel good and stimulating.

Know Your Herbs

This handout introduces some of the most useful herbs for mental health. Herbs are classified by their actions on the body and mind. Some herbs do "double duty." For example, skullcap helps with anxiety and depression in addition to relieving physical pain. The following are descriptions of key categories of herbs for you to explore as you build your knowledge of herbal medicine for mental health.

- **Adaptogens** help us adapt to stress. They restore resilience, build endurance, and reduce fatigue. They most often support adrenal and immune function. When a client is presenting with symptoms of stress, fatigue, and depression, you might start with adaptogens to regulate the stress response. Some common adaptogens include ashwagandha, licorice root, and eleuthero (Siberian ginseng).

- **Analgesics** provide pain relief and are used orally or topically. Common analgesic herbs include arnica, corydalis, skullcap, and white willow bark.

- **Anti-inflammatory herbs** are closely linked to herbs that decrease pain, heat, and other symptoms of inflammation. Common anti-inflammatory herbs include boswellia, turmeric, and white willow bark. (Keep in mind that turmeric must be mixed with a little black pepper and fat to be assimilated.) One of the benefits of these herbs is that they can reduce or eliminate dependence on pharmaceutical NSAID use, which can negatively affect liver and stomach function over time. Some herbs are both analgesic and anti-inflammatory, most notably cannabis. The THC component is anti-inflammatory, whereas the CBD is anxiolytic and more sedative.

- **Antidepressant herbs** alleviate depression and improve mood and focus. Common herbs include lemon balm (also good for agitated or anxious depression), oats, saffron, and St. John's Wort.

- **Antidipsotropic herbs** support sobriety with alcohol, including oats and kudzu.

- **Aromatic herbs** are fragrant and rich in essential oils called aromatics. They are a simple way to boost mood and they stimulate the appetite, making them useful for picky eaters, such as children or adults on the autism spectrum. Lavender, peppermint, rosemary, and sage are among the most commonly used in foods and teas. Some, like sage, are even burned.

- **Bitter herbs** are helpful for people who have digestive problems, especially if they can't digest fats well, have gallbladder and liver issues, or experience constipation. Dandelion greens and roots are among the best known.

- **Carminatives** prevent gas and bloating. Anise seed, cardamom pod, dill, and fennel seed are among the most effective. Add them to the food you are cooking or prepare a simple tea to drink just after the meal.

- **Hepatic herbs** support liver function and regeneration. They are especially helpful for clients whose livers have been affected by excessive use of drugs or alcohol, anesthesia and medications, or toxic environmental exposures. Herbs like milk thistle and schizandra, and vegetables like beet root and greens, fall into this category.

- **Hypnotic herbs** promote relaxation and sleep. Similar to sedatives, hypnotics are often more potent. My favorite is kava, which is deeply relaxing—but be careful, since kava can sometimes have a paradoxical effect and keep you awake.

- **Laxatives** help restore the natural rhythm of peristalsis, the movement of waste through the large intestine, by alleviating constipation. Bulking agents like chia, flaxseed, or psyllium husk are best for long-term use, but a pinch of cascara sagrada or senna will also help. Nonherbal laxatives include magnesium, vitamin C, or an enema. Avoid overreliance on laxatives; identifying the cause of constipation is critical. Some common causes are emotional distress, too little water or fiber in the diet, and food sensitivities.

- **Nervines** strengthen the nervous system and affect energy level. Some nervines, such as coffee and ginseng, are energizing and mood-boosting. Others promote relaxation and sleep. Relaxing nervines include peppermint, kava, lavender, St. John's Wort, oats, and passionflower. Sedating nervines include California poppy hops and valerian.

- **Rubefacients** can be used topically along with analgesics and anti-inflammatories. They increase circulation, which always aids healing, and they can be incorporated into daily use for fibromyalgia. Rubefacients include cayenne (available as a cream at the pharmacy), mustard, and stinging nettles.

- **Spasmolytic herbs** reduce spasms. The most effective herbs include chamomile, hops, passionflower, and skullcap.

- **Stimulants** boost mood and cognition, and they can be used for ADHD instead of pharmaceutical stimulants. They include ginger, ginkgo, coffee, gotu kola, and rosemary.

CHAPTER 12
Mindfulness Tools

Start Where You Are

In our modern, fast-paced world, autopilot can easily take over. We mindlessly multitask our way through the day while texting and scrolling through social media. We head from work to the gym and eat on the go. In contrast, to "start where you are" encourages you to live in the present moment. In Buddhism, this practice is referred to as *beginner's mind*, which involves cultivating an attitude of openness and a willingness to learn as if each moment is new and fresh. You develop such a state by slowing down, focusing on the sensory details of your environment, bringing awareness to your body, and noticing your breath.

To "start where you are" can become a daily mindfulness practice that builds a foundation of presence within you. You can start cultivating this practice by noticing the moment-to-moment changes in your thoughts, emotions, and sensations. Such awareness allows you recognize and attend to your emotional and physical needs *as they occur*. In this mindful pause, you learn to become curious about what best serves you right now. With this awareness, you may be more likely to put down your phone, go for a walk, reach out to a friend, or simply focus on eating your dinner without any distractions.

Mindfulness is not a religion, nor is it a forced activity. Being mindful is not about becoming enlightened, nor is it driven by an agenda. Rather, mindfulness asks you to reflect on yourself, your choices, and your interactions *without judgment*. It involves observing your experiences without labeling them as "good" or "bad." Mindfulness is about acknowledging things *just as they are*. By adopting a nonjudgmental stance, you can view your strengths and vulnerabilities with equal acceptance—with the recognition that you are imperfectly and beautifully human.

Mindfulness of the Moment

Take the next several minutes to cultivate an attitude of mindful awareness. Be curious and nonjudgmental about your experiences. What are the thoughts that you are having? Are you experiencing any emotions? What sensations are you noticing in your body right now? How is your breath moving through you? Do you feel energized or fatigued? If your mind is wandering (as minds inevitably do), notice where it takes you. Are you distracted by thoughts of the past or the future? That is okay. If possible, bring your attention back to your breath and to your sensations.

There is no right or wrong response to this practice. This is just one moment in time. No single moment can define the totality of you. Take a few minutes to write about your observations on the following lines. You can return to this practice each and every day.

_____
_____
_____
_____
_____
_____
_____
_____
_____
_____
_____
_____
_____
_____
_____
_____
_____
_____
_____

Guided Imagery

Get into a comfortable position in which you can relax. Then read through the script provided and imagine yourself in the scene. You can ask someone else to read the script to you so you can close your eyes and focus on experiencing the imagery, or you can read through it ahead of time and then close your eyes and imagine each part of the scene when you are ready. As you go through the exercise, make sure to incorporate all your senses—seeing, hearing, smelling, feeling, and maybe even tasting the situation in your mind.

Script

You are walking in a wooded area, following a dirt road that you have been assured will lead you to a beach. As you listen to the gentle crunching of your shoes on the ground, you notice that the road is somewhat sandy, which gives you hope that the beach isn't far away. You listen to the wind gently blowing through the trees and hear the cries of seagulls. Yes! The beach cannot be far away.

As you round a curve in the shady road, you see ahead of you a sandy path that slopes away from the road and down through the trees. The trees lining the path are a mix of huge pine and oak trees, and the path is not only sandy, but also coated with pine needles from the trees. The air is filled with the fragrant smell of pines, and the wind seems to be coming up the path toward you, bringing the smell of the lake as well. You move more eagerly down the incline of the shady path and hear children's voices. Two laughing children come running up the path toward you, wearing bathing suits, their wet feet coated with sand as they run up the path.

The path becomes broader and takes you down into sunshine. You come out of the shade of the trees onto a golden beach with a clear blue lake ahead of you. You see two colorful umbrellas and a few people on the beach, but what catches your eye are the magnificent white clouds floating over the lake. Their brilliant whiteness contrasts with the light blue of the sky and the darker blue of the water. The lake is so large that you can't see the shore on the other side, just the place where the light blue sky meets the water. You stand for a moment and take in the scene, listening to the calls of the seagulls as they glide on the wind currents above the lake. You see gentle waves washing up on the shore, and you walk through the sand toward the shoreline, struggling through some of the deeper sand as you go.

As you reach the edge of the beach, you take off your shoes and shake the sand off them. You walk barefoot in the dark, wet sand near the water's edge, feeling the damp sand give gently under each step you take. You turn around and notice the footprints you are leaving in the sand behind you. Then you step toward the water to get your toes a little wet, and the coldness of the water is surprising. You don't really want to go any farther into the lake.

Still, you are very pleased to have found this beach, and as you stand and feel the waves lapping on your feet, you enjoy the sights and sounds around you. You stand and enjoy the warm sun on your shoulders and face, and the breeze off the lake moving through your hair. You take a deep breath and try to take a mental picture of the beautiful scene so you can remember it when you leave to return up the sandy trail.

Mindfulness Eating

For this mindful eating exercise, you'll want to select a bite-sized piece of food, such as a grape, raisin, or Hershey's Kiss. Throughout the exercise, make sure to remain aware of your bodily sensations, thoughts, memories, and associations that come to mind. Notice when your awareness fluctuates, drifts away, or is interrupted (e.g., when your thoughts take you into the future, such as making plans or judgments like "This is silly!").

When you are ready to begin, hold your chosen food item in front of you. Pretend that you are from another planet and that you have never seen anything like this before. However, you are satisfied that this small object in your hand is, in fact, food.

Because you are observing this object for the first time, you will want to study it carefully. Pick it up, feel its weight and temperature.

Begin to inspect its exterior, taking notice of its shape, color, texture, and anything else interesting about it . . . Now, bring the item closer to your nose and begin to smell it. Try to fully comprehend the smell of this item. And while keeping its smell in the forefront of your awareness, check in with your body, noticing any reactions you may be having to the smell. . .

Now, bring your awareness to your dominant hand. Using your dominant hand, bring the item to your mouth. Place it in your mouth, but do not chew or swallow it yet. First, become aware of its textures . . . and flavor or flavors. Explore the sensations of holding this item in your mouth . . . on your tongue . . .

As slowly as possible, begin to experience its taste as you bite into it and begin to chew. Be fully aware of the sounds and the movements of your mouth as you chew . . . And when you are ready, swallow. And as you do, continue to sense its taste as it goes down your throat . . . noticing any tastes that continue to linger . . . and any sensations that you experience. Continue to observe your experience.

When you are finished, reflect on the following questions to fully process the experience:

- How was that experience for you?

- Was anything surprising about it?

- How did it differ from the way you typically eat?

- Is there some way for you to bring this quality of "awarenessing" into your life?

Riding the Waves of Change

All experiences are meant to come and go, like waves in the ocean. They rise up, crest, and release. Similarly, you can think of your emotions as "energy in motion." They are meant to surge, be fully felt, and then subside. However, sometimes you might block emotional waves before they come to the shore. When you remain cut off from your emotions in this manner, it is important to realize that there are consequences. You might start to feel rigid and constricted. You might begin to feel numb or as if you are just going through the motions of your life. Or you might feel frightened that you will be overwhelmed by a tidal wave of built-up emotion.

Blocking emotional waves is especially common when you have experienced trauma. You might fear getting flooded by memories, painful feelings, and accompanying body sensations. Perhaps these feelings are related to events that occurred many years ago. Such unexpressed emotions can build up and manifest as physical tension in your body, resulting in headaches, tight shoulders, or difficulties with digestion. You may not even be aware that you are holding on to your emotions until your body rebels.

Healing from trauma involves slowing down and attending to your pain at a pace that you can tolerate. This involves learning to surf in the shallows in preparation for riding the bigger waves. In other words, you turn toward relatively smaller stresses or losses prior to processing your most difficult traumas or worst fears. For example, you might start by working with the frustration related to an interaction with a coworker. Here you explore the skills of building tolerance for your emotions while attending to a relatively manageable event. In time, you can work up to more distressing traumatic events. Pacing yourself in this manner is especially important if you experienced repeated abuse or neglect in your childhood.

Riding the waves of change also involves letting go of accumulated emotional burdens. However, letting go is easier said than done. If you find it difficult to let an emotion go, it is important to explore why you are holding on. Once you understand the nature of your emotional burdens, it will be easier to release them. For example, you might not let go of feelings of hurt or resentment in the hope that your pain might finally be acknowledged by a family member. In this case, you might need to grieve the fact that this person is incapable of recognizing or acknowledging your pain.

Riding the waves of change isn't always easy, but the end result is that you have an opportunity to feel lighter and discover an increased sense of freedom in body and mind. As a result, it becomes easier to feel positive emotions of joy, pleasure, happiness, or excitement. Most importantly, this process awakens your authentic presence. By turning toward your emotions, you invite yourself to be raw and real. You no longer feel as though you are going through the motions of your life. In time, you begin to feel as though you are living your life wholeheartedly. Set an intention to ride the waves of your inner experiences—set your sails for a journey of self-discovery.

Build Tolerance for Your Emotions

Take some time to explore a mindfulness practice focused on riding the waves of change. On each inhale, allow yourself to notice your inner experience. What is the emotion or sensation that you are aware of right now? Honor whatever you are holding as if it is a precious gift. Imagine a wave rising up as you breathe fully into this moment, this experience. You might ask yourself if this emotion needs anything from you. How can you take care of yourself right now?

On each exhale, imagine the wave receding as you release emotion and sensation. If it feels right, imagine giving anything that no longer serves you back to the universe. Continue as long as you like, allowing yourself to observe your inner experiences as they come and go.

Complete the practice by extending appreciation to yourself, for both your willingness to hold on and the courage that it takes to let something go. Take a few minutes to write about your experience.

_____

_____

_____

_____

_____

_____

_____

_____

_____

_____

_____

_____

_____

Today is an opportunity to ride the waves of change.
All thoughts, feelings, and sensations are meant to come and go.

BE THIS Sense Grounding

BE THIS is an acronym that stands for six powerful grounding skills (Breath, Emotion, Touch, Hearing, Intentional Stretching, Sight/Smell) that put you in touch with all your senses. This lets you redirect your attention away from anxious or negative thoughts and focus on your surroundings in a more positive way.

Use BE THIS when you notice emotional overload, such as when you might rate your negative or anxious state as being in the 5–7 range (i.e., the high range) when rated on a scale of 1–7 (where 1 = the lowest negativity and 7 = the highest negativity).

The four steps to practicing the BE THIS are as follows:

1. Notice when you have gone into emotional overload, which you can do by rating your level of negativity. You don't have to wait until you reach the "high" range to do grounding. In fact, it is a good idea to start practicing early on, when you notice that your level of negativity is in the medium 4–5 range.

   Write down the clues that let you know when you are in the 5–7 range of emotional overload. In other words, what does your emotional overload look or feel like? For example, this could be a feeling you have in your body, the urge to cry, a sense of anger or helplessness, and so on. The trick is to notice this before you overreact emotionally, or during your emotional overload.

   _____

   _____

   _____

2. Look around and describe your surrounding environment in a single sentence, followed by your intention to practice BE THIS. This could be stated as "I am standing in the living room at home, and I am practicing my awareness and grounding skills." The purpose of this is to center you in the moment. Practice this right now by writing a sample intentional statement.

   _____

   _____

   _____

3. Find a place where you can spend approximately five to seven minutes to practice in peace. This can still be done with others present, but it is best when distractions are limited.

4. You will cycle yourself through the BE THIS skills. You can spend approximately one to one and a half minutes with each of the BE THIS skills. Right now, practice each of the six skills as described below.

    a. **Breath.** For the first minute, use diaphragmatic breathing to stay grounded in breathing. As you move on to the other senses, continue to keep about 25 percent of your awareness on your breathing.

       How did it feel to do this first part of the exercise?

       _____

       _____

       _____

    b. **Emotion.** For the next one to one and a half minutes, let yourself experience your emotions and feelings with a sense of acceptance, without either pushing them away or attaching to them. Just name or label your emotions as if from a safe distance—without adding any judgment of good or bad—by simply saying "feeling of anger" or "feeling of sadness." You might even say where you feel this in your body, such as "tightness in my stomach" or "clenching in the jaw." As you continue to do this, notice if the feelings are less intense or change.

       Practice by naming your present emotions and body feelings. If you're not exactly sure what name to give the emotion, take your best guess and write it down anyway. In this way you are getting to know your feelings a little more closely.

       _____

       _____

       _____

       If someone else is involved in your emotional overload, spend another 30 seconds to one minute noticing if it is possible for you to experience empathy with regard to this person. Empathy means imagining how another person feels. It doesn't mean that they are right and you are wrong, or vice versa. It just means that you could understand how they might be feeling. If you don't feel empathy, just notice that you don't feel this. When the minute is up, move on.

What thoughts came up for you while doing this portion of the exercise?

_____

_____

_____

c. **Touch.** For one minute, you will practice relaxing touch. Raise your hands to heart level, with your palms facing one another and a few inches apart. Sense any heat and pay attention to your pulse until you can feel it in your hands. Then, take three breaths, each one filling the space between your palms with positive energy. Then, slowly bring your palms together, compressing the energy. Briskly rub your palms together for a few seconds.

Next, place your hands over your eyes for a few moments, then one hand over each temple, then over the back of your head. Let the energy in your hands relax and soothe you. Next, you can place your palms over the top of your chest and slowly sweep them downward over your heart, stomach, thighs, and knees. Lastly, let your arms hang at your side and shake your hands for a few seconds to release any remaining tension.

What thoughts came up for you while doing this portion of the exercise?

_____

_____

_____

d. **Hear.** For one minute, tune into the sounds of your environment. Let yourself expand your hearing and awareness to let in as many sounds as are possible— even those you make by breathing, moving in your chair, and so on. Try listening to each without putting a name or label on it. Just notice each sound, occurring moment to moment, second to second.

Again, write down whatever thoughts came up for you while doing this portion of the exercise.

_____

_____

_____

e. **Intentional Stretching.** For the next minute, set a simple intention and follow up mindfully. You might set the intention to stretch your neck by rolling your head around from right to left in a relaxing circular movement. Or you might set the intention to raise your arms high over your head as you inhale, then lower them as you exhale. It's a good idea to think of an intention that helps you release some tension and tightness from the boy.

Write down some gentle body movements (such as those mentioned previously or others) that you could use as an intention and that would help you to relax.

_____

_____

_____

f. **Sight/Smell.** For the final minute or longer, use your visual and olfactory senses with curiosity. Do this without thinking about the function of an object, or whether you like or want or dislike it. Simply look around and notice *in detail* as many different shapes, sizes, and colors of objects as you can—noticing these with an attitude of openness, child-like wonder, and interest. Also, what different scents are in the environment?

Look around the room or environment you are in at this moment. After you have spent time exploring, take a moment to note some of your observations about the sights and scents around you:

_____

_____

_____

Congratulations on completing *BE THIS*! Now that you have completed the practice, go ahead and re-rate your level of emotional negativity on a 1–7 scale. How has the number changed?

If grounding has been helpful, write down examples of times when this practice could have been helpful in the past, as well as how you could use it in the future. Remember that *BE THIS* is like any skill. The more you practice and use it, the better you get at it!

_____

_____

_____

Optional Practice: Speed Scan BE THIS Grounding

Sometimes you don't have five or six minutes to reverse overload! Fortunately, you can scan through all of the BE THIS skills in just a minute or less. As before, rate your level of emotional negativity both before and after you do the practice.

1. **Breath:** Take one or two deep and satisfying diaphragmatic breaths.

2. **Emotion:** Quickly scan your body from head to toe, sensing for an emotion or feeling in the body. Name that feeling.

3. **Touch:** Slowly touch one thing nearby or press your feet into the ground.

4. **Hear:** Notice a single sound that is happening at this very second—even if it is the sound of your breath.

5. **Intentional Stretching:** State a simple intention to do a single stretch, and follow it up right now.

6. **Sight and Smell:** Notice one object in front of you, and take one long inhale to see what scent you can detect in the environment.

Bear Meditation

In the film *The Big Lebowski*, there is a scene where the Stranger says to Jeff Bridges' character the Dude, the following words: "Sometimes you eat the bear, and sometimes, well, he eats you."

The bear can be any difficult, unresolved situation in your life—like the pain you must endure. The interesting thing about bears is this: Your attitude toward the bear can make all the difference in the world! If you provoke the bear and try to get it to leave, it may attack you and try to make a meal of you. You might try to have patience for the bear, try to outlast it, and maybe it will move on. You could even try to befriend the bear so you can the bear can coexist. Another approach might be to just be present with compassion for both you and the bear—to "bear witness" so to speak.

So, which approach would you choose?

Follow the steps below to get help for dealing with the bear. Use this *Bear Meditation* not so much to find a solution, but more to acknowledge your willingness to be open to hearing a new perspective in dealing with it.

1. Find a quiet place where you can sit in silence as long as you need. Before starting, set the following intention: "May my higher power listen with love and compassion. May my higher power not judge me. May it point me toward a wise path filled with deeper awareness, meaning, and self-compassion."

2. Have a heart-to-heart with the higher power in your life about your pain. Spend a few moments to think about this higher power. A higher power can be anything from a belief in God to the wise, nurturing self within, or anything in between— even a wise and kind being like Mother Teresa, St. Francis, the Buddha, or any other admired individual. If you want, you can visualize your higher power seated opposite you.

3. State how the *bear* is affecting your life. Let your higher power know about your fears, worries, emotions, and concerns. As you tell your story, know that your higher power is listening intently. In addition, know that your higher power instantly came to be by your side to you right now because they care deeply about your well-being.

4. Let your higher power know that this difficulty is something that you can't easily handle on your own and that you have come to ask for help. Visualize your higher power as fully understanding and appreciating the wisdom you have in seeking assistance. Take a few moments to feel how nice it is not to carry the heavy weight and burden of dealing with the *bear* all by yourself. Feel the lightness of this.

5. Ask the higher power for courage to just "sit" with the *bear*. Do this without expectations just so you might understand the bear better. The higher power may help you here, to just give you another viewpoint, a wise way of being with this. Surrender to whatever happens. If there is sadness, give that to the higher power to hold. Whatever happens, know that the higher power is there with you, supporting you, and sending you love and compassion each moment. Sit for as long as you need.

6. You are not yet done. For now, you will do something you may have thought to be impossible. You will switch seats and positions with your higher power. This doesn't mean that you *are* this higher power, but that you can view yourself with care, compassion, and love through the eyes of the higher power. From that vantage point, see what it's like to look at you. See your courage, appreciate your strength, witness your wisdom. You only need to do this for a few seconds. Now, return your presence to your body.

7. Lastly, say a blessing of gratitude and thanks for how your higher self made itself available to you—and how it will continue to do so anytime that you need assistance in the future or whenever you want to do another meditation.

How did this meditation change your approach to the *bear*? What did you learn about it or yourself?

_____

_____

_____

What is it like to know that you can tap into your higher power when needed? How do you think this can be of use?

_____

_____

_____

Decentralizing Pain

This exercise is designed to get you thinking about pain and the experience of pain in a different way. But first, to illustrate a point, answer the following question as a full sentence. The question is this: *What food did you eat this morning and how did you like it?*

That was easy, wasn't it? Now, did you use the words *I*, *me*, *my*, or *mine* in answering that question? Of course you did! That's normal because we typically take a very personal, or "I-centric" view of things. This is how we talk about and share our world and experiences.

But what happens when we talk about "my pain"? What happens when we buy into the pain as being our own? Now, this is not to imply that you are *not* the one experiencing it. Of course you are. However, what this practice suggests is that it is possible to view and experience pain—or anything for that matter—from a more neutral and less judgmental perspective. In other words, it's like being an impartial witness who is noticing what is occurring and is just describing it without any personal stake in what is happening. Have you ever wondered how taking an "impartial witness" perspective might change your feelings about the pain?

This practice will let you experience the story of your pain from that impartial witness viewpoint. There are four parts to this exercise, which begins with a *warm-up story*.

Warm-up Story—Personal Point of View

For the next three minutes, describe a recent memorable meal that you had. It's best if this meal was shared with others and had some kind of an emotional component—either very positive or negative. Now, describe that story in detail: what you ate, how the food tasted, whether you liked or didn't like it, who you were with, whether you enjoyed or didn't enjoy the conversation, what you talked about, and the place where you had the meal. Did you eat more than you wanted? How did that feel for you? (Alternatively, write down the story here if there is no one to tell it to).

_____

_____

_____

_____

Warm-up Story—Decentralized Point of View

Excellent. You just shared a story very much from the personal "I" point of view. Now, you will share the *identical* story in a very different way. This time, you will tell the story, but without using the words *I*, *me*, *my*, or *mine* in the telling. That's right—you're going to try to decentralize your story! This is not an easy thing to do, so here are a few suggestions. When telling the story in this way, don't use a pronoun such as *he* or *she* or *this person* to represent you. That would be like using I. Instead, talk about the experiences, such as "There was the experience of *the body* walking and sitting down at the table," "*The mouth* tasted the hamburger and noticed how juicy it was," "*The eyes* saw the white tablecloth," "*The stomach* felt uncomfortably tight after eating," or "There was a conversation that was very interesting.

Do you see how it is possible to tell the same story from a third person perspective? It's important when you first practice this to tell your story to an engaged listener. The listener has a very important and specific job. The listener will not interrupt you while listening with interest. Most importantly, the listener will be paying attention for the words *I*, *me*, *my*, or *mine* that you may use without even knowing it. Upon hearing any of these words, the listener will simply raise their hand to let you know that you used the word. Then you can rephrase your story.

Again, this is not easy, and you *don't have to be perfect in not using those words*. The point of telling your story this way is to help you learn that your experience of having a meal (or of pain) can be viewed in this decentralized way. You are always able to go back to your very personal, "I-centric" viewpoint after this practice.

At this time, you will share your same meal story without using the words *I*, *me*, *my*, or *mine* for the next three minutes, and the engaged listener will keep time for you. Are you ready? Start now. (Alternatively, if you can't find someone to tell the decentralized story with, write that version of the story.)

_____

_____

_____

_____

_____

_____

_____

How challenging was it for you to tell your story without using the personal *I*, *me*, *my*, or *mine* words?

_____

_____

_____

What did it feel like to experience your story from this more neutral point of view? Was it more descriptive? Did it have less negative emotional feeling for you?

_____

_____

_____

What is one helpful or positive thing you noticed by shifting into the impartial spectator point of view?

_____

_____

_____

Story of Pain—Personal Point of View

For three minutes you will tell the very *personal* story of an experience where you felt pain. This could be the story of your morning, such as waking up. Or it could be the story of how pain limited your ability to do something you wanted to do (e.g., see a friend, take part in some activity). Use as many *I*, *me*, *my*, or *mine* words as you like! (If you don't have someone to share this story with, write down your experience.)

_____

_____

_____

_____

_____

_____

_____

_____

Story of Pain—Decentralized Point of View

You've already had practice telling a story without the words *I*, *me*, *my*, or *mine*. For the next three minutes, you will share the identical pain story that you just described, but from the very neutral, non-judging, and impartial perspective of an interested witness. Again, the engaged listener will keep time and raise their hand to let you know if you've used the words *I*, *me*, *my*, or *mine* during your story. If so, just rephrase and start again, describing the experiences in parts of the body. Even the word *pain* is a judgment of sorts, so you might consider using the word *sensation*, then describe that sensation as well as you can—such as "tightness," "vise-like," "tension," "wave-like," or whatever words describe the sensation that you felt in that moment. Remember to describe your surroundings and other experiences in detail.

By the way, you can still mention negative thoughts that were part of the pain story. From the observer perspective, you might describe that as "The mind kept repeating the negative thought that . . ." or "There was the feeling of frustration and tightness in the gut," or "The mind said the words 'I wish things were different.'" In this way, you can know what is in the mind and what is in the body. (If you don't have an engaged listener, journal your decentralized story of pain.)

_____

_____

_____

_____

_____

After having had some practice, what was it like to again tell a story from the decentralized perspective?

_____

_____

_____

_____

_____

What did it feel like to experience your story of pain from this more neutral point of view? Were you able to notice how thoughts or commentary from the mind had a role in your pain story? It can be helpful to know that just because you "have" a thought doesn't mean you have to "buy" it or decide to purchase it as your own.

_____

_____

_____

_____

_____

What is one helpful or positive thing you noticed by shifting into the impartial spectator point of view for your story of pain?

_____

_____

_____

_____

_____

How do you think this shift could be useful? When could you practice telling the story in this decentralized way—even if as a reminder that you have a choice about how to experience your story of pain?

_____

_____

_____

_____

_____

Sensing and Rating Anxiety in the Body

For this exercise, you will learn how to pay attention to sensations of anxiety that occur in the body in a whole new way. This is a portable practice that can go with you anytime you feel anxious. It is also a useful way to "drop into the body" anytime throughout the day—just to say "hello" and get more familiar with this precious gift that we all possess!

There is no better early warning system than the body for signaling to us that we may be out of balance with some situation—either past or present—in our lives. Whether the body's signal is related to old trauma, a difficult life situation, or stress, the ability to notice these warning signals can help you respond more quickly and effectively.

Remember, no one is immune from anxiety! By sensing and rating anxiety in the body, you can be present with it and cope with it in a healthy way. The practice of noticing sensations takes time, so be kind to yourself as you learn how to do this. If possible, do this practice in a quiet location so you can observe the sensations in detail.

Follow along with the six steps:

1. Begin this practice when you first notice any sensation of anxiety. If you wait until a full-blown anxiety attack is underway, then it could be difficult to even practice this technique! The more you do this practice, the more easily you will begin to notice the early onset of anxiety—whether it's just a tightness in the chest or a shallower than normal breath.

2. Bring your palms together and press your heels into the floor as a way to get grounded in the body. Press them together for about five seconds, then exhale to let go of stress.

3. Bring attention to where you are feeling anxiety in the body and answer the questions that follow. If you are alone, you can either state the answers out loud or write them down. (If you are with others while experiencing anxiety, simply state the answers mentally).

a. Where in the body is the sensation of anxiety present? Name as many different places as you can, from where there's the strongest feeling to the smallest feeling.

_____

_____

_____

How would you rate the anxiety level on a 1–7 scale, where 1 = the lowest level of anxiety and 7 = the highest level?

_____

_____

_____

b. If the anxiety sensation had a name, what name would you give it?

_____

_____

_____

c. If the anxiety sensation had a color, what color would it be?

_____

_____

_____

d. If the anxiety sensation had a shape, what shape would it be?

_____

_____

_____

e. If the anxiety sensation had a size, how large or small would it be?

_____

_____

_____

f. If the anxiety sensation had a weight, how heavy would it be?

_____

_____

_____

4. For one minute, take several slow, calming and soothing breaths. As you do this, you can visualize or imagine that this breath travels into the place where you are experiencing the sensation of anxiety. Let the breath fill up that area. With each exhale, you can visualize the sensation draining out of the body.

    Optionally, instead of focusing on your breath, you can simply observe the sensation with as much curiosity as you can! Like a surfer riding a wave, see if you can surf the anxious sensation, noticing in great detail every little change as it rises and falls—just like an ocean wave.

5. At the end of one minute, go back to step 3 and re-rate the level of the sensation on a 1–7 scale, and also answer the questions about name, color, shape, size, and weight.

6. Continue to observe the sensation for up to five minutes, noticing how it changes moment by moment, even subtly.

What did you learn from noticing and rating your sensation of anxiety?

_____

_____

_____

_____

When can you routinely schedule this practice as a way of noticing the early warning signs of anxiety?

_____

_____

_____

_____

Be the Pebble

Sometimes, stress can get our minds so active and "wound up" that they are like a choppy ocean. If you've ever gone out to sea on waters like that, you know that getting seasick is no fun. For many, having a mind that is as choppy and turbulent as that water can have very much the same effect.

But what if you were a pebble that could drop below the surface of that tumultuous water and get down to where the water was still, calm, and peaceful? The pebble wouldn't be experiencing the chaos up above. It would just be at rest, peaceful and snug on the bottom of the ocean floor. That's just what this practice can help you do when you're stressed and spinning with thoughts.

For this practice, you are going to use a word or a phrase that will serve as your "pebble" that can focus your mind and help you drop below the surface of those noisy, riotous waves. This is a gentle practice that guides you to that place of greater peace and inner hospitality. Follow along with the three steps.

1. **Choose a Word or Phrase.** To begin, you'll want to choose a word or short phrase that you can focus on and repeat in your mind, over and over. The words or phrases you can use for this practice are infinite. You could, for example, mentally repeat words such as *one*, *quiet mind*, *peace*, *shalom*, or *now*. I have found that many people like to use the word *pebble* because it is neutral and has no associations for them. You might even decide to use a prayer, such as the ancient Jesus Prayer: "Lord Jesus Christ, have mercy upon me." Feel free to get creative and use words that feel good. For example, I know an avid golfer who finds the word *bogey-free* to be calming and helpful for him. If the word you are using doesn't feel right, you can always try another one next time.

   It's also a good idea to avoid words that associate you with a particular memory. If you find that a word stimulates memory or intrudes by creating more thoughts, you can choose a more neutral word. Even using a neutral word like *one* has been shown to lower stress.

   The purpose of this practice is to release stress and gently quiet your mind by turning it away from the turbulence. You can think of this practice as dropping a pebble into rushing water. The word you focus on will gently take you beneath the choppy surface to where there are no waves; your mind and thoughts will settle down and grow quiet in the stillness beneath the waves. You can also imagine this practice as a way of calming the surface so you can float on top of the still water.

Once you begin to focus on the word, allow yourself at least 10 minutes of quiet time to reflect on your word or phrase. It helps to find a quiet place to sit, either indoors or outside. While you can do this practice lying down, it's better to sit up because it will be easier to stay awake. This is true even if you are sitting up in bed. Avoid practicing for at least one hour after a meal because you may get too drowsy to stay focused.

2. **Sit Quietly with Eyes Closed.** Now, sitting quietly, close your eyes. While repeating your word, you will be placing about 10 to 15 percent of your awareness on the breath. Make sure you breathe evenly and into the belly. As you think of your word, do not concentrate hard; this is not about forcing or creating too much effort. This is a gentle and effortless way of resting in the stillness beneath the water. Imagine that you are just *preferring or favoring* your chosen word over other thoughts. If your mind wanders off into thinking about the past or the future for a while, that's okay. Even if you get drowsy, that's okay too. Just gently return to your word again.

Sometimes, it may feel like your word has gone inward, as if it's still there even though you're not repeating it. If this happens, simply allow yourself to experience it this way. Your other senses may also intrude as you repeat your word. You may hear a noise, or you may feel a sensation in your body. Don't push these away; rather, just notice them and return to the breath and the word.

3. **Allow Negative Feelings to Pass.** Sometimes, strong feelings or emotions may occur while you are repeating your word. If you experience a strong negative feeling, see what it is like to sit with it until it passes. Your mind will naturally be drawn to it, and you don't need to explain or understand it, but let yourself notice if it increases or lessens in intensity. If for any reason it doesn't dissolve away and you get uncomfortable, you can always stop the practice by opening your eyes, distracting yourself, or just resting. Know that you can always return to this practice later.

At other times, you may experience an uplifting feeling while doing this practice. Whatever your experience may be today, the next practice session may bring totally different feelings. Give yourself permission to be open to whatever arises.

I like to think of this as a gentle practice, so if you feel the need to shift your position on the ground or chair or bed, go ahead and do so—but do so with full awareness. You may want to use a watch or clock the first few times you try this. After a while, you will sense when your 10 minutes are up. Before you open your eyes, allow yourself to just sit in the presence of your body with compassion. Then, slowly open your eyes. You may also want to end your 10 minutes of attentiveness with a short message or blessing of thanks.

How did this practice settle your mind? Were you able to stay with your pebble word(s) in an easy way, as a preference, and not have to force it?

_____
_____
_____
_____
_____
_____
_____

Try keeping track of how long you practice, such as from five to 10 minutes, for example. Make note of your stress or anxiety level before and after you practice. Use a 1–7 scale, where 7 is the highest level and 1 is the lowest. This way, you may learn what amount of time is optimal for you.

As with any other practice, this one works best when used regularly. How could you schedule this? What times of day do you think it would be most effective or helpful to reduce stress?

_____
_____
_____
_____
_____
_____
_____

Loving-Kindness Affirmation

In his book *Works of Love*, Danish philosopher and theologian Søren Kierkegaard shares some wisdom on the essence of love. He writes:

To cheat oneself out of love is the most terrible deception;

it is an eternal loss for which there is no reparation,

either in time or in eternity.

As someone grappling with pain—either physical or emotional (maybe both)—it may be hard to think about the idea of love. But the affirmation practiced in these pages is not like the love you may be thinking of. It is not the flavor of love that is romantic, sentimental, or nostalgic—dependent on one person or a specific memory. Rather, this is the deeply profound and compassionate wish for the well-being of all persons.

It is predicated on the basis that all beings deserve this non-discriminating love, that we all *need* it because all of us have struggled or suffered in some way. Even that person who seems happy and appears to have it all together will deal with loss and pain in life. And so, this practice is a form of compassion, which really means *to be with the suffering of another*.

This practice begins by developing compassion for ourselves. This is a process since you may not feel you are deserving of this deep wish for your well-being. If this is the case, you can begin by picturing the young baby, toddler, or child you once were, who was deserving of this loving meditation. State the words for that part of you.

Offering love and charity toward our neighbors is a central tenant to all wisdom traditions. Key examples of loving-kindness are found in stories of how Jesus, Buddha, and Mohammed all fed the hungry and starving, without discrimination. Whatever your background may be, this is an inclusive practice that anyone can benefit from. In addition, you can see the words here in any way that fits with your religious or spiritual background—as a blessing, a prayer, an affirmation, and so on.

As you read along with the following list, state each item to yourself over and over . . . *like you really mean it.*

1. **Begin with Forgiveness.** We've all been hurt, which is why this practice begins with forgiveness. You may be that parent, for example, who knows that you have

unintentionally wronged your children and yet hope for the grace of forgiveness. Or you may have inadvertently hurt someone because you didn't know any better. Whatever the case may be, reflect on the words. Allow forgiveness to act as a salve for your wounded spirit so that you may let go and move on. By sending forgiveness, you also open the gateway to a more awakened and sensitive behavior—alert to even the subtle consequences of your actions and thoughts. Jesus spoke to this in the Bible (Luke 6:37) when he said, "Do not judge, and you will not be judged. Do not condemn, and you will not be condemned. Forgive, and you will be forgiven."

Repeat the following words once before moving on.

May I forgive myself for hurting others.

May others forgive me for hurting them.

May I forgive myself for hurting myself.

2. **Say Loving-Kindness for Yourself.** Repeat the following words over and over. Say them until you can feel the words resonating within. This could be for 5 minutes, for 10, for 30 minutes.

May I be safe.

May I be happy.

May I be healthy.

May I be peaceful.

Optionally, add these words:

May I be free from pain, hunger, and suffering.

3. **Say Loving-Kindness for Others.** Next, you will repeat the loving-kindness affirmation for others. Picture these individuals looking radiant, healthy, and happy as you send them this deep wish for their well-being.

In the following list of groups, the top two are self-explanatory, but the "neutral persons" group refers to persons whom you may see or interact with from time to time but whom you don't really know—such as that person at the checkout stand at the grocery store, that person who lives down the street whom you wave to, and so on.

a. Teachers, mentors, guides

b.   Family members

c.   Friends

d.   Neutral persons

e.   Unfriendly persons

f.   All persons, living beings, living things without discrimination

The "unfriendly group" represents those who are difficult persons in your life. They may have even created pain and abuse. This is a group that presents the greatest challenge for sending out the loving-kindness words. If you find that you can't send loving-kindness to this group, you can stop and start sending love to yourself. Then, where you feel resonance with the words, again start sending loving-kindness to others, starting from the top of the list.

Remember that even that an abusive or difficult person in your life has suffered in some way. Even this person would benefit from such a blessing. In addition, you can know that this difficult person does not have to know you are sending these words out to them. In fact, they may not even be alive. Because loving-kindness breaks down the walls of separation between ourselves and others, saying it for others—even those who may have hurt or harmed us—is also beneficial to us.

Repeat the following loving-kindness words for each of the six groups.

May (name here) be safe.

May (name here) be happy.

May (name here) be healthy.

May (name here) be peaceful.

Optionally, add these words:

May (name here) be free from pain, hunger, and suffering.

4. **Conclude with a Final Blessing or Wish for Others.** After you have extended loving-kindness to all the six groups, end with following words.

May suffering ones by suffering-free,

May the fear-struck fearless be,

May grieving ones shed all grief,

May all beings find relief.

What was it like for you to say the loving-kindness meditation or affirmation? Was there any part of this that you found difficult?

_____

_____

_____

_____

_____

_____

_____

The loving-kindness practice takes time and patience. How do you think this could help you move toward forgiveness—either toward yourself or others?

_____

_____

_____

_____

_____

_____

_____

How could you develop an ongoing loving-kindness affirmation practice? Where would be an ideal place to practice this? Perhaps in the solitude of nature or in a place you design and dedicate to this gentle practice of cultivating peace, kindness, and compassion?

_____

_____

_____

_____

_____

_____

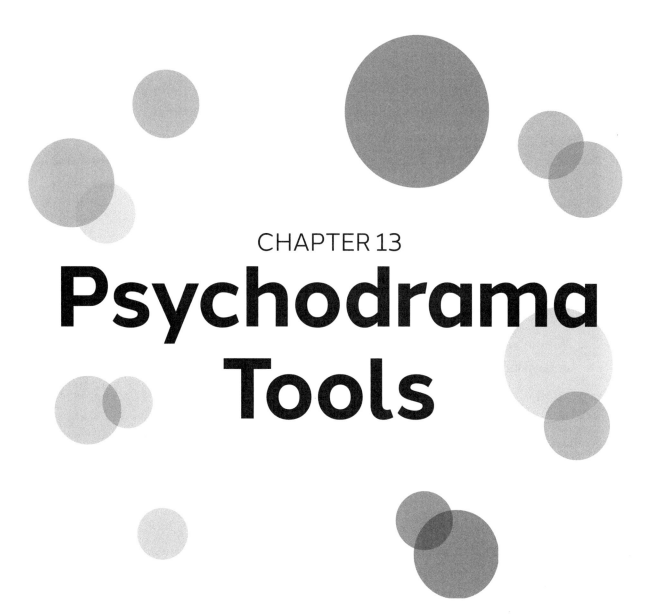

CHAPTER 13
Psychodrama Tools

Psychodrama Overview

The structure of a typical psychodrama group is developed through the use of sociometric exercises (sociometry = the science of social connections), which provide awareness to the group regarding its members' commonalties that in turn build trust, rapport, and respect. Psychodrama groups are typically brief, are solution-focused, and tend to address participants' core issues and, therefore, are often intense. Each psychodrama session runs approximately 1½ to 3 hours.

The following is a description of a typical psychodrama session:

1. A set of warm-up exercises.

2. Negotiation between the group regarding choosing a protagonist (i.e., who will "work" during the session).

3. With input from the group, the group leader picks a group member who is ready and willing to work on one of their personal problems.

4. The leader asks the protagonist to briefly state their problems. (This statement should be limited to a few sentences.)

5. The leader immediately moves the protagonist from this narrative phase into a "scene" that is relevant to and representative of the problem.

6. The protagonist is instructed to choose members from the group to play roles in this scene. (The roles cast are customarily those of significant people in the protagonist's life.) The group members who are chosen are instructed to do their best to portray the given role, usually without further clarification.

7. Sometimes the protagonist requires a "double." The double may be chosen prior to the beginning of a scene or during a scene if it becomes apparent that the protagonist (1) is unable to bring out all they need to, (2) is blocking emotion or expression, or (3) is unable to verbalize their feelings. The group leader will either instruct the protagonist to choose a double to come and speak for and through the protagonist, or designate a double without input from the protagonist.

8. The group leader calls for action, and the scene begins.

9. At certain points during the scene, the group leader should inquire about the accuracy of the roles being played. If on target, the scene continues uninterrupted. If not, the leader instructs the protagonist to switch roles with the group member playing that role. During this role reversal, the protagonist acts the part for a minute or two, thereby defining the role for the group member playing that role. This sequence is repeated as necessary, ensuring that all the actors in the protagonist's scene get to know their parts.

10. The scene plays out in this way until completion (i.e., the protagonist feels finished). At that point, the leader calls for quiet.

11. After a quiet pause, processing begins.

12. The protagonist is invited to describe the feelings they had while they were acting and/or observing different parts of the scene. The leader may ask specific questions regarding the protagonist's internal experiences (e.g., body sensations, emotions, thoughts, memories, insights).

13. The leader then moves on to the participants who played the various roles. Each participant is invited to share thoughts and feelings related to playing their respective roles.

14. The leader debriefs all the participants. Among the many ways to do this debriefing, it is recommended that each person who played a role should in some manner address the protagonist with what may seem (but is often not) an obvious statement asserting who they are and who they are not (e.g., "I'm not your mother, I'm your friend Diane" or "I'm not your brother, I'm Kenny").

15. Finally, the leader invites the audience (those in the group who were not directly involved in the scene) to provide feedback to the protagonist regarding their feelings about the scene. Prompts such as "How does what you've witnessed or been a part of relate to something in your own life?" may be offered to clarify the type of feedback that is being solicited.

The Best Gift Ever Given and Received

This two-part exercise deals with giving and receiving.

Part 1

Bring in a gift-wrapped box, place it prominently on display, and begin by drawing attention to the box. Then ask the clients to recall in their imagination the best gift they have ever received. Allow time for the memory to become vivid in all its dimensions. Instruct the group to pay attention not only to the gift, but to their sensory experience while experiencing the memory of the gift.

On the first go-round, ask each client to identify just how they feel presently, without sharing any information about the gift.

On the next go-round, ask each client to identify the following:

- What and why they felt as they did
- What the gift meant to them
- Who gave the gift
- What it was like to receive the gift

Part 2

Ask clients to once again close their eyes and then recall in their imagination the best gift they have ever given. Again, allow ample time for the memory to become vivid in all its dimensions. Instruct the group to pay attention to the gift—what it feels like knowing they will be giving it—and then to the act of giving the gift. Instruct them to pay specific attention to the receiver's reaction, along with their own sensory and emotional experience during the memory.

On the first go-round, ask each client to identify the following:

- Whom the gift was for
- Why it was so special
- How they felt at the time they were giving the gift
- How they feel presently

Finally, ask each client to contrast the two experiences.

Feelings Floor Check

This floor check helps clients build the skills of emotional literacy, regulation, and co-regulation. It can be your staple activity when you want the group to explore feelings. It also works well as a warm-up to deeper role plays or experiential letter writing.

Goals

- Expand a restricted range of affect that can be the result of trauma.

- Allow the group to become comfortable identifying, articulating, and sharing emotions and listening as others do the same.

- Allow the group to connect with each other around vulnerable emotions, share, and take in sharing and support.

- Teach and develop emotional literacy and emotional intelligence.

- Help clients learn to tolerate and talk about positive and self-affirming emotions so that they are less likely to relapse over them.

- Introduce structured, welcoming, and safe processes that can even feel playful or gamelike.

- Mobilize each group member's self-engagement system in a relational context for a repeated experience of self-regulation and co-regulation.

Steps

1. On separate pieces of paper, write feelings words such as angry, sad, mistrustful, anxious, despairing, self-conscious, content, hopeful, ashamed, guilty, frustrated, desperate, happy, serene, genuine, lonely, excited, empowered, or helpless. Have at least one paper marked "other" so clients can choose their own emotion.

2. Place the papers a couple of feet apart from each other, scattered around the floor.

3. Ask participants to stand on or near the feeling that best describes their mood in this moment.

4. Say, "Whenever you are warmed up, share a sentence or two about why you are standing where you're standing."

5. After all who wish to have shared, you can choose to repeat the process and ask participants to stand on another feeling that they are also experiencing. (Learning to hold more than one feeling at a time helps clients tolerate living in gray rather than black and white.) Then have them share as before.

6. At this point you can vary the criterion questions. For example:

    a. "Which feeling do you avoid feeling?"

    b. "Which feeling did your family of origin avoid feeling?"

    c. "Which feeling did your family of origin struggle with or get stuck in too much of the time?"

    d. "Which feeling did you have trouble with in your family of origin?"

    e. "Which feeling state triggers you when you encounter it in someone else?"

7. If you want to build resilience, you can include criterion questions such as:

    a. "Which feeling do you like to be near in someone who is a friend or partner?"

    b. "Which feeling would you like to experience more of in your life?"

    c. "Which feeling used to drag you down, but you have learned how to manage it better?"

8. If you'd like to extend the process further, you can say, "Place your hand on the shoulder of someone who shared something with which you identified. Now tell them why you chose them." The entire group can do this at once, which can create a nice feeling of connectedness or even a bit of a buzz.

9. If the group seems warmed up to do more work, you can invite them to do a role play. Or you can have them simply sit down and share about the entire process and what came up throughout.

Basic Spectrogram

This exercise allows you to quickly learn how much or how little of a feeling, symptom, or issue the group members are experiencing. It is useful for developing emotional regulation, getting people involved in the group process, developing group cohesion, and facilitating bonding as group members open up and connect with each other. You can modify the criterion questions to suit anything you wish to explore in the group.

Goals

- Provide a floor graph that group members can step into to represent the degree and intensity of a particular emotion, symptom, or issue.

- Help clients learn and practice the skills of emotional regulation.

- Help clients learn and practice the skills of emotional literacy and build emotional intelligence.

- Create group cohesion and build trust.

- Give everyone in the group a chance to feel involved in experiential work.

Steps

1. Designate an area in the workspace and explain to the participants that each end of this area represents an extreme—for example, one end of the workspace represents 0 percent and the opposite end represents 100 percent. Next, draw an imaginary line bisecting the area, representing the midpoint (50 percent).

2. Ask a criterion question and invite the participants to move to whatever point along the continuum best describes their response to the question. For example:

   a. "How comfortable are you in group right now?"

   b. "How satisfied are you with your progress in healing from relational trauma?"

   c. "How comfortable are you when feeling your intense emotions, such as anger, need, or love?"

d. "How comfortable do you feel around others when they are feeling intense emotions, such as anger, need, or love?"

e. "How comfortable are you with adult intimacy, such as partnering, parenting, or close friendship?"

f. "How comfortable are you around the people you grew up with?"

g. "How vulnerable do feel when opening up about your feelings?"

h. "How good do you feel about your work life or other responsibilities (such as your education or caregiving responsibilities)?"

i. "How good do you feel about your hobbies or other pursuits outside of your work or responsibilities?"

j. "How comfortable do you feel about your body?"

3. Allow people to share, either with the full group or in dyads or clusters with the people nearest to them. (They are already sociometrically aligned from moving in response to the question, so sharing with those standing next to them is an excellent way to create moments of identification and connection.) Invite them to share a sentence or two about why they're standing where they're standing (e.g., "I'm at about a 50 percent comfort level in group; I'm glad I'm here, but I'm a bit anxious about what's to come"). This encourages the participants to reflect on, regulate, and share their feelings, then listen as others do the same.

4. After you have explored as many questions as you wished to or the group has reached its saturation point, you can invite them to return to their seats and continue to share or begin a role play, if someone has warmed up to do so.

Shame Floor Check

The kinds of relational dynamics that engender trauma can engender shame too. When in the throes of feeling shame, the brain responds as if it were actually facing physical danger. The feeling generates a sympathetic flight/fight/freeze response in the nervous system, which is why it can make someone red in the face, sweaty, and anxious.

Goals

- Introduce and normalize shame.
- Bring clients' shame responses to consciousness.
- Help clients understand what triggers them.
- Help clients share triggers so they feel less toxic and immobilizing to the self.

Steps

1. Write the following shame responses on separate pieces of paper:

    a. Feeling frozen or in a fog, unable to act

    b. Lack of spontaneity

    c. Wanting to hide or disappear

    d. Feeling like you have little impact

    e. Being a perfectionist/hard on yourself/self-critical

    f. Feeling like an outsider or that you are different or left out of normal groups

    g. Feeling suspicious, anxious, or like you can't trust others

    h. Wanting to shut people out or withdraw from connection

    i. Sympathetic activation, like blushing cheeks, increased body temperature, sweating, or queasiness

    j. Feeling that you can't be your authentic self/loss of identity

    k. Feeling inadequate

  l. Sunken body posture or not looking people in the eye

 m. Other

2. Place the papers a couple of feet apart, scattered around the floor.

3. Ask any of the following criterion questions, or come up with your own. After each question, invite the participants to share with each other.

  a. "Walk over to a manifestation of shame that is pulling you now."

  b. "Walk over to a manifestation of shame that you have long denied."

  c. "Walk over to a manifestation of shame that your family experienced."

  d. "Walk over to a manifestation of shame that you are here to work on."

  e. "Walk over to an effect of shame that you feel you have come a long way in mastering."

4. If you would like to give the participants practice in reaching out to others, say, "Walk over and place your hand on the shoulder of someone who shared something with which you identified. Share with them why you chose them."

5. Depending on what the group is ready for, you can sit down and share about the entire process or move into future projection psychodramas, inviting the clients to talk to themselves in the future after having moved forward in some of these areas.

Emotions Anatomy Floor Check

Becoming comfortable identifying disequilibrating body states and talking about them is an important part of healing trauma. Developing emotional literacy through translating problematic inner states into words, making them conscious, reflecting on them, and talking about them allows a client to manage difficult feelings and sensations rather than act them out unconsciously, or self-harm or self-medicate over them. It is part of developing a recovery-oriented skill set.

Goals

- Allow the body's inner states and emotions to become embodied, experiential, and vocal.

- Allow clients to become comfortable identifying, articulating, and sharing about how emotion manifests for them in their bodies.

- Allow group members to connect with each other around vulnerable inner states, share, and take in sharing and support.

Steps

1. On separate pieces of paper, write inner body states such as frozen, numb, pins and needles, tight, loose, intense sensation, dead, adrenalized, collapsed, balanced/calm, breathless, weary, and energized. Have one paper marked "other" so clients can choose their own emotion/sensation; you may also leave a few pieces of paper blank for the group members to write in their own words.

2. Place the papers a couple of feet apart from each other, scattered around the floor.

3. Ask the participants to stand on or near the state that best describes their experience of the moment.

4. Say, "Whenever you are warmed up, share a sentence or two about why you are standing where you're standing."

5. At this point you can vary the criterion questions. For example:

   a. "Which state do you avoid, or self-medicate or self-injure around?"

b. "Which state do you fear will become bigger if you let yourself feel it?"

c. "Which state do you want to experience more of? How can you take steps toward that?"

d. "Which state do you have trouble tolerating in someone else?"

e. If you want to build resilience, you might ask, "Which state used to drag you down but now you have learned how to manage it better?"

6. If you'd like to extend the process, you can say, "Place your hand on the shoulder of someone who shared something with which you identified. Now tell them why you chose them."

7. Role plays may emerge at any point in this process.

8. Or invite the group to sit down and share about the entire process and what came up throughout.

Addiction and Relational Trauma Spectrogram

This spectrogram starts to bring awareness and regulation around the extent to which addiction and relational trauma have impacted a client's life. It brings up some of the feelings that clients may have trouble talking about so that they can share these with the identification and support of their fellow group members. The fact that they can immediately share the feelings that are getting triggered or warmed up inside of them helps to make the exercise healing. And as they share, they feel witnessed and held by the energy of the group, which allows them to expand their own internal container.

Goals

- Create awareness as to how much growing up with addiction and dysfunctional family patterns have impacted the client's inner world and relational habits.

- Allow group members to see hidden emotions and thoughts to come to the surface.

Steps

1. Designate an area in the workspace and explain to the participants that each end of this area represents an extreme—for example, one end represents 0 percent and the opposite end represents 100 percent. Next, draw an imaginary line bisecting the area, representing the midpoint (50 percent).

2. Ask a criterion question that explores the participants' experience of self-medication or living with or growing up with addiction and relational trauma, and invite them to move to whatever point along the continuum best describes their response to the question. For example:

   a. How much sadness do you feel relative to this?

   b. How much anger do you feel relative to this?

   c. How much shame do you feel relative to this?

   d. How much loss do you feel relative to this?

   e. How much confusion do you feel relative to this?

    f. How derailed do you feel your life has been by addiction?

    g. How much regret about the past do you feel relative to this?

    h. How much anxiety about the future do you feel?

    i. How vulnerable do you feel opening up about your self-medication?

    j. How much hope do you feel?

    k. How much strength or personal growth do you feel?

    l. How much faith do you have?

3. Allow people to share, either with the full group or in dyads or clusters with the people nearest to them (those they are sociometrically aligned with). Invite them to share a sentence or two about why they're standing where they're standing.

4. You can also ask, "Did anyone say something that particularly resonated with you? Or is there someone you feel you could learn something from? If so, walk over to that person, place your hand on their shoulder, and share why you choose them."

5. After you have explored as many questions as you wished to or the group has reached its saturation point, you can invite them to return to their seats and continue to share. You can also begin a role play; participants may wish to talk to another person, a part of themselves, a feeling or concept (e.g., hope, despair, recovery), or the addictive substance or behavior itself (e.g., alcohol, food, the internet, money).

Process Addictions Floor Check

Over the past two decades, what people think of as addiction has broadened considerably. With an increasing body of research connecting the brain's dopamine production with behaviors such as sex, eating, work, and internet use, we have a growing understanding of how we can stimulate and manipulate these pleasure chemicals with behaviors. This floor check is a way to bring awareness around the various ways that people might be self-medicating C-PTSD pain, beyond using drugs and alcohol.

Goals

- Help clients understand how unresolved trauma manifests in other addictions and process disorders.

- Gain awareness of the extent to which substances or behaviors are being used to self-medicate.

- Allow for open and honest sharing about compulsive behaviors.

- Help clients become aware of any secondary addictions that may have affected their family dynamic and influenced their own addiction.

Steps

1. On separate pieces of paper, write examples of process addictions or other forms of self-medication that clients may fall into, such as:

    a. Food

    b. Sex/porn

    c. Spending/debting

    d. Frenetic activity/adrenaline

    e. Cigarettes

    f. Work

    g. Exercise

    h. Technology/internet

    i. Other

2. Place the papers a couple of feet apart, scattered around the floor.

3. Ask the group members to stand on or near a form of self-medication that they currently use or that they believe they could fall into.

4. Invite the group members to share with each other, saying a sentence or two about why they are standing where they are standing.

5. Next, invite the group members to stand on or near a form of self-medication that they feel was present in their family of origin, either in a particular person or in their family as a whole, that created problems. (This may well be the same form of self-medication currently used by the client, which would illustrate the intergenerational nature of addiction.) Invite them to share again.

6. Ask the participants to stand on or near a form of self-medication that they feel they may once have slipped into, or could slip into, and share how they found their way through it, or how they keep themselves from going there.

7. Invite them to walk over to someone who shared something that made sense to them, or someone they feel they could learn something from, and ask that person for their insight, support, or advice.

8. At this point the group may be ready to sit down and share about the experience so far or move into another process. Clients may wish to use role play or experiential letter writing to talk to the form of self-medication that they are using or abusing.

Grief Spectrogram

Both trauma and grief are on a continuum, and clients will vary considerably as to how they experience the same traumatic episode or relational dynamic. Consequently, the level of grief, sadness, anger, disruption, and so on will depend upon the individual. This spectrogram helps clients to identify and understand their experiences of grief. The use of a grief spectrogram is an adaptation developed by Ronny Halpren, MSW, bereavement coordinator for the Carbini Hospice in New York City.

Goals

- Help clients access their experiences and symptoms of grief.

- Allow for identification, support, and bonding among group members.

- Provide a safe context in which clients can open up and be vulnerable about their grief.

Steps

1. Designate an area in the workspace and explain to the participants that each end of this area represents an extreme—for example, one end represents 0 percent and the opposite end represents 100 percent. Next, draw an imaginary line bisecting the area, representing the midpoint (50 percent).

2. Ask a criterion question that explores the participants' experience of grief, and invite them to move to whatever point along the continuum best describes their response to the question. Grief is complicated and messy, so reassure them that they are free to change their minds and move around as the sharing progresses. Possible questions include:

    a. "How much unresolved emotion do you feel surrounding this loss?"

    b. "How much yearning do you feel?"

    c. "How much sadness, depression, or regret do you feel?"

    d. "How much anger or resentment do you feel?"

    e. "How much self-recrimination, shame, or embarrassment do you feel?"

f. "How blocked are you from getting in touch with your genuine feelings involved in this issue?"

g. "How much has grief disrupted your daily routine?"

h. "How much trouble are you having organizing yourself?"

i. "How much is your sleep affected?"

j. "How tired do you feel?"

k. "How uninterested in your life do you feel?"

l. "How much fear of the future do you feel?"

m. "How much hope do you feel about your life and the future?"

n. "How much do you feel your grief has contributed to your becoming a deeper person?"

o. "How much old, unresolved grief is being activated and remembered as a result of this current issue?"

p. "How vulnerable do feel when you're experiencing grief-related feelings?"

3. After each question, allow people to share, either with the full group or in dyads or clusters with the people nearest to them (those they are sociometrically aligned with). I sometimes let the group choose how they would like to share by simply asking, "Would you like to share in the large group or subgroups on this one?" Invite them to share a sentence or two about why they're standing where they're standing.

4. You can also ask, "Did anyone say something that particularly resonated with you?" or "Is there someone you feel you could learn something from?" and invite them to "Walk over to that person, place your hand on their shoulder, and share why you choose them."

5. After you have explored as many questions as you wished to or the group has reached its saturation point, you can invite them to return to their seats and continue to share. You can also move into a role play or experiential letter writing.

Disenfranchised Losses Floor Check

There are many losses in life that go unnamed and ungrieved. By this I am not saying that a full grief process is necessary for each and every loss, simply that it is important for the client to acknowledge their loss and feel all their feelings around it rather than trying to make it go away by pretending it isn't there. When losses that deserve time and attention go unseen and unmourned, they are referred to in the grief vernacular as *disenfranchised*. These losses live in unmarked graves within people and family systems who often avoid discussing them. The pain becomes covert rather than overt—that is, unexamined feelings surrounding the loss still affect the client, who may not be aware of the way in which they are impacting their life and relationships. This floor check helps clients identify, honor, and begin to process their disenfranchised losses. They also get to receive the identification and support of their fellow group members.

Goals

- Help clients understand the types of losses that often go unrecognized and unmourned.

- Help clients identify and begin to mourn these types of losses in a supportive container.

Steps

1. On separate sheets of paper, write the following types of disenfranchised losses:
   a. Loss of a connection to the self
   b. The grief of the inner child who lives inside of the adult
   c. Loss of safety in family relationships
   d. Loss of an unencumbered childhood
   e. Divorce or breakup
   f. Loss of a trusted and dependable loved one (e.g., due to addiction or illness)
   g. Parental estrangement, abandonment, or visitation changes

h. Socially stigmatized death (e.g., AIDS, suicide, murder, DUI, overdose)

i. Death of a pet

j. Infertility, miscarriage, or abortion

k. Disabling condition or other health issue

l. Brain injury, dementia, or cognitive deficit

m. Mental health issue

n. Moving or loss of a home

o. Job loss or retirement

p. Other

2. Place the papers a couple of feet apart, scattered around the floor.

3. Ask criterion questions and invite the participants to stand on or near the type of loss that represents their response. Possible questions include:

a. "Which type of loss is pulling you now?"

b. "Which type of loss do you feel you most need to work on?"

c. "What is a kind of loss that you feel your family experienced (either family of origin or progenitive)?"

d. "Is there a type of loss that you feel you have come a long way in working through?"

e. "Which type of loss have you denied?"

f. "Which type of loss did your family deny?"

g. "Which type of loss do you keep hidden or have trouble talking about?"

h. "Which type of loss makes you feel like a victim?"

4. After each question, invite the group members to share a sentence or two about why they are standing where they are standing. You may have them share with the full group, with those standing on the same type of loss, or a combination of these.

5. Say, "Walk over to someone who shared something that you identified with or that moved you, stand next to them, and share with them what moved you" or "Walk over to someone from whom you feel you could learn something and ask them for help."

6. Invite the group to sit down and share about the experience as a whole. Or, if they are warmed up for further work, you can move into a role play or another process.

Forgiveness Spectrogram

This exercise is meant to flush out some of the complicated and complex emotions that come up around the notion of forgiving someone who has hurt the client or forgiving themselves for hurting someone else. It offers a way to bring some awareness and regulation around each feeling, to really look at how much or how little they're experiencing it. And it gives space to put some language around these emotions so they can be reflected on and communicated.

Goals

- Bring regulation to difficult feelings.
- Provide an experiential format for dealing with forgiveness issues.

Steps

1. Invite the group members to think of a forgiveness issue that has come up—this might be in relation to forgiving themselves, forgiving someone else, or hoping for another person's forgiveness.

2. Designate an area in the workspace and explain to the participants that each end of this area represents an extreme—for example, one end represents 0 percent and the opposite end represents 100 percent. Next, draw an imaginary line bisecting the area, representing the midpoint (50 percent).

3. Ask a criterion question that explores the participants' forgiveness issues, and invite them to move to whatever point along the continuum best describes their response to the question. Possible questions include:

   a. "How blocked are you from getting in touch with your genuine feelings involved in this issue?"

   b. "How much do you feel this issue is affecting your inner peace today?"

   c. "How much fear are you feeling at the thought of honestly addressing your feelings around this issue?"

   d. "How much anger or resentment are you feeling associated with this issue?"

e. "How much hurt or sadness are you feeling associated with this issue?"

f. "How much self-recrimination, guilt, or shame do you feel around this issue?"

g. "How much hope do you have that you can work through your feelings surrounding this issue?"

h. "How vulnerable do feel at the thought of forgiving someone?"

i. "How vulnerable do feel at the thought of forgiving yourself?"

j. "How undeserving of others' forgiveness do you feel?"

k. "How much of your energy do you feel is being absorbed by this issue?"

l. "How much do you feel this issue impacts your relationships today?"

m. "How much do you feel this issue has impacted your ability to move into future relationships comfortably?"

4. After each question, allow people to share, either with the full group or in dyads or clusters with the people nearest to them (those they are sociometrically aligned with). Invite them to share a sentence or two about why they're standing where they're standing.

5. You can also ask, "Did anyone say something that particularly resonated with you? Or is there someone you feel you could learn something from? If so, walk over to that person, place your hand on their shoulder, and share why you choose them."

6. After you have explored as many questions as you wished to or the group has reached its saturation point, you can invite them to return to their seats and continue to share. You can also move into a role play or experiential letter writing.

Granting Forgiveness to the Self

People sometimes have a harder time forgiving themselves than forgiving others. Feelings of shame, unworthiness, and guilt can make them feel that forgiving themselves is somehow not okay. If they can't forgive themselves, their self-recrimination can turn into anger toward someone they've hurt; in this case, forgiving themselves is better for that person too. When the client can forgive themselves, in a humble way, and they're not using self-forgiveness as a way to cancel someone's pain, then forgiving themselves is healthy and helpful for both themselves and others.

Goals

- Give the client a concrete way of experiencing self-forgiveness.
- Free the self.

Steps

1. Ask the protagonist to choose someone to play the self they want to forgive.

2. Invite the protagonist to begin the scene by telling that part of themselves why they want to forgive them, or why they are having trouble forgiving them, or to say anything they wish to say to that part of themselves.

3. Let the scene progress, and use role reversal, doubling, and whatever other techniques feel appropriate. This part of the role play can go back and forth. Role reversal interview can also be used by asking questions of the protagonist in role reversal:

   a. "Do you think they deserve forgiveness?"

   b. "Tell us a little about the part of yourself that seems unforgivable."

   c. "Are you in any way afraid to forgive that part of yourself?"

   d. "Why do you think that part of you wants forgiveness so much?"

4. When the scene seems to be coming to natural closure, ask the protagonist to end it. Say, "Say the last things you'd like to say for now to this part of yourself."

5. Have the role players return to their seats for deroling and sharing. (Deroling allows the role players to brush off those roles and become themselves again.) Or you can do several role plays, one right after the other, and move into sharing after this.

Resilience Floor Check

It's so important that clients not only get in touch with their pain and anger, but also identify their special gifts and let them be seen by others. This floor check offers a way to claim and consolidate some of those personal strengths. Let this be lively and fun—let the group members brag a bit and bond over their strengths as well as their problems. Encourage them to share about how they mobilized or discovered their inner and relational qualities of resilience in getting their lives to work.

Goals

- Educate clients on the qualities and characteristics of resilience.

- Provide a format through which clients can choose for themselves which qualities they feel they experience in their own lives and relationships.

- Create opportunities to lay claim to personal strengths and consolidate the gains of growth and recovery.

- Encourage connection, engagement, and bonding.

Steps

1. On separate sheets of paper, write these characteristics of a resilient self, which are based on the Connor-Davidson resilience scale (Connor & Davidson, 2003):

    a. I am able to adapt to change.

    b. I can have close and secure relationships.

    c. I believe sometimes fate, God, or another higher power can help.

    d. I can deal with whatever comes.

    e. Past successes give me confidence for new challenges.

    f. I see the humorous side of things.

    g. Coping with stress strengthens me.

    h. I tend to bounce back after illness or hardship.

i. I believe things happen for a reason.

j. I make my best effort no matter what.

k. I can achieve my goals.

l. When things look hopeless, I don't give up.

m. I know where to turn for help.

n. Under pressure, I can focus and think clearly.

o. I prefer to take the lead in problem-solving.

p. I am not easily discouraged by failure.

q. I think of myself as strong person.

r. I can make unpopular or difficult decisions.

s. I can handle unpleasant feelings.

t. I can act on a hunch/intuition.

u. I have a strong sense of purpose.

v. I am in control of my life.

w. I like challenges.

x. I work to attain my goals.

y. I have pride in my achievements.

z. Other

2. Place the papers a couple of feet apart, scattered around the floor.

3. Ask the participants to stand on or near a characteristic that describes them—a way that their resilience manifests in their life.

4. Invite them to share a sentence or two about why they are standing where they are standing. You may have them share with the full group, with those standing on the same characteristic, or a combination of these.

5. Repeat this process with additional criterion questions—for example:

a. "Which quality do you have that you feel really proud of?"

b. "Which quality do you feel you gained in 'the school of hard knocks' or through struggling?"

c. "Which quality do you lean on the most when you feel down to get you through?"

d. "Which quality do you feel is most present in your family?"

e. "Which quality do you feel might get you far in your life?"

f. "Which quality do you feel you do not possess?"

g. "Which quality do you want to develop more of?"

6. Say, "Walk over to someone who shared something that you identified with or that moved you, stand next to them, and share with them what moved you," or "Walk over to someone from whom you feel you could learn something and ask them for help."

7. When the group is saturated, invite them to sit down and share about the experience as a whole. Or, if they are warmed up for further work, you can move into role plays.

349

Posttraumatic Growth Floor Check

The field of positive psychology looks at the kinds of personal strengths people can develop in meeting life's challenges. The posttraumatic growth inventory was developed by psychologists Richard Tedeschi and Lawrence Calhoun (1996) to bring awareness to and measure some of these gains. I have adapted their categories into an experiential group process so that group members can drop down into themselves and really feel, unpack, share, internalize, and consolidate some of these gains.

Goals

- Consolidate gains made through facing life challenges and trying to overcome them.
- Acknowledge and celebrate clients' personal growth.
- Help clients set goals for more growth.

Steps

1. On separate pieces of paper, write these outcomes of posttraumatic growth:

    a. I changed my priorities about what is important in life.

    b. I have a greater appreciation for the value of my own life.

    c. I developed new interests.

    d. I have a greater feeling of self-reliance.

    e. I have a better understanding of spiritual matters.

    f. I more clearly see that I can count on people in times of trouble.

    g. I established a new path for my life.

    h. I have a greater sense of closeness with others.

    i. I am more willing to express my emotions.

    j. I am more confident that I can handle difficulties.

    k. I am able to do better things with my life.

    l. I am better able to accept the way things work out.

    m. I can better appreciate each day.

n.   New opportunities are available to me that wouldn't have been otherwise.

o.   I have more compassion for others.

p.   I put more effort into my relationships.

q.   I am more likely to try to change things that need changing.

r.   I have a stronger religious faith.

s.   I discovered that I'm stronger than I thought I was.

t.   I learned a great deal about how wonderful people are.

u.   I better accept needing others.

v.   Other

2. Place the papers a couple of feet apart, scattered around the floor.

3. Say, "Walk over to a statement that draws you and share a sentence or two about why you choose it." You may have them share with the full group, with those standing on the same statement, or a combination of these.

4. Repeat this process with a few additional criterion questions, such as:

    a.   "Walk over to a statement you feel you have come a long way in mastering."

    b.   "Walk over to a statement that represents your growing edge."

    c.   "Walk over to a statement that you feel trauma took away from you and you are getting back."

    d.   "Walk over to a statement that you look forward to expanding in the future."

    e.   "Walk over to a statement that inspires you in your recovery."

    f.   "Walk over to a statement that makes you think of a parent, grandparent, mentor, or role model."

5. Say, "Walk over to someone who shared something that you identified with or that moved you, stand next to them, and share with them what moved you," or "Walk over to someone from whom you feel you could learn something and ask them for help."

6. When the group is saturated, invite them to sit down and share about the experience as a whole. Or, if they are warmed up for further work, you can move into role plays or experiential letter writing, inviting the participants to either thank someone else for their love and support or thank the self for making good choices and trying to get life to work.